The Pulitzer Prize

The Pulitzer Prize

The Inside Story of America's Most Prestigious Award

by J. Douglas Bates

A Birch Lane Press Book
Published by Carol Publishing Group

A Birch Lane Press Book
Published by Carol Publishing Group
Birch Lane Press is a registered trademark of Carol Communications, Inc.

Editorial Offices: 600 Madison Avenue, New York, N.Y. 10022
Sales & Distribution Offices: 120 Enterprise Avenue, Secaucus, N.J. 07094
In Canada: Musson Book Company, a division of General Publishing
Company, Ltd., Don Mills, Ontario M3B 2T6

Queries regarding rights and permissions should be addressed to Carol
Publishing Group, 600 Madison Avenue, New York, N.Y. 10022

Carol Publishing Group books are available at special discounts for bulk
purchases, for sales promotions, fund raising, or educational purposes.
Special editions can be created to specifications. For details contact:
Special Sales Department, Carol Publishing Group, 120 Enterprise Avenue,
Secaucus, N.J. 07094

Manufactured in the United States of America

10 9 8 7 6 5 4 3 2 1

Library of Congress Cataloging-in-Publication Data

Bates, J. Douglas.
    The Pulitzer Prize : the inside story of America's most
prestigious award / by J. Douglas Bates.
        p. cm.
    "A Birch Lane Press book."
    Includes bibliographical references and index.
    ISBN 1–55972–070–0
    1. Pulitzer prizes. 2. Pulitzer, Joseph, 1847–1911. I. Title.
AS911.B38   1991
071'.3—dc20   91–13659
                                                        CIP

To Jim Dwyer,
Claire Spiegel, and Tamar Stieber

Contents

Acknowledgments

THIS BOOK WOULD NOT have come about if it weren't for the contributions of three people: my older brother, Tom Bates, who nudged me and introduced me to agent Richard Pine, who challenged me harder and put me in touch with editor Hillel Black, who pushed hardest of all while providing immeasurable insight and professional guidance. If there were a Pulitzer Prize for journalistic encouragement, all three would be contenders.

Many others helped with advice, information, support, and inspiration. Foremost at the start of the project were my younger brother, Dan Bates, along with Teresa Carp, Arnold Ismach, Bob Keefer, Brian Lanker, Mike Thoele, and John Thompson.

Near the end of my undertaking, I received invaluable support at the *San Diego Union* from Karin Winner, Doug Hope, Bernie Jones, Bill Hodge, and the entire news desk.

The three heroes of this book—Jim Dwyer, Claire Spiegel, and Tamar Stieber—have my lasting gratitude. Their trust and openness were indispensable.

Special thanks go to Gloria Jean Bates, my wife. Her able assistance and unwavering faith in the project helped keep it moving forward. She never quit believing that the story behind the prizes was a tale worth telling.

The Pulitzer Prize

1

"The Academy Awards of Journalism"

2:45 P.M.—April 12, 1990

RESTLESS REPORTERS FIDGET a little as they await their annual news handout at Columbia University. Some of them chatter self-consciously in small groups; some gaze out the dirty windows at the sideshow on Broadway. Others continue to arrive, one by one, with their notebooks and tape recorders and city-desk instructions. Now all they need are their press releases so they can call in to the glass cages where editors are waiting anxiously—or in some cases with smug anticipation—to hear who won the 1990 Pulitzer Prizes.

As journalism goes, this is light duty. These reporters will be handed their news. All they are expected to do is phone in the winners. But deadlines weigh heavily this late in the day, and those editors back in the newsrooms are watching the clock with far more intensity than normal. This is the one day of the year when American newspaper executives suspend their usual

3

objectivity and overplay a self-interest story— if *their* papers, not their competitors', win Pulitzers. So nerves grow increasingly taut until one of the assembled journalists—a reporter at the front of the room, wearing khaki pants and a pseudo-safari jacket—steps up to a bronze bust and grabs it by its prodigious nose.

"Pull it, sir? Okay!"

With a feigned tug, he yanks on Joseph Pulitzer's metallic beak.

"Honk!"

That lightens things up a little, drawing one belly laugh and a few smiles from some of those who saw it. Pulitzer's dusty bronze likeness just keeps staring, somewhat fiercely, at the media event that's ready to unfold in the cavernous World Room in Columbia's Graduate School of Journalism.

Altogether, thirty-two reporters are gathered here for the yearly ritual glorifying Pulitzer, the nineteenth-century newspaper publisher. In their restless banter, some of the scribes have made a common error, mispronouncing the great man's name. It's *PULL-it-sir*, not *PEW-lit-sir*. Hence the fellow in the Banana Republic getup recites the old Pulitzer nose joke, an offensive pronunciation gimmick dating all the way back to the Civil War. Young Joseph—"Joey the Jew" and "Jewseph Pulitzer," as fellow Union Army soldiers called him—endured such anti-Semitism throughout his early adulthood.

Eighty years after his death, Pulitzer remains a powerful force—in some ways still the most influential figure in American publishing. Only he, among all publishers past and present, could attract the media muscle that has massed here in the World Room. In death, as in life, he remains a master of manipulation and self-promotion. And this drama on a sunny Thursday afternoon in Manhattan, April 12, 1990, is the genius's masterstroke: Pulitzer Prize Day—the annual announcement of "the Academy Awards of Journalism," as columnist Jack Anderson once described the Pulitzer in a speech after winning one.

Anderson could have expanded that remark. The Pulitzer Prize is the Academy Award of almost all American writing, including fiction, drama, biography, history, general nonfiction, and poetry as well as music. These prize announcements, just moments away, will send Joseph Pulitzer's power surging through the lives and careers of nearly two dozen U.S. writers and journalists. Champagne corks will pop, emotions will soar, egos will bloat, and otherwise intelligent women and men will shout and laugh and carry on like Hollywood celebrities who have just been handed those strange, faceless metallic statues.

Today's event, though, resembles nothing like Oscar Night. Pulitzer Prize Day is about as glitzy as the drab building where the event takes place. The gray, corrosion-stained structure was built with Joseph Pulitzer's wealth in 1912, the year after his death. The money he left for upkeep was depleted years ago. Despite some recent interior painting and remodeling, the seven-story hall still looks run-down, reflecting a sense of diminished prestige.

Litter lies strewn on the entry steps and continues into the dingy lobby. A blob of pink ice cream—probably fallen from a sugar cone purchased on Broadway—lies melting on the green marble floor. A custodian will soon clean it up, but right now he's downstairs in the men's lavatory, swabbing a mess left by a man who spent the night there.

"They hide in here sometimes," the janitor says. "They'd rather sleep in a toilet stall than one of them shelters."

The building's shabbiness is relieved by one striking exception: the Gannett Center for Media Studies. It's the journalism think tank that opened on the building's ground floor in 1985 under a $15 million grant from the Gannett Foundation. Each year, twelve to fourteen senior journalists and educators come here under a scholar-in-residence program to do research on communications issues. The center is administratively and financially independent of the university, and the schism shows. Walking into the handsomely decorated, richly furnished Gannett Center, after visiting the building's upper floors, can be slightly disorienting.

"You should have seen the upper floors a year ago," says one of the Gannett fellows, Joann Byrd, executive editor of the *Herald* in Everett, Washington. "They've actually spruced it up a little. Before, it looked like something in a third-world country."

And Gannett has sealed its borders; no homeless man will ever sneak into the lavatories in the think tank's part of the building. It is tightly secured by electronic locks, with admission only by special key or by remote-controlled lock-release from within.

The center is so separate from the journalism school, in fact, that Byrd and other newspaper executives who are working there this particular afternoon are surprised when told it's Pulitzer Prize Day.

Meanwhile, on the seventh floor, Robert Christopher gets ready to go downstairs to meet the press. Christopher is the sixty-six-year-old adjunct professor and former magazine editor who serves as administrator of the Pulitzer Prizes. Part of his job each year is handling the announcements of winners. He keeps the event decidedly low-key.

"The university tries hard to avoid any Oscar hoopla," he tells a visitor.

Four floors down, the probable reasons for Christopher's edginess—the thirty-two reporters representing some of the most influential news organizations in the Western Hemisphere—are waiting for him to hand out press releases and answer questions. That might seem easy, but it's actually the trickiest part of Christopher's job. Almost without fail, one or more of the Pulitzer Prize Board's decisions each year result in controversy. Most of these flaps are minor and receive little attention outside the trade press. Others become national news. The most notorious example involved the 1981 prize to Janet Cooke of the *Washington Post* for a fabricated feature story on a nonexistent eight-year-old heroin addict. In such crises, Christopher is responsible for damage control, trying to keep the prizes as untarnished as possible.

"Almost every year, somebody demands that some prize be withheld," Christopher says. "Nobody has ever been stripped of a Pulitzer Prize, although the *Washington Post* would have been if they hadn't returned Cooke's."

Christopher, an urbane, respected former senior editor at *Time* and executive editor at *Newsweek*, took this job shortly after the Janet Cooke scandal. So far, in eight years of administering the prizes, he has not had to deal with any public relations nightmares of that magnitude. But as he reaches for another paper clip on his desk, his hand shakes slightly.

Downstairs, it is quite clear why the university avoids any

"Oscar hoopla." None is needed. The *New York Times,* the *Wall Street Journal, Newsday,* the *Village Voice,* and the *Daily News* have all sent reporters. So have the Associated Press, United Press International, the Canadian Press, Reuters, the U.S. television networks, several New York television and radio stations, the Voice of America, some of the nation's major newspaper chains, and a handful of industry journals, including *Editor & Publisher,* bible of the newspaper business. In a post-cold-war wrinkle, the prize announcements have even attracted a Soviet newspaper reporter, Alexander Shalnev, New York correspondent for *Izvestia.*

They are gathered in the World Room, the journalism building's largest lecture hall, named after Joseph Pulitzer's defunct New York newspaper, the *World.* Decades ago, the room's ornate woodwork, high ceilings, and soaring windows probably gave it an elegant look. Today, the room is powder blue with cheap brass chandeliers and industrial beige carpeting which give it the appearance of an aging matron who outfitted herself at Woolworth's.

Old-world elegance on a third-world budget.

Through the sooty windows on the west side of the World Room, some of the waiting reporters look out at Broadway, where Joseph Pulitzer's brand of journalism is languishing on the newsstands. Tabloids screaming CABBIE KILLER! and TAXI BANDIT SLAYS NO. 5, piled in tall stacks, sell slowly to strolling students, stripped down to T-shirts and tank tops in the early spring sunshine. Most of them glance at the garish headlines. Who could possibly fail to notice TAXI TRIGGERMAN in three-inch boldface? Broadway's sidewalks have buzzed all afternoon with chatter about the string of cab-driver killings.

New York's crime-of-the-week clearly fascinates these Columbia students, but not quite enough to make many of them plunk down money for newspapers. On this day, the students appear more interested in contributing their spare change to Broadway's panhandlers and pretzel-cart vendors. The ice cream shops are doing well, too. Winter was rough in the city this year, and now that the chill is suddenly off, ice cream is big.

Bigger, at least, than newspapers.

Like their peers all across the nation, these young adults do not read newspapers—not habitually, anyway. It is a deep, powerful, immensely important trend, one that you won't find reported in newspapers themselves. Combined with declining advertising and rising costs, this trend is brewing profound change in the American newspaper, which some gloomy analysts think is heading for the same fate as the American passenger train. Others vociferously disagree—particularly the owners of newspapers. There is no dispute, though, that the trend helps explain in part why New York's leading purveyors of sensational journalism, the *Post* and the *Daily News,* are losing money in their life-and-death struggle for survival.

Just down the hallway from the World Room, however, two very different newspapers have found their way into young readers' hands in the student lounge. One is the *New York Times,* which has buried the cabbie-killer story deep inside. Topping the front page is a rather staid report on U.S. Census woes.

The other paper is the recent April Fool's Day issue of the student daily, the *Columbia Spectator,* which calls this charming special edition the *Columbia Masturbator.* Its pages are filled with sleazy ethnic slurs and seemingly endless bathroom humor (edited by Fart Director Angelic Dicks, along with Karen Holdmyrod, Kneel Towardit, and Feelmy Fineballs). The *Masturbator*'s spoof sports page is called "Spurts." You get the idea. So do the young woman and man who are mirthfully perusing it. They seem to find it funny, but it is hard to imagine Joseph Pulitzer feeling anything but disappointment in the sensibilities of some of the aspiring young journalists in his school in 1990.

The prizes, though, are a different story. As *Time* media writer Thomas Griffith puts it, the Pulitzers have turned into "the most valuable American awards there are." He refers not to the modest $3,000 check that accompanies each prize, but to the startling cachet that goes with it.

In newspaper journalism, the prize works a form of magic that defies logic or easy explanation. No other newspaper award—and there are at least three hundred—comes close to the high stakes of the Pulitzer. Its intoxicating power can be traced to newspaper ownership, which views the Pulitzer as good business. Winning it is useful in boosting a newspaper's circulation and in promoting a positive image among readers. The prize also enhances a paper's relationship with stockholders and directors. And it polishes a company's industry-wide reputation, enabling the paper to lure more top-drawer talent to its newsroom.

Thus, for a reporter, photographer, columnist, editorial writer, or cartoonist, winning the Pulitzer can jump-start a career. Winners at smaller, lower-paying, less-prestigious newspapers, for example, suddenly find they can join the staffs of larger, higher-paying, more respected organizations. Those already employed at big papers discover it is easier to win promotions, improved assignments, or special working arrangements not available to fellow employees. There can be tangential rewards as well: book contracts, free-lance opportunities, speaking engagements, reputation-padding publicity, and invitations to join the Pulitzer Prize hierarchy as judges.

Rewards also await the editors who supervise such winners. The prize can build editors' reputations outside their companies and give them "publisher protection" within. Particularly for controversial editors embroiled in creating change—disturbing the comfort level of their publishers and staffs—a Pulitzer Prize can have the effect of validating that change and defusing unrest in the boardroom and in the newsroom, at least temporarily.

Vertically, the entire newspaper establishment has a vested interest in the prizes. They are aggressively sought and lavishly publicized—to the point that "Pulitzer Prize winner" has become an American cliché. And riding on the coattails of this self-serving news coverage are the Pulitzer Prizes for books and plays, which on occasion would have remained obscure if not for the newspaper industry's fascination with the journalism prizes.

For a book publisher, the Pulitzer can mean greatly enhanced publicity for a book and its author, sometimes resulting in improved sales. A book's shelf life in stores can be significantly prolonged by a well-timed Pulitzer Prize. Money can be at stake, so some of the big houses flood the Pulitzer competition each year in a shotgun approach. Alfred A. Knopf, for example, entered fifty-eight books in this year's competition—almost 10 percent of the 590 books entered by all publishers combined. In part because of aggressiveness like that, but also because of the high quality of their authors, no one should be surprised that Knopf books won more Pulitzer Prizes—eleven—during the 1980s than any other publishing house.

Even when winning fails to improve sales significantly, the prize can improve the new contract a writer gets for a forthcoming book. Recognition, too, awaits a winner. Occasionally, the prize can transport an author overnight from obscurity to the front page of the *New York Times Book Review*. That, in fact, is what will happen after Columbia announces on this day that the 1990 prize for fiction goes to a little-known New York writer, Oscar Hijuelos, for his second novel, *The Mambo Kings Play Songs of Love*, one of twenty books submitted for 1990 Pulitzers by Farrar, Straus & Giroux.

For a play, winning the Pulitzer can mean the difference between box-office success and failure. That has become so much the case that Broadway producers have begun adding incentive provisions to playwrights' contracts, offering them profit bonuses if their shows garner the Pulitzer (and, in some cases, the Antoinette Perry Award—the Tony). The Pulitzer can rescue a foundering production or revive one that has closed. And the prize can help propel a play into a movie deal, as acknowledged by Richard and Lili Zanuck, producers of the film version of Alfred Uhry's Pulitzer-winner, *Driving Miss Daisy*.

For playwrights, like authors of books, winning the Pulitzer can be a shortcut to money and recognition. That will be the case in the 1990 competition, when August Wilson is awarded his second Pulitzer Prize, this one for *The Piano Lesson*. With perfect timing, it will open on Broadway two weeks after today's prize announcements. The theater will be packed for every performance. And some of the more generous critics will begin mentioning Wilson in the same breath with Eugene O'Neill, generally regarded as America's greatest playwright, and winner of four Pulitzer Prizes—a feat matched only by Robert Frost, winner of four Pulitzers for poetry.

Winning the prize can mean financial gain even for the struggling poet, that least-recognized and most ill-compensated of American writers. The poetry prize sometimes brings a windfall of travel stipends and honoraria for readings and enhanced pay for future published verse.

In literature, the Pulitzer has become America's version of the Nobel Prize.

The similarities are not coincidental. Pulitzer stole the idea.

Alfred Nobel, the Swedish chemist, made a far-reaching discovery in his laboratory in 1867. He combined nitroglycerin with an absorbent substance, creating the first high explosive that could be handled and shipped safely. He named his invention "dynamite." It quickly made him one of the world's richest men. It also contributed to a severe nervous disorder in his later years. He suffered from profound guilt at having profited from substances that caused so much carnage, including the death of his younger brother, Emil, and four other persons who perished when Nobel's explosives factory blew up, before he had perfected his creation. The inventor also abhorred the thought that his dynamite and a later invention, blasting gel, were being used in war when he had created them for peace. When he died in 1896—fifteen years before Pulitzer—his will directed that the interest on his $9 million fortune should be given each year to the winners of five awards. They were to be in five fields: chemistry, physics, medicine or physiology, literature, and, fittingly, work toward international peace.

Creation of the Nobel Prize was an act of contrition by a sensitive, guilt-wracked man.

So was creation of the Pulitzer Prize, to some extent, although the American publisher probably aimed more at manipulating history than assuaging his guilt.

Like Nobel, Pulitzer was an inventor who made his fortune quickly. His invention was sensational journalism. He also introduced the first newspaper comic, a hugely popular strip called "The Yellow Kid," which gave birth to the appellation "yellow journalism" for Pulitzer's style of newspapering, the CABBIE KILLER variety being peddled out on the street. While building his fortune, he routinely exaggerated the news, ran scare headlines, sharply slanted his political coverage, and published fabricated news stories. With equal culpability by rival William Randolf Hearst, Pulitzer helped incite the nation into the Spanish-American War. It killed almost five thousand Americans and untold numbers of Spaniards and Cubans in

1898—all in the interest of selling more papers in a circulation war with Hearst.

For all his frailties, though, Pulitzer had greatness in him. He was the first of the crusaders, the champion of modern investigative reporting. His newspapers tirelessly pushed for social reform and fought corruption in government and big business. He was a complex, contradictory man whose noble contributions to journalism and the nation, later in life, certainly outweighed his venal past.

Ensuring that historians would remember the positive side was perhaps Pulitzer's cleverest triumph. He did it at his death in 1911 through two astonishingly visionary acts: leaving $1.5 million to establish Columbia's Graduate School of Journalism, and bequeathing another half-million endowing the prizes— the first national awards for books, drama, music, and journalism.

Pulitzer, like Nobel, suffered a debilitating nervous disorder during the latter years of his life. Never diagnosed, the illness left him nearly blind and hypersensitive to noise. As his condition worsened, so did his feelings of guilt, and by the turn of the century, his morning *World* had abandoned the yellow journalism that had made him wealthy.

"Our Republic and its press will rise or fall together," the repentant publisher wrote soon after the beginning of the twentieth century. "An able, disinterested, public-spirited press, with trained intelligence to know the right and courage to do it, can preserve the public virtue without which popular government is a sham and a mockery. A cynical, mercenary, demagogic, corrupt press will produce in time a people as base as itself."

Those lofty words—carved in marble in the lobby of his journalism school—helped make Pulitzer a hero in newspaper history. But it should be noted that his *World* moved away from sensationalism only after it had ceased being profitable and after the paper began to feel the competition of a young upstart publisher named Adolph Ochs who had taken over an ailing journal called the *New York Times*. Ochs threw out the comics and gossip and began publishing an intelligent, ethical, serious-minded product. The *Times* soon began making inroads on Pulitzer's *World,* which Ochs derided as "freak journalism." It should also be noted that Pulitzer eschewed sensational journalism only in his flagship paper. His evening street edition, serving the lower classes, continued to peddle such banner headlines as LOVE AND CIGARETTES CRAZED HIM.

Establishing the Pulitzer Prizes turned out to be a clever, if not original, idea, but creating the journalism school proved to be brilliant.

Pulitzer's Graduate School of Journalism at Columbia became the nation's second such professional school, preceded only by the University of Missouri's. Part of the mystique of Pulitzer's school was that he made it part of the most prestigious university in New York, the city that was—and still is to lesser extent—the media capital of the nation. His school opened up a whole new field of academic endeavor, endearing Pulitzer forever to the journalism educators who were beholden to him. Thereafter, in their struggle to win academic respect and to overcome the newspaper industry's deep-seated anti-intellectualism, they would remember Joseph Pulitzer as "the father of modern journalism," as opposed to the sleazier and richly deserved "Citizen Kane" image that would cling forever to Hearst, his bitter rival.

Pulitzer's journalism school, and the prizes it would award every year, helped cleanse his historical image. For $2 million—about $26.5 million in 1990 dollars—he bought himself a form of everlasting respect.

This day's prize announcements will unleash a torrent of media attention. Pulitzer's name will appear in almost all of the nation's sixteen hundred daily newspapers, with a combined circulation of more than sixty million and read by at least one hundred twenty million people. The broadcast media will feel compelled to report the story. So will the news magazines, and *People,* and all the trade journals. So will many of the overseas news media of the Western world. And this year, so will *Izvestia.*

If Pulitzer were alive, he would be pleased. His prizes have rendered a level of global immortality exceeding anything imaginable to a man just after the turn of the century—even to a visionary such as he.

And if William Randolph Hearst were alive, he would only

be annoyed that he failed to think of the prizes first. Today, there are Hearst Foundation awards every year. The public seldom hears about them.

In the two publishers' long and acrimonious rivalry, the battle for posthumous respect turned out to be no contest.

Joseph Pulitzer won.

2

Three Finalists Await Their Fate

3 P.M.—Eastern Standard Time

WHILE REPORTERS BUZZ AT COLUMBIA, butterflies flutter in an apartment a few dozen blocks to the north, in Manhattan's Washington Heights district. These are figurative butterflies, of course, winging their way around the upper digestive tract of thirty-three-year-old Jim Dwyer. Any minute now, he knows, his name will be in the news. Today Columbia University reveals the Pulitzer Prize finalists—and those among them who are the actual prize winners.

Jim works for *New York Newsday*. For nearly four years, he has been writing a thrice-weekly column targeted at the 3.5 million people who ride the city's subways every day. *Newsday* editors think so highly of Jim's work that they've entered some of it—a collection of columns highlighted by an exposé of subway safety neglect—in the Pulitzer Prize competition.

And thirty-six days ago, behind closed doors at Columbia, Jim Dwyer was selected as a finalist for one of the news-reporting prizes. This selection is supposed to be a secret, but Jim knows about it. Word was leaked to him, almost a month ago, through Donald Forst, his editor. Forst had been quietly tipped off by one of the Pulitzer Prize Board members, David Laventhol, president of the Times Mirror Company, which owns *Newsday*.

In the labyrinthine, secretive, two-tier Pulitzer judging process leading to the announcements, eighty-six men and women served as "jurors" on screening committees that nominated slates of finalists for the various prizes. An additional sixteen men and women served as judges on the elite Pulitzer Prize Board that decided which of the finalists would get the awards. Board policy requires all 102 of these people involved in the judging to keep decisions confidential until the formal announcements on Pulitzer Prize Day. In practice, however, many of the judges—particularly in the journalism competition—surreptitiously leak word about the prizes to their news organizations. And some of the most generous sources of these leaks are the high-powered people at the top: board members such as Laventhol.

Which explains why Jim Dwyer knows he's a finalist. The question: Did he win?

In one sense, yes, he did, no matter what—even if he will be named only a runner-up. Becoming a finalist for a Pulitzer is no small achievement. Jim is one of 1,770 entrants in this year's journalism competition, and only forty-five have been named finalists for the fourteen newspaper prizes.

Jim has made it onto a select list, and he knows it. So he is understandably anxious as he peers into the monitor of his home computer. He has set it up in a rented room he uses as an office in the same Fort Washington Avenue building where he and his wife, Cathy, and their four-year-old daughter, Maura Jean, live in a modest, two-bedroom apartment. Jim has been working out of this home office for almost three months on a leave of absence from the paper. *Newsday* granted him the ninety-day leave so he could write a book about the subways under a contract with a New York publisher.

But Jim is not working on the book now as he taps the keyboard of his computer, linked by modem to the *New York Newsday* office in midtown Manhattan. He is scanning the

Associated Press wire and other news services, looking for bulletins on the Pulitzer Prizes. Even though it is 3 P.M.—the scheduled hour of the announcements—there is nothing about them on the wires, so far.

Jim imagines what winning the Pulitzer might mean to him. It certainly could be a well-timed boost for the subway book. Not to mention his newspaper career. The prize could elevate him into the ranks of New York's celebrity journalists. He might be the next Breslin.

As a boy growing up in New York in the late sixties and early seventies, Jim was a devoted reader of rival tabloid columnists Jimmy Breslin, writing then in the *Daily News*, and Pete Hamill, in the *Post*.

"I loved the way those guys wrote," Jim says. "Pete Hamill, especially, was writing prose poems every day, and I was very impressed with them. I knew that's what I wanted to do."

A combination of encouragement at home, prodding at Jesuit schools, and determination on his own part helped make the young dreamer's wish come true. Today Jim Dwyer is a co-worker of Breslin, now at *New York Newsday*, and an acquaintance of Hamill, now at *Esquire* magazine. And Jim has become a poet of sorts himself, writing lyrically about life on New York's subterranean trains. British journalist and author Bernard Levin, in a *Sunday Times of London* piece on New York, described Jim as "the reporter/philosopher/poet of the subways." His pieces are filled with humor, sensitivity, and compassion for society's less-privileged. Occasionally his columns rage against the power structure in a manner that one Pulitzer Prize judge described, with respect, as "cowboy journalism." A reader can almost visualize this columnist strapping on his six-shooters, saddling up, and riding out to bring the bureaucrats to justice.

Walking down the streets of his neighborhood, though, Jim looks more like a longshoreman than a cowboy. He's not a tall man, but he's sturdy with a broad face and easy smile, clear eyes, and rosy complexion. He has a dark beard, thinning hair, and a waistline gently suggesting a man who enjoys a beer along with his Monday night football.

The son of Irish-born immigrants—a school janitor and a nurse—Jim Dwyer has climbed a long way up the so-

cioeconomic ladder, from childhood on the cusp of Spanish
Harlem, to Columbia University, to one of the best jobs at 2
Park Avenue. His *Newsday* columns, always championing the
people near the bottom of that ladder, reveal a rising journalist
determined to remember his origins.

But Jim is not satisfied with his accomplishments. He feels
he has exhausted the subway beat. When he goes back to the
newspaper at the end of his leave, he'll take on a new role as a
general columnist. For a newspaper writer, he receives a
respectable salary, about $65,000 over the past year, but he
hopes to do better. Living in New York can be expensive. He
and Cathy want to have another child. They would like to buy a
larger apartment. They wish they could afford a secure place
for their Toyota, which they now park out on the street, hoping
it's still there when they go out to use it. Their neighborhood is
relatively safe, with automobile break-ins the most frequent
crime, but the area is still part of the 34th Precinct, the
homicide capital of New York. The windows on the east side of
their apartment look out at the slums of Harlem; eventually,
Jim would like to move.

A Pulitzer Prize, he thinks, might help that day come sooner.

Like most outstanding reporters, Jim has already won some
awards. His subway columns received Columbia University's
1988 Meyer Berger Award, given each year to recognize
distinguished reporting about New York. That's a notable
honor, but outside the newspaper industry few people have
heard of it.

Just as Americans are infatuated with glittering, big-name
prizes—Pulitzers, Oscars, Emmys, Grammys, and Tonys—the
nation is benumbed by all the rest of them. And no wonder. A
directory of awards published by Gale Research lists over
12,500 American awards—271 of them in journalism alone.
Some of them, such as Jim's Meyer Berger Award, enjoy
respect. And many of them—especially in journalism—are
junk, hopelessly tainted by special interests using prizes to
promote their products, services, causes, and political biases.
In days gone by, favorite examples included a tobacco-industry
cash prize for the "most outstanding" newspaper photograph
each month depicting someone smoking a cigar. In the 1990s, a

typical example is the annual $1,000 prize for "distinguished environmental reporting," offered by a chain-saw manufacturer. Ethical journalists neither seek nor accept such shoddy awards.

The Pulitzer is another matter. Although it has been rejected over the years by at least two writers—novelist Sinclair Lewis in 1926 and playwright William Saroyan in 1940—no journalist has ever turned down the prize.

And Jim Dwyer says, with a smile and twinkling eyes, he has no intention of being the first news reporter to reject it.

As Jim scrolls through the news wires on his computer, hoping to spot a bulletin on the prizes, he does not think about potential monetary and career-boosting rewards that a Pulitzer could bring. He's fantasizing about the people he would want to thank if he were to win. And he decides the first person he would acknowledge is a small-town New Jersey newspaper editor, Richard Vezza, who helped get him started in the business. Jim realizes this wish sounds a bit sappy for a supposedly tough New York newspaperman, but he isn't ashamed to reveal such private thoughts.

He admits he's a romantic and a sentimentalist.

Jim Dwyer does not fit any of today's newsroom molds—not that of the hard-bitten hack, the cynical hipster, the aloof yuppie, or the ambitious office politician. If you saw him on the subway in his denims and windbreaker, you might take him for a blue-collar worker, heading home from the docks or the factory. And then, when he pulls out his notebook and jots something down, a slight smile at the corners of his mouth, you might change your mind and decide he's a dreamy poet, scribbling down a thought that just came to mind.

In a way, you'd be right on both counts.

Noon—Pacific Standard Time

Far away in another Manhattan, three time zones to the west, sunshine burns away low morning clouds along the coast of Southern California. A gentle April breeze scents the air with fragrance of hibiscus and bougainvillea and star of jasmine, blooming in all the yards of the $500,000-and-up homes along Grandview Avenue in Manhattan Beach. The day is turning out to be stunningly gorgeous—perfect for tennis or wading in the Pacific Ocean, just four blocks away—but Claire Spiegel is indoors, watching television, anxiously flipping channels.

Tanned, trim, and athletic, this thirty-seven-year-old woman does not normally watch daytime TV. Or much TV at all. Today, she's riveted to it, looking for news. The networks are no help: nothing but soaps and game shows. So she clicks back to Cable News Network and leaves it there. Maybe CNN will have something.

Like Jim Dwyer on the opposite coast, Claire Spiegel is a finalist for a Pulitzer Prize in news reporting. And like Jim, she knows it. Word has been leaked to her, too. She was tipped off by Shelby Coffey, editor of the *Los Angeles Times,* where Claire works as a news reporter. And just like Jim Dwyer's editor at *Newsday,* Coffey received the confidential information from David Laventhol, the Pulitzer Prize Board member whose Times Mirror Company owns the *Los Angeles Times* as well as *Newsday.*

Claire is acutely aware that this is Pulitzer Prize Day, with the announcements of finalists and winners just moments away. And in still another quirky parallel to Jim Dwyer, Claire also is home from the newspaper on a leave of absence—a maternity leave, in her case.

The baby, Leslie, born four months ago, is with her nanny, Amy Caffee, in another part of the two-story house—a warmly elegant showplace designed for Claire and her lawyer husband, Brad Brian, by a local architect. By newspaper-reporter standards this is upscale living, from the vaulted ceilings and grand piano indoors to the lusciously laden orange trees in the subtropical garden out back, where Claire's older daughter, four-year-old Allison, is playing with a running garden hose.

Bright, precocious Allison comes to the doorway, seeking a little attention. She says she's coming inside. And she's bringing the running hose. "No, Honey!" Claire yells, trying to deal with this mini-crisis without leaving the CNN broadcast. But here comes Allison, along with the gushing water. So Mom leaps up and intercepts her, heading off a major mop-job on the hardwood floors. Claire takes one last hopeful look at the TV, then retreats outside with Allison to turn off the water.

That's been Claire's story in recent years—mastering the

classic juggling act of motherhood and career. Even with ample financial resources, it's been tough for Claire. She has juggled expertly—brilliantly, perhaps, considering the aura of happiness and success surrounding her home and the fact that she is minutes away from being named at least a runner-up for a Pulitzer Prize.

But Claire isn't entirely satisfied with her juggling prowess. And she can't help imagining how a Pulitzer Prize might help smooth things out. She's been working up her nerve to ask the newspaper for some favors: extending her maternity leave for the rest of the year, and then allowing her to return to her job on a three-day workweek. Big favors, indeed, requiring the kind of employee-relations flexibility that many newspapers, being among the most conservative businesses in America, are not known to cherish.

"I could get raped, so to speak, in terms of my job," she says. "I mean, they could say, 'Sure, we'll implement a three-day workweek for you, but we'll take away your medical [insurance], we'll change your beat, we'll make you work nights.' They could be nasty about implementing it."

Claire is particularly worried about keeping her news beat, health services, a recently created assignment at the paper. She loves it. Claire also has become impressively skilled at it. Like Jim Dwyer, Claire is an award-winning reporter. Among her honors are a *Los Angeles Times* Editorial Award for in-depth project reporting and a first-place Greater Los Angeles Press Club award for investigative reporting, both in 1985. Some of her more recent articles—a hard-hitting series exposing medical malpractice at a public hospital—have brought her to the brink of a Pulitzer Prize. Her beat is viewed as one of the plum jobs at the *Los Angeles Times,* and Claire, though born into privilege and affluence, had to work hard to deserve the assignment.

Like Jim Dwyer, Claire attended Joseph Pulitzer's journalism school at Columbia and learned news reporting on the streets of New York. Beyond that, however, the string of coincidences begins to fade. Born and raised in Berkeley, the daughter of a successful corporate lawyer and a well-educated homemaker, Claire lived a childhood as sheltered and WASPish as Jim's was unbridled and Catholic.

When Jim was a twelve-year-old being mugged on the subway, Claire, then fifteen, was being bused to an exclusive all-girls school. While he learned how to sink jump shots and avoid being attacked on the playground, Claire took tennis and ballet lessons. While Jim worked on his junior-high-school paper, already set on becoming a journalist, she was a high-school exchange student in Indonesia, thinking about becoming an anthropologist.

As an adult, Jim is as rough-hewn and earthy in his speech and mannerisms as she is genteel and circumspect. He, with his broad, careworn face and urban persona, could play an undercover cop on "Hill Street Blues"; she, with her crisp demeanor and light brown hair trimmed in a no-nonsense career-woman's style, could play an attorney on "L.A. Law."

Their career goals couldn't be less alike, either. While Jim admits he hopes to advance in the newspaper business and improve his family's standard of living, she remains content and hopes to preserve her current status by working out her conflicts between career and parenthood.

Somehow, though, these two very different people grew up with some shared values, reflected in their work that was entered in the Pulitzer competition. While Jim probed a subway-system breach of safety that put scores of lives in danger, Claire investigated a mismanaged trauma center that was endangering patients in L.A.'s Watts district. The reporting by both journalists reveals a gut-level distrust of the political establishment and a sincere affinity for people ill-served by it.

Those values have propelled both Jim and Claire down a long, twisting road to this moment on Pulitzer Prize Day: Waiting on the brink of The Big One, wondering what it might mean to their lives and careers. And, in Claire's case, juggling those thoughts with parental duty, trying to keep little Allison from coming through the door with that gushing garden hose.

1 P.M.—Mountain Standard Time

As Jim Dwyer searches the news wires on his home computer and Claire Spiegel watches for TV bulletins, Tamar Stieber lunches on gefilte fish and matzo in her tiny adobe apartment in Santa Fe, New Mexico. Outside, cirrus clouds make this a slightly gray day. It's windy and quite chilly; winter hangs around longer in this city at seven thousand feet in the Sangre de Cristo Mountains, still powdered with snow.

Tamar checks her watch. Thirty minutes remain before she has to start her reporting shift at the *Albuquerque Journal*'s Santa Fe bureau. She tries to relax, blissfully unaware that she's a finalist for a Pulitzer Prize and that the winners are about to be announced at Columbia University.

Her editor, Tim Coder, knows she was named a finalist in the secret judging thirty-six days ago. Word was leaked to him, just as it was to Jim's and Claire's editors. Coder, the *Albuquerque Journal*'s Santa Fe bureau chief, heard it from the paper's assistant managing editor, Rod Deckert, who heard it from his boss, assistant editor Kent Walz. Walz heard it from an editor at another newspaper a week before Pulitzer Prize Day while both were in Washington, D.C., attending a convention of the American Society of Newspaper Editors. Walz says the other editor, whom he declines to identify, was not involved in the judging but had heard the news from a third editor who *was* involved.

The *Albuquerque Journal* editors, however, have not passed on the leaked information to Tamar. Mercifully, they have spared her the emotional distraction that Jim and Claire have experienced for much of the past month, waiting for Pulitzer Prize Day.

Instead, Tamar's thoughts at this moment are on her recent brush with death on the freeway between Santa Fe and Albuquerque. The terrifying accident that demolished her car four days ago, on the eve of Passover, should have killed her.

"The Angel of Death passed me over, one day early," she tells co-workers. "Nobody could look at that car and believe I came back alive."

Never a religious person, Tamar has decided to observe Passover this year. So there's no leavened bread for lunch today, just gefilte fish and matzo, and the Jewish tradition gives her much-needed comfort. This has been a trying year.

Winning the Pulitzer could make life a little less trying for Tamar Stieber. Aside from the career-boosting power of the prize, the $3,000 in cash that goes with it would be welcome by itself. Tamar is broke. Her credit cards are maxed out. She's wallowing in $25,000 of personal debt—mostly academic loans—and she's having trouble digging her way out on her $484-a-week salary.

That's not even half of what Jim Dwyer and Claire Spiegel are making at their newspapers. But even though all three reporters are in their mid-thirties, Tamar is still a beginner. She is a late arrival to newspaper journalism, a career she began only recently after years of dead-end jobs, a divorce, off-and-on schooling, world travel, and a tumultuous childhood in New York.

Like Jim Dwyer, she is a native of the city, born in Brooklyn. And like his parents, hers were lower-middle-class immigrants, working ferociously during her childhood to raise the family's socioeconomic status to "middle-middle," as she puts it. Tamar's parents, though, weren't Irish Catholics like Jim's; hers were Eastern European Jews.

She describes herself as their "dilettante daughter" who dabbled at life for many years before applying herself and getting serious about a profession. This is only her second year at a daily newspaper. Moreover, her *Albuquerque Journal,* with a circulation of 118,000, is much smaller than Jim's *Newsday* (circulation 700,000) or Claire's *Los Angeles Times* (1,113,000). It's a general axiom that the smaller the paper, the lower the pay.

So Tamar is an entry-level reporter receiving beginner's wages at a paper not known to be among those most generous in compensation. And her economic status is reflected in her home, which she admits is extremely cramped. It reminds her of her college apartments, with books and record albums and papers stacked everywhere in an eight-foot-wide living room-kitchen, connected to a tiny bedroom where box springs rest on the floor without benefit of bed frame. But the place is "a steal at $325 a month," she says. Vacant apartments are hard to find in Santa Fe these days, and anything less than $600 is considered a bargain. After arriving in town, Tamar was forced to spend her first four months living in the homes of generous co-workers, sleeping in kids' beds and even on floors. Finding her own tiny apartment, just a few blocks from the newspaper office, was a major triumph for her, satisfying one of her two major goals. Her next one is clawing her way out of debt.

Winning the Pulitzer could give her a welcome nudge toward that end. The prize, however, would come as a much bigger payday for struggling writers and journalists such as Tamar Stieber if the competition had kept up with inflation over its eighty-year history. In 1911, Joseph Pulitzer set the news reporting prize at $1,000. In 1990 dollars, that is the equivalent of $13,290, according to the U.S. Bureau of Labor Statistics. Thus the prize isn't nearly the cash windfall that it was originally.

Meanwhile, the Nobel Prize, which inspired Pulitzer in the first place, has fared better over the decades. In 1901, the initial year of the Nobel Prizes, a winner received 150,800 Swedish kronor, which translated at the time into about $40,000 in U.S. dollars—a turn-of-the-century fortune equivalent to about $530,000 in 1990 dollars. Today, a Nobel winner receives about 4 million kronor, which roughly translates into $700,000.

Thus, from a strictly pecuniary point of view, receiving the Nobel Prize is like winning the lottery, while winning the Pulitzer Prize is more like receiving a modest but unexpected company bonus.

As Tamar Stieber nibbles on her lunch, occasionally checking on the time, money and prizes are the farthest things from her mind. She hasn't a clue that this is Pulitzer Prize Day. Five months ago, of course, she was aware that her editors had entered some of her work in the competition—stories exposing a link between a rare blood disorder and a common, over-the-counter dietary supplement called L-Tryptophan. And she felt extremely flattered her bosses would do this. Even though she's thirty-four years old, she knows she's still a neophyte, unlike Jim Dwyer and Claire Spiegel, who have been reporters for years. Tamar has never won a journalism award. Forgetting all about the Pulitzers is easy for her. She knows she has no chance against the more experienced journeymen who typically win.

Besides, she thinks, good things like that do not happen to Tamar Stieber. They happen to other people.

3

Unasked Questions

AT 3:01 P.M. NEW YORK TIME, one minute after the
Pulitzer Prizes were supposed to have been announced, two husky Columbia University students are still
trudging across the campus yard, lugging cardboard boxes
filled with well over one hundred pounds of elaborately
prepared press kits.

The two young men are accompanied on foot by Nancy
Carmody, office manager for the university's public information department. She supervised the printing and assembling
of the bulky press kits over the past twenty-four hours amid
tight security in a production room in the Low Memorial
Library building. Carmody is responsible for guarding the
confidentiality of the list of finalists and winners, and she
approaches the task with military precision and efficiency.
Each year she drills her office workers on the need for strict
secrecy in handling the Pulitzer Prize material. No
unauthorized people are allowed in the production room; no
material—not even waste paper—may be removed from the

room before the announcements are delivered to the journalism building. And only under her watchful eye are these two students allowed to transport her important cargo.

Each of the seventy-five press kits weighs about 1.5 pounds and contains forty-two pages of typed information, including the identities of all forty-five individual finalists for the 1990 Pulitzer Prizes. On one of those pages—announcing the prize for specialized news reporting—the three 1990 finalists are identified as Jim Dwyer, Claire Spiegel, and Tamar Stieber. And one of the trio is identified as the Pulitzer winner; the other two are runners-up.

Also included in each press kit are black-and-white glossy photographs of either Jim, Claire, or Tamar, along with pictures of the other twenty-three finalists who won the prize. Back in February, every entry in the competition had to be accompanied by a photo, and a brief written biography, so the material could be provided instantly to the news media on this announcement day.

As Carmody and her two helpers hurry toward the journalism building, Robert Christopher, the prize administrator, surveys the crowd of restless reporters in the World Room. He checks his watch. It is 3:02 P.M. Five minutes ago he came downstairs from his office, looking distinguished in a sharply tailored gray business suit. Now he strides to the head of the room, stopping just inches from the bust of Joseph Pulitzer, and raps on a wooden table.

The babbling continues. He raps again.

This time the room goes quiet. All eyes are on Christopher, who begins to speak.

"In just a few minutes, staff members of the university's public information office will arrive with press kits announcing the 1990 winners of the Pulitzer Prizes."

He explains that there is a limited number of the kits, and they will be distributed first to "working journalists." Then, if there are any left, other people may help themselves. And that's it, for now. The room begins buzzing again.

Bud Kliment, Christopher's assistant, notices a flourish that has been overlooked. He steps up to an electrical panel near the room's doorway and throws one of the switches. It illuminates a system of fluorescent lights behind an impressive showpiece at the head of the room—a big stained-glass image of the Statue of Liberty, flanked by two hemispheric views of the world. The colorful display was moved to the journalism building when Joseph Pulitzer's World Building on Park Row was torn down.

Reinstalling the stained glass in the World Room was a fitting touch, for the Goddess of Liberty was Pulitzer's most famous circulation-building gimmick—perhaps the grandest newspaper promotion of all time. Few people today, however, are aware that the nation's most celebrated symbol of freedom might never have reached U.S. shores if it had not been for Pulitzer. In 1884, the huge, unassembled statue—France's gift to the United States—was corroding in crates in Paris while private U.S. organizations struggled unsuccessfully in a fund drive to pay for shipping the colossus and erecting it in New York Harbor. Not many Americans were enthusiastic about the statue. They couldn't visualize its possibilities. But Pulitzer could, and he brilliantly seized the opportunity. Instead of just underwriting the statue's delivery, which he could have accomplished with the stroke of his pen, he took over the fund drive. Using the power and attention of his newspaper, he fanned patriotic passions and raised the needed money from his readers, in thousands of contributions ranging from a nickel to $250.

Pulitzer's enormously successful campaign, marked by vigorous self-advertisement and soaring circulation figures for his *World,* climaxed in the dedication of the Statue of Liberty in 1886—very much a *World* promotional event. Thereafter, Pulitzer never let his readers forget the paper's crucial role in bringing the Goddess to America. He reminded them of it every day with a likeness of the statue, flanked by two faces of the globe, on the newspaper's front-page nameplate. And if that wasn't enough, he had the stained-glass display installed in his newspaper building for everyone to see and admire.

After Kliment flips the fluorescent lights on, several of the assembled reporters turn to gaze at the display. One of them, a woman who obviously knows the connection between the statue and the late publisher, explains it to the others. Unfortunately, her knowledge does not extend to pronunciation of the man's name. She calls him *PEW-lit-sir.*

How could anyone fault her, though? The mangling of *PULL-it-sir* has become part of the nation's pop vernacular, and anyone questioning that assertion need look no farther than the motion picture *Batman*. The box-office record-breaker, seen by more people worldwide in 1989 than any other film, features an ambitious free-lance photographer, Vickie Vale, who tries to talk a Gotham newspaper reporter into teaming up with her and going after an exposé on the batlike crime-fighter. The screenplay by Sam Hamm and Warren Skaaren includes the following line, spoken somewhat lustily to the skeptical reporter:

VICKIE VALE
My pictures, your words—Pulitzer Prize material!

On screen, when the line is uttered by actress Kim Basinger, it comes out "*PEW-lit-sir* Prize." And she repeats the error once more before the comic-book movie ends.

Abruptly, at 3:08 P.M., heads start turning in the World Room as Nancy Carmody marches through the doorway, trailed by her two perspiring volunteers with their heavy boxes.

Robert Christopher raps the table again. Instantly, the room goes quiet. He announces that telephones are available for reporters' use throughout the building, and he says he will remain in the World Room to answer questions. Then, with no further fanfare, he nods at Carmody, who starts passing out the press kits. For a moment, the scene turns chaotic. Reporters mob the woman and her two helpers, then dash for the phones. Other reporters—those with more leisurely deadlines or less-anxious editors—wait more patiently, then take their press kits to chairs or quiet corners of the room to examine them.

Carmody's boss, Fred Knubel, Columbia's public relations director, observes the activity with a satisfied look. Yes, the announcements came off a few minutes behind schedule, and there was something slightly tacky about handing out the press kits from cardboard boxes. Knubel is an affable former newspaperman who has helped with the Pulitzer Prize announcements for twenty-five years. He says the university is pleased by the absence of pomp and ceremony.

"I suppose you might say we're a little proud of it," he declares. "The prizes don't need to be boosted that way."

Across campus, back at Knubel's PR headquarters in the Low Memorial Library building, his staff busily transmits the lists of winners by FAX machine to the Associated Press and United Press International.

And eighty blocks south on Broadway, at Times Square, a much more traditional form of electronic communication is being used to notify all the prize winners. Western Union is sending them telegrams. Claudia Stone, the Pulitzer Prize office assistant, went to Times Square during the noon hour with a neatly typed stack of messages to be released at precisely 3 P.M. That's the system the Pulitzer Prize administration has been using for decades, but today Stone ran into an unexpected snag.

"For some reason," she says, "the Western Union office wouldn't accept them [her typed messages]. All they accept there now is money from people who want to wire it somewhere. They gave me a phone number and said I had to *call* in the information. I protested because we've always prepared the announcements ourselves and hand-carried them to Times Square. That way, we know if any mistakes are made, they're Western Union's mistakes, not ours. But I was told we can't do it that way anymore."

Exasperated, Stone returned to the university, dialed the designated phone number and spent most of an hour laboriously dictating the prize announcements to a Western Union operator.

Now, shortly after three o'clock, Western Union is transmitting the telegrams to almost every corner of the country, where couriers have begun delivering them to the newsrooms, offices, or homes of the winners. And Stone's worst fears are coming true: The Western Union operator did make a mistake while taking all those dictated messages by telephone. At this moment, Charles Simic, winner of the prize for poetry, is being sent a telegram that formally congratulates him on winning the 1990 Pulitzer Prize for biography.

After a few minutes, reporters start coming up to Christopher with questions. Many of them reveal a startling lack of preparation.

"How, exactly, does the judging work?" asks one young reporter who plainly did no homework. Christopher replies with admirable patience, explaining how the nominating juries met at Columbia in March—in this very room—and picked slates of finalists for the journalism prizes. And he outlines how the arts and letters nominating juries deliberated by telephone. He adds that the Pulitzer Prize Board convened in April—just three days ago, again in this room—and chose the winners from among the various slates of finalists, called "nominees."

It's a complex, arcane system, and the young reporter's eyes glaze over during the long-winded explanation. Christopher, too, despite his reservoir of patience, can't completely hide his boredom with the task. He has had to explain this thing more times than he would care to admit.

Another ill-informed reporter has a question: "Altogether, how many gold medals were given out?" Again, Christopher patiently explains there is only one gold medal each year, given to a newspaper rather than to an individual, for meritorious public service. Winners in all the other prize categories receive $3,000. The 1990 gold medal, he says, is shared by the *Philadelphia Inquirer*, for an investigation of the American blood industry, and by a little North Carolina paper, the *Washington Daily News*, for revealing that the city of Washington, North Carolina, had failed to disclose contamination of the water supply with high levels of carcinogens over an eight-year period.

Another reporter speaks up: "Did the Pulitzer Prize Board overrule any of the nominating juries this year?"

Recognition glints in Christopher's eyes. Now here is a question from a reporter who *did* do her homework. She is clearly aware that almost every year the board throws out a slate of finalists nominated by one or more of its juries and gives the prize to someone else. That understandably frustrates the jury members, who sometimes complain loudly and pub-licly, creating a media stir that brings negative attention to the prizes. Christopher essentially side steps the question by replying that it's inaccurate to say that the board "overrules" a jury. There was "some juggling of nominations in a couple of the journalism categories" this year, but no juries were overruled, he says.

A second well-informed question is posed: "Did the board refuse to give a prize in any category this time?"

"No," replies Christopher, who seems to have anticipated this question, apparently an annual one. He directs the reporter to the press kit, which includes a full page listing all the years and the categories in which the board decided to make no award. The list reveals that the last such year was 1986, when the board declined to give a drama prize. Nonawards like that invariably generate negative publicity. But there will be none of that this year, and Christopher's professional demeanor is betrayed by a look of relief.

"Several prizes this year seem to involve disasters, natural and man-caused," another reporter observes. "Would you agree this was a common theme in the 1990 Pulitzers?"

"Yes, of course," Christopher replies. He notes that many of the 1,770 journalism entries this year resulted from catastrophes such as the California earthquake, Hurricane Hugo, and the *Exxon Valdez* oil spill. There also was an environmental theme among the entries this year, as exemplified by the North Carolina paper's gold-medal winner on contaminated drinking water.

Christopher smiles. All of the reporters' questions are like this—strictly softball. He relaxes, appearing to enjoy his role. This makes it an unusual year; Christopher almost always finds himself in the middle of a squall over at least one of the prizes each April. Some years are more like a typhoon.

Such was 1988, when three different journalism prizes attracted withering criticism. The *National Journal* and *Harper's* magazine demanded that a reporting prize to Tim Weiner of the *Philadelphia Inquirer* be withdrawn because part of Weiner's series on the Pentagon's "black budget" was based on information and graphics published earlier in the two magazines. Meanwhile, conservative Reed Irvine of Accuracy in Media, a press watchdog group, demanded that *Washington Post* television writer Tom Shales's prize be withdrawn because of alleged unethical relationships with his sources. And several press critics, including the *Washington Journalism Reviews,* lambasted the awarding of a Pulitzer to the *Lawrence* (Mass.) *Eagle-Tribune* for what the magazine branded a "one-sided, sloppily reported" series on Willie Horton and prison furloughs.

The Pulitzer Prize Board, with Christopher acting as front man, rejected the demands for stripping two of the controversial prizes and ignored the criticism of the third one.

The 1990s appear to be getting off to a mellower start, as the reporters continue serving up gentle lobs to Christopher.

"It looks like a lot of the winners were from the West," a reporter says, flipping through his press kit. "Is that right?"

"Yes," Christopher responds with a smile. He seems pleased that somebody asked this question. "Half of this year's journalism prizes went to newspapers in the Western states. I think that's a first."

Several reporters jot down that quote. One who doesn't, however, is Alexander Shalnev, the correspondent for *Izvestia.* He simply observes, wearing a look of keen interest. Shalnev is particularly curious about American news coverage of the past year's upheaval in the Communist world and whether any Pulitzer Prizes will flow from it. Another detached observer steps beside him and asks him what he thinks of all this.

"The Pulitzer Prizes?" Shalnev replies, pronouncing it *PEW-lit-sir.* "I think it's an orgy of self-congratulation."

That may be a harsh judgment by the Soviet reporter, but his words carry a glimmer of truth. Rarely does a newspaper spare a drop of ink going beyond such superficial reporting and raising questions about the administration of the Pulitzer Prizes. It seems likely that establishment journalists simply have a blind spot where the prizes are concerned.

One notable exception is David Shaw, media reporter for the *Los Angeles Times.* Shaw, who is perhaps the industry's most respected newspaper-employed press critic, took a hard-nosed look at the Pulitzer Prizes in a lengthy series published by his paper in 1980. His findings, updated and condensed into a chapter in his 1985 book *Press Watch,* included statistical verification of a longstanding complaint: an Eastern bias pervades the prizes.

"It's a self-perpetuating cycle," Shaw wrote. "Predominantly

Eastern board members pick predominantly Eastern jurors, who send predominantly Eastern prize-nominations back to the predominantly Eastern board, which picks predominantly Eastern prize-winners."

Thus, there is genuine significance in Robert Christopher's remark that in 1990, for the first time, half of the journalism winners were from Western states.

In a more positive finding, Shaw concluded that the prize board's legendary reputation for logrolling and other political machinations may have been accurate a generation ago but not any longer. He also found that small newspapers fare better in the competition than is widely perceived, that some of the board's decisions are "remarkably quick and casual," and that the board is dominated by "elder statesmen of the journalism establishment"—primarily change-resistant white males with an average age of fifty-six.

Shaw broke considerable new ground with his reporting on the prizes. He couldn't have known it at the time, but his most important revelation was the fact that the board had over-turned at least one jury recommendation every year. He discovered not one year had passed when that had not hap-pened. Pulitzer Board members undoubtedly saw that refer-ence in Shaw's 1985 book. Since then, there have been two years in which the board has stuck faithfully to all of the jury selections. It is easy to believe that Shaw's reporting brought about this enhancement in board humility.

Even the venerable Shaw is not immune to the allure of these prizes. He admits he was delighted in 1989 to discover he was a Pulitzer finalist and then disappointed when he failed to win—and then delighted all over again in 1991 when he finally received the prize for criticism.

Meanwhile, questions remain that thoughtful reporters such as Shaw could be asking about the Pulitzer Prizes. For example, aren't the Pulitzer Board members somewhat haphazard in handling their personal conflicts? Members recuse themselves from deliberations in which their own newspapers are being considered for prizes. So why don't they similarly recuse themselves when their direct competitors are being consid-ered? And how can a board member justify voting prizes for books bearing the imprint of the member's own publisher?

Doesn't that amount to doing a grand favor for a company with whom the board member has a financial relationship?

Some questions mix ethics with finances: Who bankrolls the competition, now that its costs have ballooned far beyond the revenue from Joseph Pulitzer's endowment? Why does the prize board accept anonymous corporate contributions? Should journalists accept cash awards from sources that are kept, in part, a closely guarded secret?

How well has Joseph Pulitzer's money been managed? Why has the true cash value of his prize declined over the decades?

Other questions arise from strained credulity: How does a brilliant journalist such as I. F. Stone or a gifted composer such as Leonard Bernstein die without ever winning a Pulitzer? How hard do Pulitzer Prize Board members really work at the task? Do these tremendously busy executives, all with high-pressure careers, honestly read all fifteen books that are nominated as finalists each year? Do they really listen to all of the lengthy tape recordings nominated for the music prize? And what makes this board—dominated by journalists who have never composed music or published a poem or written a play—qualified to make such awards in arts and letters?

Why does the board insist on doing all its deliberating behind closed doors, with no observers allowed and no formal record of how members vote?

Isn't such secrecy inappropriate for a profession dedicated to getting at the truth and reporting it—not just in government but in business, education, science, medicine, the arts, and every other facet of society, both public and private?

Doesn't the clandestine nature of the contest debase the efforts of journalists who often must battle heroically against such secrecy to report their prize-winning stories?

And what about the desirability of even having such prizes in journalism and literature? Isn't there far too much emphasis on them? Are they truly a wholesome thing, or do they introduce a corrupting influence? Maybe novelist Sinclair Lewis, who rejected a Pulitzer for *Arrowsmith* in 1926, was tiptoeing around the edges of truth when he wrote that "all prizes, like all titles, are dangerous."

On Pulitzer Prize Day in the World Room at Columbia University, no reporters are raising these issues. Such questions may not even occur to them or to the editors who assigned them to cover this event. Sadly, their blind spot—like the prize board's secrecy—subtly mocks and demeans the accomplishments of people such as Jim Dwyer, Claire Spiegel, and Tamar Stieber. Anyone who traces the paths of these reporters' work from the first germ of an idea all the way to national recognition on this day in New York can come away with answers to many of the unasked questions. And the quest leads to an unmistakable conclusion: Just as the Pulitzer honors these journalists, they in turn ennoble the prize.

4

Jim Dwyer:
Don't Take the A Train

AUGUST CAN BE HOT in Manhattan—blistering,
sometimes, on the street.

Below ground, in the subways, where the tunnels might be
expected to offer cool, cavern-like relief, the air can get even
hotter from the exhaust of hundreds of air-conditioned train
cars. Giant fans, capable of gusting fifty thousand cubic feet of
air per minute, are installed at strategic locations to ventilate
the tunnels. But the fans' control mechanisms are electronically
complicated and frequently break down; a full 25 percent of all
New York subway ventilation fans have been known to be out of
order at the same time. Sometimes, entering a subway can feel
like stepping into an oven.

That was the case on August 1, 1987, a stifling afternoon
when northbound and southbound A trains were sharing part
of the same track because of construction at Chambers Street.
The big exhaust fans were doing their usual unreliable job, and
the air conditioning was not working in the Chambers Street
train tower. Ashton Clarke, the tower operator, later estimated

that the temperature in his booth must have been about one hundred degrees when he accidentally sent two A trains—crowded with commuters, tourists, and shoppers—streaking toward each other on a head-on collision course.

The subterranean carnage that loomed was the kind of disaster that would shock the nation—not just because of the terrible loss of life, but because New York's A train is legendary. Duke Ellington, the jazz great, gave the subway route immortality through the swing classic, "Take the A Train." Bluesman Billy Strayhorn composed the piece in the thirties as an ode to the subway, which at that time was an express train to Harlem. But it was Ellington who made the composition famous—along with the A train—when his band recorded it in Hollywood in 1941. "Take the A Train" became Ellington's trademark and perennial theme, and the tune's namesake became a permanent fixture in the American consciousness.

Beginning its thirty-five-mile journey at Far Rockaway on a Queens peninsula, the A train travels north across Jamaica Bay, past JFK Airport, and through Howard Beach, then veers east and goes all the way through Brooklyn before going under the East River and coming out in the financial district of downtown Manhattan. Then it turns north again at the World Trade Center and passes Greenwich Village, Chelsea, Columbus Circle, Central Park, Columbia University, and Harlem before reaching the end of the line in Washington Heights, Jim Dwyer's neighborhood.

Every day, Jim takes the A train to and from the offices of *New York Newsday* in midtown Manhattan. His wife Cathy rides it, too, to her part-time job at an advertising agency, where she develops computer software for the company and its clients. Often, the couple take the A train together when they go out, sometimes with four-year-old Maura tagging along.

The famous subway is so much an everyday part of the Dwyer family's life that Jim was stunned when he learned what happened shortly before 2 P.M. on that sweltering August day in 1987. The pair of four-hundred-ton A trains, placed accidentally on a collision course, screeched to a stop less than two hundred feet apart. Catastrophe was averted only because a motorman on one of the trains saw a safety light turn red. He stopped and radioed frantically as he stared into the approaching headlights of the other squealing, braking train.

Miraculously, no one was hurt. But Jim had no trouble personalizing the near-disaster. It would have killed and maimed scores of passengers. He could have been one of them. So could his wife and daughter. How, he asked himself, could something so unthinkable come so close to happening?

The Metropolitan Transit Authority quickly fixed the blame on human error. Ashton Clarke, the tower operator, was held at fault. Urine testing cleared him of any alcohol or drug involvement, but he was suspended for "inattention to duty."

None of this was reported right away by the New York media. Jim, in fact, didn't learn about it until the story was old news, more than a week after the near-tragedy had occurred. He discovered it only because he had begun changing his approach to his column.

"In the early going," he explains, "my job as the subway columnist didn't involve hard news. I was to be kind of an impression reporter. I saw the job, at first, as an opportunity to exercise my writing muscles, rather than my reporting muscles. Since I had gotten into journalism I'd been doing a lot of very detailed investigative reporting, to which I found I was naturally bent, but in doing that I had kind of choked off a part of my brain—the part that would sit in and eavesdrop on conversations on subway trains and write them up into nice stories. And that was what the subway column was for me at first."

But riding the subways, hours on end, in his columnist role, he had become intrigued by the bungling of the bureaucrats who ran the Transit Authority. And he had started writing about it.

He wrote, for example, about what he described as the Transit Authority's mean-spirited decision to close, rather than repair, a subway station that robbers had torched during a holdup in a South Bronx neighborhood. Jim's columns reported that the closure decision was based on grossly inflated estimates for repairing the station. And he pointed out that the poor neighborhood, once forgotten, was making a comeback that would be crippled by the Transit Authority's decision.

Under pressure from Jim and his newspaper, transit officials met with Bronx borough leaders and worked out a deal to save the station.

On another occasion he revealed that Robert Kiley, head of the Metropolitan Transit Authority, was being chauffeured daily between home and office, at public expense, while seeking a raise in his $150,000 salary. (Jim's column suggested that Kiley skip the raise and start catching the Lexington subway, only two blocks from the official's home.)

Another column by Jim exposed a phony story put out by Transit Authority officials after thousands of passengers were trapped for several hours in a stalled train on one of the hottest days of the summer. The Transit Authority said the train locked up because a rider pulled an emergency cord. Jim reported what really happened—an electrical component had exploded under the train—and forced officials to admit the truth.

In investigating such stories, Jim had begun examining the system's weekly reports.

He says, "I'd discovered that the bureaucracy generated 100 to 150 pages a week on trains that go bad, accidents and near accidents, breaches of rules, everything from a door being stuck to a canary being loose in a car. I'd plugged into people who would supply all these documents to me once a week, and I would sit down and review them."

In mid-August of 1987, while scanning a document called a Train Trouble Control Report, Jim discovered the near-collision of the A trains. The fact of the accident disturbed him, of course, and so did fixing the blame.

"Inattention to duty." That official explanation troubled Jim. It sounded lame and incomplete to him. It set off that little alarm bell that every good investigative reporter has buried somewhere deep inside. He decided to look into the incident.

When he approached Transit Authority officials, they stuck with the "inattention to duty" conclusion. Transit Authority president David Gunn insisted to Jim that the near-disaster was entirely the fault of the tower operator, whose job involves pushing buttons to move track switches. In a later column, Jim would quote Gunn's explanation:

"The number of moves is very repetitive. You got uptown,

downtown. Uptown, downtown. It can get boring, is what I'm telling you. I think that's what the word 'inattention' meant."

But Jim wasn't satisfied with that explanation. He decided to talk to the suspended tower operator, Ashton Clarke.

"I had a hell of a time finding him," Jim recalls. "I couldn't get my hands on his phone number, but I tracked down his address in the Bronx. I went to this weird apartment house. Nobody was home at his address. The neighbors were kind of buggy; they didn't want to help me. All I could do was leave my card under his door."

Eventually, Clarke called Jim at *Newsday*. But Clarke, a veteran of two decades with the Transit Authority, didn't want to talk about the matter. He was defensive "and felt a little ambushed by my questions," Jim says. "But he was mad that he got suspended, and that was my way in—sympathy for his situation, which I genuinely felt."

And Clarke helped steer the columnist to a different explanation for the near-collision: fatigue. Clarke had been drowsy that day in the enervating heat of the subway tower, working the second leg of a double shift. Jim later wrote about it in a *Newsday* column:

> Shortly before 2 P.M., in his 14th hour of work, Clarke received a message from another tower: Instead of the alternating pattern they had used all day (because of the construction), they would now send two trains uptown.
>
> Uptown, downtown, uptown would be changed to:
> Uptown, uptown.
> It didn't register with Clarke.
> Instead, he followed the routine of the previous 14 hours: He brought a downtown train onto the track approaching the station—while an uptown train already was there.
> Clarke had put the two trains on a head-on collision course...

In his interview with the suspended tower operator, Jim discovered Clarke's fatigue wasn't simply a result of his working a double shift. The man was on his twelfth straight day of work. And each of those twelve days had been a double shift.

Jim was astounded. Ashton Clarke wasn't just tired when he failed to switch the trains to "uptown, uptown." The man was punch-drunk with fatigue—dangerously so. Not a word about fatigue had appeared in the accident report.

Jim could not have known it at the moment, but his discovery put him on his own collision course, like a four-hundred-ton subway train, head-on against the power structure behind the biggest mass-transit bureaucracy in the world. Also unbeknownst to him, the revelation put him on the path to being nominated for a Pulitzer Prize.

* * *

"Jim Dwyer grew up riding the New York subways, standing in the front cars of trains, watching the headlights dance on the walls of the darkened tunnels, listening to the steel wheels screech against the rails…"

So stated *Newsday* editor Anthony Marro in a letter accompanying the formal entry of Jim's work in the 1990 Pulitzer Prize competition. Marro, however, did not write the colorful letter. Like so many such letters submitted to the prize judges, written in persuasive language and signed by top executives, this one was actually written by an underling, Tom Curran, *Newsday's* investigative projects editor. Lower-echelon people such as Curran are typically asked to ghostwrite these letters because the CEOs are, euphemistically, "too busy." The real reason, however, as nearly everyone in the newsroom knows, is that many staff members can write better than the man or woman at the top. And the Pulitzer Prize entry letters, aimed at catching the attention of the judges, are considered too important to receive anything except the paper's best shot.

But Marro's letter, written by Curran, was totally honest in its content about *Newsday's* Pulitzer Prize candidate. Jim Dwyer did indeed grow up riding the New York subways. He was born in Manhattan and lived his entire childhood in a working-class neighborhood on the Upper East Side. His parents, Phil Dwyer and Mary Molloy, immigrated separately from Ireland—he from Kenmare Bay, County Kerry, she from Ower, County Galway— shortly after World War II and were married in New York after meeting at an Irish dance hall. They rented a third-floor walkup apartment, where they still live today, and began having babies—four of them, all boys. Jim was the second, born in 1957.

For Jim and his brothers, 95th Street was their playground. "We'd play out there 'til eleven at night—football, stickball, punchball, stoopball—all the street games," he says. The subway was their means of freedom, their equivalent of the suburban youngster's bicycle. The brothers rode the trains everywhere, often alone, and rarely with any problems. New York City and its subways felt safer in the sixties. Jim was mugged only once on the trains, in 1969. While he was heading home from "Cap Day" at Yankee Stadium, a gang of older boys stripped twelve-year-old Jim of his new Yankee cap and his sunglasses. He was not a passive victim, however. "They did not get my mitt, which I had carried to the game hoping to catch fly balls," he says.

Many years later, Bernard Levin, the British writer who labeled Jim "the poet of the subways," changed some of the facts of that boyhood incident. He told Jim his British readers wouldn't understand Yankee "Cap Day," so he wrote that the gang of toughs had taken Jim's "fishing rod." That bit of journalistic license gave Jim a good laugh. But he was sorry he had mentioned the ball-cap incident. "It was no big deal," he says. "I wasn't hurt. Much worse has happened to far more vulnerable people than me."

Some boys who grew up with Jim Dwyer in their urban setting turned out troubled, but not the young Dwyers. "We, my brothers and I, were a little better off than some of the kids—probably because we were white, basically, and most of the others were not."

The Dwyer brothers had a few other things going for them, though. Foremost was a pair of extremely hard-working parents who realized the importance of education. They sent their sons to demanding Catholic institutions, "schools for smart poor kids," as Jim puts it.

"Our junior high was called Monsignor Kelly School. It was a place where everybody was encouraged to write, and write a lot."

Jim's early writing was influenced by what he read at home, including daily newspapers. The publications his parents brought into the home did not include the sophisticated *New*

York Times. They bought the tabloids, the working people's papers: the *Post* and especially the rival *Daily News.*

"We used to go get the early *Daily News,*" Jim recalls. "It was a ritual in our neighborhood, waiting for the paper to come up."

The Dwyer family looked forward to the paper strictly for its news and sports content. Among their neighbors, though, the evening anticipation had more to do with gambling. The *Daily News's* 7 P.M. bulldog edition contained the parimutuel results at the race tracks, the basis of the illegal numbers games. That helps explain why the paper sold four million copies a day back then, before the era of legalized, state-operated lotteries.

Reading the tabloids, young Jim was exposed to the breezy newspaper prose of Breslin and Hamill, and he became enchanted with idealistic notions about the so-called fourth estate.

"It seemed to me that journalism was doing good things for the world," he says. "Since then I've been disabused of that a little bit, but I liked it. I got a kick out of it."

Jim later was active on the student paper at Jesuit-operated Loyola High School. There, he got his first intoxicating taste of press freedom.

"That high school paper was a real First Amendment monument, in a way," he recalls. "It never went to a printer. It went straight onto a mimeograph machine. A friend and I would type onto the stencils that day and then go right up to the mimeograph machines with any damn thing we wanted to put into the paper."

Somehow, the Jesuits tolerated this behavior. They evidently saw something hopeful and promising in the stocky young Irish-American who took so much delight in putting out the paper, and they did not want to spoil his enthusiasm.

Talent and financial need combined to bring Jim a full four-year scholarship to Fordham University. There, he also worked on the school paper, the *Ram,* an experience that showed him the flip side of press freedom. He and fellow staffers offended the college administration one too many times, and Fordham officials shut down the *Ram.*

"So some of us got a few hundred bucks together and went down to this Commie type-shop, a typesetting collective, in lower Manhattan and hired out their machines," Jim recalls. "Since we could no longer put out the *Ram,* we put out an alternative paper, the *Lamb*. There wasn't a thing the school could do about us. We had a lot of fun."

By the time he graduated from Fordham, Jim had begun to think seriously about newspapering. While his equally motivated brothers went off to pursue careers in law and engineering, Jim enrolled in Joseph Pulitzer's Graduate School of Journalism at Columbia University.

"It was after I got to Columbia and started wandering around New York writing stories for the school that I realized that I'd really found what I wanted to do," Jim says. "I remember many times walking back from being out on a story for Columbia and breaking into a smile. I'd feel this silly grin on my face.

"If you watch Irish step dancers, essentially doing the same move thousands of times, you'll see their feet finally taking over. And after they've found the step, clomping away, thousands of steps a minute, they all of a sudden break into these silly smiles. And that was how I felt back then at Columbia, that I had found the step. I was doing what I liked to do. And I still feel that way.

"Sometimes I'll be riding around on the subway, and I'll have the makings of a good column in my notebook in my pocket. It makes me smile; it makes me happy."

His remark reveals just how fortunate the newspaper industry is in luring such talented beginners into the business. The Jim Dwyers of America don't go into journalism for the money. His initial job, directly out of Columbia, paid him $147.50 a week. That was across the river at the *Dispatch* of Hudson County, New Jersey, where Jim began his career on June 16, 1980.

Richard Vezza, publisher of the money-strapped little daily, remembers Jim warmly.

"He was sort of an editor's dream, tenacious and single-minded about his career and journalism. He had a good education, he wanted to learn and he was willing to work hard, to throw himself into it one hundred percent. Right from the beginning, you could see that he was going to be a topnotch reporter and writer."

Jim and the seven other low-paid reporters working for Vezza unleashed some astonishing investigative reporting. In a two-year period, the paper's digging brought down two mayors, the chief of police, the head of the board of education, and the director of the housing authority.

"It was a slaughter," Jim recalls. "And it was all the result of investigative reporting done by this little paper in this crooked little town."

Vezza credits young Jim Dwyer with being the moving force behind the newspaper's investigatory success.

"Jim, for example, got tipped off once that the county vocational school was buying chemicals, floor wax, rock salt, snow shovels, and so forth from a company that was owned by a local councilman. It looked like a set-up deal, but we were afraid that if we went there and started looking at the records one at a time, they'd clean the files out. So we took every reporter on the staff and sent them down there on a Monday morning. And Jim organized them and showed them what to look for and what notes to make and what company names to look for.

"And sure enough, they found there was a scheme going. The school had about three or four phony companies set up that were bidding against this local company, which was always winning and selling things to them for absolutely outrageous prices. At one point we figured out they were selling fifty-five-gallon drums of ammonia to them for twice as much as you'd pay if you went down to your local A&P and bought it by the pint bottle. And as a result, some of them [local officials] got indicted and sent to jail.

"Jim worked on a number of those kinds of stories that uncovered a lot of things."

Jim idolized Vezza for having the courage to take on the town's establishment.

"You know, Rich would walk down the street and everybody knew him and hollered and hooted at him," Jim recalls. "And he just walked along and kept his head up. It used to be a very corrupt paper, in fact. It used to take money from the politicians, and Rich changed that. He basically staged a coup and threw out all the rascals at the paper first, and then he started throwing the rascals out of government. He was terrific."

Two years after Jim began that first job, Vezza took over the *Daily Journal* in Elizabeth, New Jersey, and Jim followed him.

As much as he liked working for Vezza, though, Jim could take only six months of "this polluted, grimy, unbelievably foul little town in the heart of the chemical stink zone of northern New Jersey." So he left to join the *Record* of Hackensack, New Jersey, and toiled there for a year and a half before the first significant break of his career came along. That flowed from a Times Mirror decision that *Newsday* of Long Island, New York, needed to grow. Long Island is on New York's coast, out in the Atlantic Ocean. As Jim puts it, "If they go east, the next stop is Portugal."

So *Newsday* expanded to the west, which meant invading Queens, Brooklyn, and Manhattan, the nation's most competitive newspaper market. Times Mirror realized that this market could not be cracked through mere creation of a New York edition of *Newsday*. Instead, the company launched a whole new newspaper and called it *New York Newsday*. That huge investment added more than 250 news-editorial jobs in the city. Jim Dwyer won one of them when the paper made its debut in 1984.

Jim's work in the trenches of New Jersey journalism prepared him well for the new tabloid that was striving to be both breezy and serious in tone. He covered the courts for a while, did a little investigative reporting, and handled some odd jobs in general assignment.

That went on for a couple of years, according to his editor, Donald Forst, and all the while Jim was showing the kind of aggressiveness and flair that *Newsday* valued. Forst saw something special in the scrappy kid—maybe the same thing the Jesuits saw back at Loyola High School.

"Our editors know that when Jim Dwyer goes out on something he's going to report the hell out of it," Forst says. "And nine out of ten times it's going to be awfully good. Every once in a while there's a clinker and a stinker, but everybody's entitled to that. Jim's average is very high, and his energy level is way, way up there. He's not only a work horse, he's a thoroughbred."

Forst, like Jim's former boss, Richard Vezza, describes the hard-driving Irishman as smart, fast, funny, and somewhat rumpled in personal appearance—a man of messy desks and banged-up, unwashed old cars.

"He has a cluttered desk but an uncluttered mind," Forst

adds. "He is a good writer. He has good breadth. He's got a genuine intellect, and like any good columnist he has a point of view."

Forst decided in 1986 to reward Jim with a challenge: the newly created subway column, three times a week.

To an outsider, writing about the subways may not sound like much of a reward. But at *New York Newsday*, the assignment was a genuine plum.

It was unique. No other paper was doing it.

It was high-profile. The fledgling tabloid was promoting it vigorously.

It was important to readers—the throngs of New Yorkers for whom the subways are a major facet of life.

And best of all, the column was important to the boss. Don Forst was a subway rider. He conceived the subway column. His idea for it was the kind of imaginative brush stroke that "Mother *Newsday*" hired him to come up with when he was put in charge of *New York Newsday* in 1985 after a successful career as a newspaper doctor at ailing dailies in Boston and Los Angeles. *Newsday* wanted somebody exactly like Forst—shrewd, inventive, tough, and used to working in a competitive environment—to run the new show in Manhattan.

Forst had another plus: He was a New Yorker, somebody with a native sense of the city. So it was only natural he would come up with content as original as the subway column.

"The idea works in New York because the subway is one of the true common denominators of this diverse city," he says. "There are very few things in New York that touch everybody the way the subway does."

It seemed logical for Forst to offer the column to another native New Yorker, someone who shared the editor's vision of it. And Jim needed no time to think it over. This was the job he had dreamed about since his stickball days on 95th Street.

In June of 1986, three months after he and Cathy had become parents of a baby girl, Jim began the new assignment, hardly able to believe his good fortune. Here he was at age twenty-nine, a family man at last, with a promising new job and modest raise, still riding the subways, but now being paid for it.

* * *

A year and a half into the new position, Jim wrote a column about the near-collision of the A trains. Five months later, he produced a second column on another fatigue-related accident—a train crash in which a new $1.1 million subway car in its first day of service was rammed. "Two guys drove a flatbed work train into the side of the new car and peeled it open like a tin can," Jim recalls. "They were in their fourteenth straight hour of work. One of them had also worked fourteen hours the day before."

Jim reported that workers in both accidents had been ordered by the Transit Authority to work the double shifts but had gladly complied because they wanted the lucrative overtime pay. Two of the workers acknowledged they were putting in as many hours as they could because retirement was near and their pensions would be based on their earnings in their final years.

"I was not outraged that these people were making $50,000 a year," Jim says. "That's not a lot of money to live on in New York. A lot of transit workers live in public housing, because they're making only $30,000 or $35,000. That might be decent money elsewhere, but it's not enough to get a house or anything like a house in New York. Basically, these were just hardworking people putting in a lot of time—too much time—in safety-sensitive jobs."

That's what Jim wrote in February of 1988. "And it was a terrible column and I knew it," he says. "Well, actually, I didn't know it. My editors told me. And I was really stung."

Forst was among those who pointed out to Jim that his column raised more questions than it answered. Were these two fatigue-related accidents isolated occurrences or part of a pattern? How prevalent was overtime and double-shifting among subway workers? Were any safety laws being broken?

"I realized my column was poorly written and underreported, and I felt really bad," Jim recalls. "So I decided to do the best possible story I could do on the subject."

Comprehending what Jim Dwyer was about to attempt requires some grasp of the size and scope of New York's subway system. It operates on a scale of enormity that is staggering.

The 3.5 million riders each day are more than the total served by all other U.S. mass-transit systems combined. More than 50,000 people work on the New York subways. They run around the clock, 6,800 trains a day—550 during the rush hours alone. The system has twenty-six routes. Each one by itself is huge. The A train route alone carries nearly three hundred trains a day transporting some 200,000 passengers.

Obtaining even such basic ridership figures from the Transit Authority can be frustrating. A caller can expect to be passed around, from one wrong department to another, until finally being transferred to a surly receptionist in the Transit Authority's public information office. The receptionist refuses to provide any statistics unless the caller first explains the reasons behind the request. Refusing to identify herself at first, and later only as "Melvina," the receptionist also flatly declines to put her supervisor on the line. Instead, she rudely orders the caller to explain the request one more time. Then she sighs, mutters "Wait a minute," and brusquely places the caller on hold, where he is ignored for several minutes before finally being cut off.

The Transit Authority is not a government agency that provides information about itself with a smile. Yet these are the public servants Jim Dwyer was required to deal with in looking into subway safety. And he wasn't seeking such simple facts as the number of routes and riders. He wanted to examine the system's payroll records—including employee time cards—and compare them with the accident reports, which consistently failed to address workers' hours and whether fatigue was a factor in subway mishaps.

Jim knew the payroll documents were public records and that he—or anybody on the street, for that matter—was entitled to examine. But he also was experienced at dealing with bureaucracies, so he wasn't surprised at what happened next. Transit Authority officials had read Jim's column about subway worker fatigue. They could see what he was fishing for. Not only did they refuse to let him examine the pay and hours records, they also stopped letting him inspect the accident reports that he had been getting access to.

Jim responded by filing formal requests under the federal Freedom of Information Act, and the fight was on.

A legal tug-of-war over public records can take a lot of time if a bureaucracy wants to dig in. Sometimes that tactic works. Arrogant government officials have little to lose by stalling. In many cases, keeping potentially embarrassing information from being published serves their own self-interest. Their refusal to cooperate with a news organization seldom results in a public backlash, because Americans distrust the press just about as much as they distrust the government. And if the fight goes to court, the officials are spending the public's money, not their own, on the legal battle.

Meanwhile, newspaper publishers have to spend their own money on such protracted legal disputes. Some publishers, wincing at the costs, may lack the commitment and back off or settle for a compromise. Other times, the government agencies' tactics may work because the reporters requesting public records lack the necessary aggressiveness or faith in their publishers.

Neither of those descriptions fits *Newsday* or Jim Dwyer. The newspaper's appearance can be deceiving. It is a tabloid, and its front page is often as shrill and gaudy as its rivals on the street. On the inside, though, *Newsday* is a serious newspaper, three-time winner of Pulitzer Prize gold medals for public service (in 1954, 1970, and 1974). Few other newspapers have matched that record, and no other New York tabloid has *ever* received a gold medal.

"Mother *Newsday*," as New York staff members call the parent edition published in Nassau County, Long Island, has a rich, fifty-year tradition of scrappy investigative reporting and journalistic combativeness, including its recent battle for circulation on the streets of New York City. Fights for public records are routine at *Newsday* The paper, like all good ones, does not compromise when a government agency digs in. As a matter of principle, the records will be sought, regardless of how much money and time it takes, even if the sought-after information is useless by the time it is received. A news organization doing anything less than this only encourages officials to try withholding public records the next time.

New York Newsday, the company's six-year-old offspring, shares the same feistiness and principles as "Mother *Newsday*." Their combined circulation of more than 700,000 makes

Newsday the eighth-largest newspaper in the nation. Unlike the more sensational tabloids, *Newsday* enjoys robust financial health, overall. The fledgling New York edition reportedly still operates in the red, but that seems likely to change as the other Manhattan tabloids struggle for survival. *New York Newsday* has rather quickly emerged as a powerhouse in New York City journalism, so one might suspect that Transit Authority officials, unfamiliar with *Newsday*'s tradition, may have misjudged it. More likely, though, is the possibility that Transit Authority officials underestimated Jim Dwyer. That's what Cathy, his wife, suspects.

"Jim is one of these people who comes across as being a little disheveled, like somebody who doesn't have everything quite together. He is not an egomaniac at all, and I think that can mislead certain people. His desk, for example, is never going to be neat. But the amount that he can accomplish is incredible. He is a very single-minded person."

The Transit Authority didn't flat out reject Jim's request for the documents. That would have abruptly sent the fight into the courtroom, where the agency would be certain to lose. Instead, the Transit Authority dragged its feet. Officials told Jim the request remained "under consideration." Weeks, then months went by with no action. By now, it was becoming clear to Jim that the agency was counting on his losing interest or being reassigned to a different news beat. Sometimes, if enough time passes, an issue like this one simply goes away.

Jim, however, repeated his request. Still no action. Frustrated, he remembered a lawyer named Robert Freeman, who had been a visiting lecturer on public records in one of Jim's journalism courses at Columbia. Freeman was executive director of New York's Freedom of Information Committee. Jim telephoned him.

"This guy," Jim says, "is just excellent—a lawyer with great sympathy and affinity for openness in government. They ought to give *him* a Pulitzer Prize. He is the archangel of public information in this state."

Following Freeman's advice, Jim appealed the inaction on his request, calling the delay—now exceeding a year—"a de facto denial." Unfortunately, under New York State records laws, such appeals must be made not to a neutral power but to the head of the agency that withholds the records. So Jim had to deliver his plea to the head of the Metropolitan Transit Authority, Robert Kiley, whom Jim had skewered in the column about Kiley's habit of taking chauffeured cars to work instead of the subway.

But Jim's appeal was airtight. He had followed sound advice from the "archangel," Robert Freeman.

"He advised me and guided me through all the legal steps and told me what the precedents were, and I cited them and basically rattled our sabers and laid the groundwork for going to court."

Jim and his newspaper did not have to go to court. Late in 1988, the records were turned over to him.

But something was terribly wrong.

"While delaying my request, the Transit Authority officials had changed their procedures for filling out accident reports. They started deleting names and identifying their train crew members as 'Conductor A' and 'Motorman B,' so I couldn't look up their time records."

Jim filed a new appeal, complaining that the names could not legally be deleted from the records. Transit officials responded that the accident reports weren't "final" yet and that state records laws applied only to "final" reports.

So Jim filed another appeal, arguing that the reports were essentially final, just awaiting the board's routine approval. He complained that the board was delaying such approval so it could justify omitting workers' names from the documents.

Meanwhile, the Metropolitan Transit Authority Board adopted the agency's legislative agenda for the coming year, 1989. Among the bills the board wanted introduced in Albany was one that would eliminate transit employees' names from accident reports.

"It was breathtaking, it was so bad," Jim says.

At home, Cathy could see that her husband was under some kind of strain. He had a fierce, driven look about him, and his usually razor-sharp wit was unusually subdued. Some of it she attributed to Jim's despondency over a highly personal matter, their attempts to have a second child. Cathy had experienced her second miscarriage recently, and it was particularly devastating to Jim. He had a tendency to blame himself for the problem.

Jim was not used to failure of any kind, Cathy says. He was an achiever, an underdog who enjoyed exceeding others' expectations of him. That was the Jim Dwyer she had married in 1981. That had come five years after they were introduced to each other by a mutual friend at Harry's Hub, a popular watering hole for Fordham students, while both were attending the university. She was a serious-minded Long Island girl, studying music and computer science, and he was the perfect opposite, an extroverted, streetwise kid who was alternately extremely funny or absorbed in his work.

That's how she found him—intensely absorbed—late in 1988, when Jim's public records dispute with the Transit Authority was on the brink of going to court, which would mean considerable further delay in getting the information he needed. But on the advice of Robert Freeman and his editors, Jim decided he first needed to warn the Transit Authority he had his "hand on the nuclear bomb."

"Basically, I told the Transit Authority officials that if they'd like a front-page story saying they wouldn't say what motorman was driving a train that ran into another train, I'd write that story, unless they came out with those records. And so they did."

Abruptly, sixteen months after the fight had begun, it was over. Jim was given access to everything he had sought. But so much time had passed that he had to make additional requests for the new accident reports and payroll records that had piled up during his long battle. By late February of 1989 he received those, too.

Jim was poring over the newly acquired documents during the last week of that month when he was approached by his paper's Sunday editor, Barbara Strauch. She told him the rival *Post* was starting a new Sunday edition on March 5, and *New York Newsday* editors wanted a real "ass-kicker" of a paper that day to outshine the competition.

"Do you have anything in your pocket?" she asked him.

Jim was known in the newsroom for almost always having

more good stories than he could write. He told her about the subway accident reports and the link he was making to worker fatigue.

"Can we have it for March 5?" she asked.

He gulped. Here he was, just starting to analyze these records after battling a year and a half to get them. And now he was being asked to turn out the story in just one week. Common sense told him to say no.

"Sure," he replied.

"Then go for it," she said.

Over the next seven days, Jim unleashed a flood of energy that astonished even his wife, who was used to his occasional bursts of frenzied work. Cathy, who was pregnant again at the time, speculates that the journalistic challenge might have helped Jim take his mind off his fears of another miscarriage. Or perhaps he was simply venting the year and a half of frustration that had built up during his fight for the subway documents. Whatever the reason, he "threw himself into that story like he was possessed," Cathy recalls.

Jim studied the documents, interviewed, and wrote nearly nonstop, with sleep amounting to little more than short naps, and he produced not one story, but a series that began in *New York Newsday* on Sunday, March 5, and ran for three days. Using the public records to document his conclusions, he presented an alarming picture of the New York subways, operated by "transit workers who routinely stay on the job as long as eighty hours per week, toiling in a transit system that forbids drugs and booze in the name of safety, but pays good money for people to work punch-drunk tired, as dulled by fatigue as they would be by liquor."

His series documented case after case of subway crashes, derailments, and near-collisions caused by weary workers who were putting in outrageously long hours in safety-sensitive jobs. He listed five train operators—all over age fifty—who were each earning $70,000 a year by averaging up to thirty-eight hours in overtime every week. He listed five conductors, each averaging up to twenty-nine hours of weekly overtime. He itemized millions of dollars in damage to public property, all resulting from subway accidents linked to worker fatigue.

Almost miraculously, none of the accidents had resulted in loss of life, but the series clearly demonstrated that the fatigue problem was a calamity waiting to happen.

Nobody in the work force or in management had blown the whistle on this dangerous situation because it was benefiting both camps.

"There were strong incentives for both sides," Jim says. "Workers, especially the older guys, were pushing themselves very hard to pad their pensions, and younger guys were getting forced into it. And from management's perspective it was cheaper to hire one guy and pay him overtime than it was to hire two guys and pay additional benefits. So the Transit Authority was actually cutting corners on the number of people in safety-sensitive jobs."

Jim quoted a retired motorman, Ernest Wright, who aptly summarized the conclusion of the series:

"We had a saying down there in the subways, that the big one is coming. The only thing I hope is that I'm not involved, that no one I know is involved or gets killed."

Reaction to the series was swift and measurable. The inspector general of the Metropolitan Transit Authority began an investigation that confirmed Jim's reporting. And the chairwoman of the New York Assembly's mass transit committee introduced legislation to regulate the hours of subway workers in safety-sensitive jobs.

Much later, that bill would get bogged down in political maneuvering and fail to pass, much to Jim's disgust. But for a while, life was a giddy, exhilarating ride for the poet of the subways. Adding to the hopeful excitement of Cathy's pregnancy, the young couple were happy to be homeowners for the first time, having just purchased their Washington Heights apartment.

Jim's career brimmed with promise. His co-workers, editors, and readers were heralding the excellence of his work. *Newsday* was promoting his column heavily, with pictures of Jim on posters in subway cars and train stations, and on billboards and bus-stop benches all over the city. He was filmed for a series of *Newsday* television commercials. He soon found himself being wooed over cocktails and power lunches by editors from the other New York papers, including the prestigious *Times*. His own paper responded with a lucrative contract offer and the promise of a new, general column in the near future.

Jim, somewhat dazed by it all, accepted the *Newsday* contract. At age thirty-two, the janitor's son was hardly able to believe his good luck.

In May, though, less than ten weeks after his series was published, Jim learned just how fragile good fortune can be.

Cathy suffered her third miscarriage, and they lost their unborn child.

5

Founder of the Prizes

J OSEPH PULITZER UNDOUBTEDLY would have admired Jim Dwyer and his reporting for *New York Newsday*. The subway exposé was exactly the kind of snappy writing and crusading journalism Pulitzer espoused, and Dwyer was the type of dogged reporter he prized most.

"I believe in self-made men," Pulitzer wrote in the bequest creating his prizes. Just as Jim Dwyer fits that description, so did Pulitzer—to a degree. He emigrated to the United States in 1864 on a grimy ship crowded with desperate European refugees. Upon arrival, he spoke little English and had hardly any money in his pockets or any contacts or social status in his chosen new land. But within seven years he was publishing his own newspaper and was on his way to becoming fabulously wealthy.

A self-made man? Certainly, by conventional definitions. But a frank look at Pulitzer's early years in the United States suggests that he did not entirely fit the romanticized, heroic image of the rags-to-riches immigrant.

Pulitzer did not start at ground-zero. He arrived in the New World with advantages most other immigrants would envy.

Born on April 10, 1847, in Hungary, Pulitzer grew up in Budapest amid affluence and aristocratic privilege. His father was a prosperous grain merchant of Magyar-Jewish descent, and his mother was an Austro-German and devout Catholic who groomed Joseph's younger brother, Albert, for the priesthood.

Any hardships the young Joseph Pulitzer endured were only the result of his own bold adventures. He attended the most expensive schools in Budapest and benefited from extensive private tutoring. He spoke flawless German and French. Early in childhood, he began cultivating tastes for the finest of European arts and letters and music, and he became skilled at all manner of the leisure pursuits of the intelligentsia, such as chess, which would give him a surprising boost more than once in America.

While Joseph was in his teens, his father died and his mother remarried. The boy despised his new stepfather, so he left home at seventeen and tried in vain to enlist in the Austrian Army, the French Foreign Legion in Mexico, and the British Army in India. In each attempt he was rejected for his poor eyesight, physical frailty, and youth. Determined to become a soldier, he discovered that U.S. recruiters were in Germany, enlisting almost anyone willing to fight for the Union Army in the Civil War. So Pulitzer went to Hamburg, signed up, and quickly found himself on a ship sailing for Massachusetts.

Upon arrival in Boston, Pulitzer made a move that revealed his contradictory personal ethics. Although he had received free passage to America from recruiters who would collect a bounty for enlisting him, he decided he wanted the money for himself. So he dived into Boston Harbor at night, swam to shore, took a train to New York, and joined the Lincoln Cavalry, pocketing the enlistment bounty.

Pulitzer's principal biographers treat that episode lightly, using it to illustrate what a daring young man he was. They fail to recognize the ship-jumping as a signal of how Pulitzer would behave throughout his career. He set rigidly high moral standards for others, but he personally seldom hesitated to cut an ethical corner if it served his purposes.

Pulitzer survived the remaining few months of the Civil War without taking part in any battle. His closest brush with danger came when he struck a junior officer who had tormented him with anti-Semitic insults about his nose. Pulitzer was rescued from serious trouble by a captain who admired the hot-tempered lad's chess game and needed an able partner.

After the war Pulitzer drifted, searching for work until he ended up in St. Louis, at that time the nation's fourth-largest city and the home of a large German colony. He worked for several months at a variety of menial jobs such as mule hostelry, and he spent countless hours studying law and English at the public library. There, he became a favorite chess partner of two St. Louis men who published the *Westliche Post*, a German-language newspaper. Impressed by the twenty-one-year-old Joseph's astonishing intellect, they eventually offered him a job as a reporter.

Thanks to his chess game, Pulitzer had received his first big break in the Land of Opportunity. He didn't take long to exploit it. Working sixteen-hour days as a routine, he quickly established himself as a determined, tremendously energetic dynamo with a crusading zeal. Before long, the bedazzled publishers made him their capital correspondent in Jefferson City.

Pulitzer did two notable things there. He got himself elected to the Missouri legislature, and he shot a man.

In those days, holding elective office while covering the news was not viewed as a professional conflict. Pulitzer served as Republican legislator and capital reporter with equal gusto, constantly challenging corruption and dishonesty in his legislative oratory and in his *Post* dispatches. Before long, he changed parties, becoming a full-fledged Democrat.

In one of his crusades he attacked a corrupt contractor named Edward Augustine. He was a huge bull of a man who confronted Pulitzer in a Jefferson City hotel lobby and called him a "damned liar." His cheeks blazing crimson, Pulitzer stomped out of the hotel, marched to his room in a boarding-house a few blocks away, returned with a four-barreled Sharp's pistol, and approached Augustine, calling *him* a liar. Augustine responded by calling Pulitzer a "puppy" and started toward him. Pulitzer drew the pistol and fired twice, one shot missing and the second striking Augustine below the knee.

Writing about the incident later in the *Post,* Pulitzer gave an evasive version of the shooting and strongly suggested that Augustine had brandished a gun. In fact, Augustine had been unarmed. Pulitzer obviously had committed a felonious assault, but he received help from influential friends and eventually got off with a $100 fine for breach of peace.

There is no record of Pulitzer ever shooting a man after that scrape with the law, but his violent temper would remain with him the rest of his life. His colleagues would never have to guess whether Pulitzer was annoyed. His normally pink cheeks would flush, his blue eyes would blaze, his thin, six-foot-two frame would tense, the veins in his forehead would throb, and his tiny chin (which he hid with a beard after age thirty) would quiver. Then he would verbally explode, cursing profusely. At least one historian has speculated that Pulitzer probably suffered from Gilles de la Tourette's syndrome, a nervous disorder symptomized in part by uncontrollable outbursts of sulphurous profanity.

In 1872, Pulitzer's fourth year as a journalist, his march to wealth began when the financially distressed owners of the *Post* decided that the young man had become indispensable to the paper. They offered him a controlling interest in it. There is no record of how much he paid or where he obtained the money. His biographers speculate that Pulitzer received the stock on credit, but it seems entirely possible that he obtained the money from his wealthy family in Europe. That possibility seems even more plausible when one considers that the *Post* owners probably needed cash, which might have been their primary motive for offering Pulitzer the stock.

For whatever reason, and by whatever means, Pulitzer at age twenty-five became an American newspaper publisher. He quickly reinvigorated the paper, sacrificing a little of its dignity for much more profitable sensationalism, and within a year sold back a majority interest to the original publishers for $30,000.

Pulitzer shrewdly and ruthlessly began parlaying his windfall into greater fortune. He first purchased another struggling St. Louis paper, the German-language *Staats-Zeitung*, for a few thousand dollars under the owners' assumption that he would continue the operation. Instead, he ran it for one day before selling off its precious Associated Press franchise to the *St. Louis Globe* for a sum variously estimated at $27,000 and $40,000. Then he added to that profit by peddling the newspaper's machinery to a group starting up another German-language paper that would soon fold. By killing off the *Staats-Zeitung* for a quick profit, Pulitzer did no favor for the paper's employees or the city's German community, but he certainly made himself rich enough to retire, if that had been his desire.

He invested his money profitably in a variety of non-newspaper enterprises and embarked on a five-year hiatus from his publishing career. During this period he traveled the world, studied law, and was admitted to the bar in Washington, D.C.

On one of his Washington visits he met Kate Davis, a distant relative of Jefferson Davis, the Confederate president. Joseph and Kate were married in 1878 in the Episcopal Church of the Epiphany in Washington. That is the only occasion on record that Pulitzer ever went to a house of worship, except for his son Ralph's wedding in Shelburne Episcopal Church in Vermont—and his own funeral at St. Thomas's Episcopal Church in New York. If not an atheist, Joseph Pulitzer was at least irreligious, forbidding anyone to talk of religion in his presence. And he did not tell Kate about his part-Jewish ancestry until after they were married. W. A. Swanberg, author of the definitive Pulitzer biography, wrote that it was "virtually impossible for a Jew to attain any standing in the eyes of such narrow and socially conscious families as the Davises." Swanberg speculated that Pulitzer kept his secret from Kate "doubtless fearing that he would be rejected out of hand."

Later, when she learned the facts, "she was greatly upset" but was able to accept her husband's ancestry. "Nevertheless," according to Swanberg, "anti-Semitism was a factor that both of them would have to cope with for the rest of their lives."

After a ten-week European honeymoon, the newly married couple settled in St. Louis and Joseph began deliberating over whether to begin a new career in law or return to journalism.

The decision came to him instantly late in 1878 when he learned that the *St. Louis Dispatch,* a dying evening paper, was facing bankruptcy and a forced sale. Pulitzer sent an emissary to the auction—a secret proxy whom no one in St. Louis would be likely to recognize—who picked off the dying paper for a mere $2,500 while Pulitzer himself watched with amusement from the rear of the hall. His unnecessarily furtive approach to the purchase provided a glimpse of how he would relish secrecy throughout his career.

Shortly after he acquired the *Dispatch,* the publisher of another struggling English-language daily, the bland and bookish *St. Louis Post,* saw merger as a path to survival and proposed it to Pulitzer, who accepted.

As co-publisher of the *St. Louis Post-Dispatch,* Pulitzer quickly dominated and drove off his partner, John Dillon. Then, as sole proprietor, Pulitzer began to do the same to his competition. He succeeded by rapidly building circulation, and his tools were sensationalism and the newspaper crusade. Both, he discovered, sold newspapers. Both also came naturally to Pulitzer, especially the crusading. The man was an ideologue and a born reformer. He was a compulsive criticizer who still would have battled for social reform had he chosen law or politics instead of journalism. In his first year at the newspaper's helm, he crusaded against a crooked gas company, a lottery racket, a horse-car monopoly, and an insurance fraud.

And what a marvelous discovery crusading must have been for the young publisher. He quickly learned that by setting up his *Post-Dispatch* as a watchdog against privilege and a champion of "the people," he could advance his own interests by defending the public's.

Pulitzer did not invent the newspaper crusade, but he perfected it. No other editor of his time could match his knowledge of an issue or his zeal for attacking it, regardless of risk.

The same could be said for sensationalism. He wasn't the first publisher to try it, but he refined the controversial practice to an unprecedented level of success. No other paper of his day, for example, had the audacity to do what Pulitzer did when a prominent businessman died in a hotel room with a woman who was not his wife. The *Post-Dispatch* carried a full account of the scandalous death and headlined it A WELL-KNOWN CITIZEN STRICKEN DOWN IN THE ARMS OF HIS MISTRESS.

Sometimes Pulitzer would blend sensationalism with crusading, as when he produced a shocker gleaned from a grand jury report listing substantial St. Louis citizens who owned local buildings being used as houses of prostitution.

Some called it smutty news reporting, but readers went for this type of journalism in a big way. Pulitzer rationalized that his mission was to hook readers, then educate them later on. Besides, he liked a juicy story as much as any of his thousands of readers. Occasionally, his compulsion for the lurid story would lead him to exaggeration or even fabrication of news, as when his paper published a fake report of a revolution in Afghanistan, just to lay a trap for a news-thieving rival paper, the *Star*. Sure enough, the next day the *Star* published its own version of the faked story, and Pulitzer had a grand time exposing the theft in his *Post-Dispatch*.

Judged against the breezy standards of his era, Pulitzer's early willingness to exaggerate or even fabricate news may seem colorfully quaint—even humorous. But years later, after he became a national opinion-shaper, his commission of those journalistic sins helped push the nation into a disgraceful war.

In St. Louis, Pulitzer's brand of journalism made enemies, so many that he felt compelled to carry a pistol. But his formula also attracted readers, and in two years the *Post-Dispatch* circulation soared from 2,000 to nearly 9,000. Along with those readers came advertising. By 1880, Joseph and Kate Pulitzer were among the wealthy elite of St. Louis. They built a three-story mansion, hired servants, and bought a luxurious carriage. The second and most promising of their seven children—a daughter they named Lucille—was born that year, and the couple entertained often as important new arrivals in St. Louis society.

In this blissful period, there was no way they could know that hard-driving Joseph was wrecking his health, that two of their children, including Lucy, would die young, and that looming professional disaster would destroy their life in St. Louis.

By 1882 the *Post-Dispatch* circulation had mushroomed to over 22,000, and Pulitzer's domination of the city's newspaper market was nearly complete. The paper's four-year march to preeminence was a journalistic wonder, which Pulitzer did not accomplish entirely by himself. One of the components to his success was his passionately held belief in hiring the most capable people he could find and then paying them handsomely so they would stick with him. That strategy had led Pulitzer to a nationwide search for the best editor he could find, ultimately leading him to John Cockerill, the dashing, aggressive, thirty-four-year-old editor of the *Baltimore Gazette*.

Pulitzer lured the like-minded Cockerill to St. Louis, and it turned out to be an inspired move. Cockerill was the perfect editor, sharing his publisher's vision of the *Post-Dispatch*. Together, they built the paper into a powerhouse, accumulating readers—and enemies—in a hurry.

Late in 1882, one of those enemies, Col. Alonzo Slayback, a hot-tempered lawyer-politician whom Cockerill had attacked in an editorial, stomped into Cockerill's office and threatened him. The editor pulled a pistol from his desk drawer and shot the man dead. When police were called, they found a gun in the dead man's hand, but there were suspicions that the weapon had been placed there before officers arrived. The truth will never be known, but the resulting furor over the killing of Slayback made national news and forced Pulitzer to cut short a much-needed vacation and return to St. Louis to stand by Cockerill.

Even though Slayback and his wife had been part of Pulitzer's social circle and even guests in his home, the publisher vigorously defended his editor. After seven weeks of lobbying and heavy editorial campaigning by Pulitzer, a grand jury found that Slayback had been armed when he invaded Cockerill's office. No indictment was returned.

However, the public firestorm over the killing continued to build. Rival newspapers kept up a relentless attack on the *Post-Dispatch*, while Slayback's widow filed a lawsuit against Cockerill and the St. Louis social set turned against the Pulitzers. The *Post-Dispatch* suddenly began losing subscribers and advertisers at an alarming rate. Pulitzer, chagrined, felt he had no choice but to fire Cockerill, which he did with assurances that he would someday make amends.

The paper's circulation continued to decline, however, along with the social status of the Pulitzers. Joseph and Kate realized they were no longer welcome in St. Louis. The strain on Pulitzer had been immense throughout the ordeal, and his frail health was deteriorating. On doctor's orders, the couple planned a voyage to Europe for a six-month rest.

On the way, they stopped in New York. There, in social conversations with fellow publishers, Pulitzer overheard a rumor that set all his travel plans on hold: Financier Jay Gould was thinking of ridding himself of a money-losing little daily newspaper called the *New York World*. Pulitzer instantly sensed a fantastic opportunity. New York was seemingly overcrowded with newspapers—some of them successful, such as the *Herald, Times, Sun,* and *Tribune,* some of them failing, such as the *World,* and some of them just getting by, such as the *Morning Journal,* published by Joseph's brother, Albert, who had avoided the priesthood and had followed in his sibling's footsteps.

Despite the host of competing papers, Joseph Pulitzer astutely observed that they were overwhelmingly Republican or independent. There was no powerful Democratic newspaper such as his *Post-Dispatch.* If his editorial formula made money in St. Louis, he reasoned, it ought to make a fortune in New York.

Pulitzer met with Gould and negotiated to purchase the *New York World* for $346,000, an exorbitant sum for a newspaper with a bad name, shabby facilities, and only 15,000 circulation. After striking the deal, Pulitzer had grave second thoughts and decided to back out, but Kate laughed at his doubts and encouraged him to go with his first instincts.

That was the end of their European trip. Had they sailed instead, it is possible that Pulitzer might have escaped the nervous breakdown that was heading his way. Regardless, history would have been altered in many ways we can only guess: no Sherman Antitrust Act, no Spanish-American War, no Statue of Liberty on American soil, no such phrase as "yellow journalism," and no Pulitzer Prizes.

On May 11, 1883, in his first edition of the *World* —Pulitzer dropped "New York" from the name—he published the following promise to readers:

> There is room in this great and growing city for a journal that is not only cheap but bright, not only bright but large, not only large but truly democratic—dedicated to the cause of the people rather than that of purse potentates—devoted more to the news of the New than the Old World—that will expose fraud and sham, fight all public evils and abuses—that will serve and battle for the people with earnest sincerity.

True to his word, the *World* under its new proprietor was indeed "cheap" at two cents a copy and "bright" with headlines such as A FORTUNE SQUANDERED IN DRINK, IN PRISON FOR HIS BROTHER'S CRIME, and WHILE THE HUSBANDS WERE AWAY.

Above all, Pulitzer's newspaper was indeed a "truly democratic" crusader for what he deemed to be the best interests of "the people." Six days after publishing that promise, the paper announced these new doctrines for the *World* :

1. Tax luxuries.
2. Tax inheritances.
3. Tax large incomes.
4. Tax monopolies.
5. Tax the privileged corporation.
6. A tariff for revenue.
7. Reform the Civil Service.
8. Punish corrupt officers.
9. Punish vote-buying.
10. Punish employers who coerce employees in elections.

Pulitzer later changed his mind on the revenue tariff and dropped it from his paper's doctrine. But he stayed with the other nine, and during his lifetime they all became embodied in the laws of the nation.

In St. Louis, meanwhile, Pulitzer brought back his former

partner, John Dillon, to run the *Post-Dispatch,* and Joseph and Kate left Missouri for good. Thereafter, the St. Louis newspaper would continue to prosper, adding to the family fortune while maturing into one of the most prestigious daily journals in the nation.

New York was Pulitzer's new arena. The market was huge, ruthlessly competitive, and far more sophisticated than St. Louis. But Pulitzer went immediately to work applying the same editorial formula he had refined in the frontier city. He hired the best talent he could find, beginning by keeping his promise to the disgraced St. Louis editor, John Cockerill, who was brought to New York to edit the *World.* Pulitzer paid top wages, set high standards—"Accuracy! Terseness! Accuracy!" was the slogan plastered on his newsroom walls—and drove his people hard. He lived his job and expected employees to do the same.

The *World's* overnight shift to sensationalism and crusading brought instant results. Within one week, Pulitzer received complaints that the public—especially New York's swarms of newly arrived Irish, Germans, Italians, and Jews—couldn't find enough copies of his paper. After three months, his initial circulation of 15,000 was up to 39,000.

The next ten years brought the most astonishing success story in American newspaper journalism. By the early 1890s, *The World* had morning, evening, and Sunday editions with a combined circulation of 625,000, largest in the nation. The paper was operating by 1890 out of its own new twenty-story skyscraper—at that time New York's tallest building, on Park Row near the Brooklyn Bridge and City Hall.

During those years, Pulitzer cemented his status as the champion of freedom by mounting the successful campaign to the Statue of Liberty transport and erect. He battled the oil trusts until Congress reacted by passing the Sherman Antitrust Act. He got himself elected to Congress and meanwhile successfully pushed New York's Democratic governor, Grover Cleveland, into the United States presidency.

Pulitzer was bored and restless in Congress and resigned within four months. He decided he was much more interested—and effective—in running his newspapers and getting others elected to carry out his vision of democracy. He spent the remainder of his life striving, with mixed success, to use his editorial influence to elect like-minded presidents.

On his editorial pages, Pulitzer frequently attacked the super-rich and their pretenses of aristocracy. "The new *World,* " he once wrote, "believes that such an aristocracy ought to have no place in the republic—that the word ought to be expunged from an American vocabulary." One of his editorials blasted the city's wealthy class for putting on a "show of shoddy aristocracy" by riding ostentatiously plumed and gilded carriages to the theater district.

Ironically, and perhaps hypocritically, Joseph and Kate Pulitzer lived like royalty on East 73rd Street, in their four-story mansion with its seventeen servants. The couple also had luxurious vacation homes in Bar Harbor, Maine, on a Georgia island, and on the French Riviera. In their New York social life, the couple mixed not with the working-class people whom Joseph championed in his papers, but with the affluent elite whom he continually battled.

Such was the contradictory nature of the man. He raged against government and corporate secrecy, while relishing it to an irrational extent in his own affairs. He preached noble journalism but practiced sleaze when profits were threatened. He could be tender, kind, generous, optimistic, confident, and full of joy one moment and an hour later be paranoid, cruel, miserly, pessimistic, and full of self-doubt and despair.

Various biographers have described Pulitzer as "a sick man," a "helpless megalomaniac," and a "Napoleon of journalism." He was "neurotic," "driven," "humorless," "manic-depressive," "intense," "profane," "self-pitying," and "thin-skinned."

With each passing day, Pulitzer's nerves seemed to grow more frazzled, making him increasingly difficult to be near. As John Cockerill put it, "He was the damnedest best man in the world to have in a newspaper office for one hour in the morning. For the remainder of the day he was a damned nuisance."

Pulitzer tempted disaster by working at the *World* from dawn to midnight. His frail mental and physical health was already in serious jeopardy when personal crises began piling up in 1886. The couple's two-year-old daughter, Katherine Ethel, died of pneumonia—a heartbreak that sent Joseph burying himself all the more in his work. Seven-year-old Ralph and six-year-old Lucille also were sickly with symptoms of typhoid. Away from home their father's depression was deepened by his crushing disappointment in the shabby performance of Cleveland, the president he had done so much to elect.

Pulitzer experienced frightening rages, sometimes directed at employees—such as a burly reporter who found himself in a fistfight with the boss in the middle of the newsroom—and sometimes even at Kate, who described his emotional explosions in her diaries. In one entry, after he had savagely lashed out at her as an unfit wife and ordered her out of a room, she wrote: "When will these scenes end or when will I be at rest?"

The answer began taking shape in 1887 when a final crisis pushed Joseph over the edge—and to considerable extent out of her life.

It was a year of particularly bitter acrimony in the New York newspaper wars. Charles Dana, aging publisher of the Republican *Sun*, had feuded with the Democratic *World* since the upstart young Pulitzer had begun his campaign to dethrone the *Sun* as the city's leading morning paper. As Pulitzer's circulation skyrocketed, Dana's declined. The old man took it personally. In editorial-page skirmishes between 1883 and 1887, Dana tried in vain to discredit Pulitzer by making fun of his skimpy war record and his early years in St. Louis. He dredged up the Slayback shooting and frequently commented on Pulitzer's failure to attend the synagogue or participate in any Jewish activities.

In March of 1887, Dana launched an evening edition that quickly reached 40,000 circulation. Pulitzer retaliated by bringing out his own *Evening World*, a wildly sensational sheet that sold for a penny. It quickly surpassed the *Evening Sun* and was selling 75,000 copies daily within a few weeks.

Dana apparently became emotionally unstrung over his inability to defeat Pulitzer's *World*. The older publisher's frustration spilled into print in late 1887 as the two papers battled editorially over candidates for city district attorney. Dana, aware of New York's large Jewish vote, unleashed a "renegade Jew" attack on Pulitzer, calling him "a Jew who does not want to be a Jew" and urging voters to reject the *World*'s candidate for district attorney.

The vitriolic Dana could not have hit his rival in a more

vulnerable spot. Abnormally sensitive to begin with, Pulitzer seemed uncomfortable with his Jewish ancestry and reacted to Dana's slurs as if he had been horsewhipped. To his credit, Pulitzer refused to respond in his own paper to the *Sun's* vicious attacks, but they left him devastated, his many neuroses and anxieties stampeding out of control. Swanberg, the biographer, analyzed Pulitzer's vulnerability this way:

> Quite possibly the "Joey the Jew" taunts in St. Louis and the jests about his nose had left permanent wounds. His withholding of his pedigree from Kate, if comprehensible on the ground of his fear of losing her, had placed him under the impossible obligation of guaranteeing her against the anti-Semitism which she had never bargained for. Her own staunch Episcopalianism in turn had made it possible for Jews to misinterpret his religious skepticism as a denial of his race.... Though he was never anti-Semitic and numbered Jews among his friends and employees, he tended to recoil from racial or religious discussions....Later in life he sent money for the relief of victims of pogroms, but it was said that he asked his companions never to discuss Jews or Jewishness.

Dana hammered on this theme with brutal repetition. Throughout the election campaign, the *Sun* excoriated Pulitzer as "Jewseph Pulitzer," "the wandering Jew," and "Judas Pulitzer."

The tactic worked. Besides tormenting Pulitzer to suicidal fits of depression, the editorials united many Jews who spurned Pulitzer's apparent heterodoxy. Just before the election, Dana galvanized the anti-Pulitzer sentiment with his most savage attack:

> The Jews of New York have no reason to be ashamed of Judas Pulitzer if he has denied his race and religion....The shame rests exclusively upon himself. The insuperable obstacle in the way of his social progress is not the fact that he is a Jew, but in certain offensive personal qualities....His face is repulsive, not because the physiognomy is Hebraic, but because it is Pulitzeresque....Cunning, malice, falsehood, treachery,

dishonesty, greed and venal self-abasement have stamped their unmistakable traits....

Jewish citizens have the same interest as all other intelligent, self-respecting and law-abiding people in the defeat of Pulitzer and his young dupe.... The Jewish vote will contribute very largely to that effect.

And it did. The attorney general candidate endorsed by Pulitzer was crushed at the polls. Dana celebrated his personal triumph on the *Sun's* front page, running the election result with a picture of a crowing rooster. And on his editorial page, he once again called Pulitzer a "wandering Jew" and told him it was time he got out of New York just as he had left St. Louis.

A typical, tough-minded tycoon might have shrugged off such attacks, but not Pulitzer. He took the election outcome as personally as his rival did, and Dana's shameless barbs went right through the younger publisher's thin skin.

Physical calamity struck within two weeks of Pulitzer's humiliation. One morning in his office, after demanding to see the editorials and being handed the galley proofs, he was stunned to discover he could hardly see the print, let alone read it. Without a word to colleagues, he put on his coat and took a carriage home. There, his physician diagnosed a broken ocular blood vessel in one eye and severe deterioration of the other. Pulitzer, at age forty, was rapidly going blind. The doctor was also appalled at his patient's other symptoms: chronic indigestion, insomnia, asthma, exhaustion, and depression. The psychosis that probably lurked at the bottom of all these ills was never diagnosed. The doctor prescribed six weeks in bed in a darkened room.

During Pulitzer's confinement, Dana kept up his devious form of anti-Semitism in the *Sun,* reprinting the "Jew who does not want to be a Jew" editorial three times a week, each time with the same headline: MOVE ON, PULITZER!—REPUDIATED BY HIS RACE. Every day, the *Sun* published "letters from readers"— quite transparently composed in the *Sun* office—demanding that Pulitzer get out of New York.

Dana must have been delighted when Pulitzer did exactly that. At the end of his six weeks in bed, the sick publisher left New York to search for medical specialists who might restore his health. In torment, he traveled compulsively from spa to spa in California, Colorado, London, Paris, Nice, Weisbaden, Naples, Constantinople, St. Moritz, and elsewhere around the world in a frenzied hunt for a cure.

He never found it. His illness grew only worse—to the point that Pulitzer could not tolerate any noise. Even the slightest annoying sound, such as a colleague eating toast, could destroy his nervous disposition for an entire day. So he spent most of the rest of his life apart from Kate and the children and the clamor of family life. And he never worked another day in the newsroom of his beloved *World*.

Pulitzer's breakdown, however, did not mean victory for Dana and the *Sun*. Shortly after the Jew-baiting episode, Pulitzer took revenge from his sickbed by striking a deal to erect his towering new World Building directly across Franklin Street from the *Sun's* unimpressive four-story building. Dana tried desperately to block the real-estate transaction, but Pulitzer prevailed, laying out $2 million in cash for the land, building, and new presses. For many months thereafter during construction, the hoisting of every steel girder was a visible humiliation to Dana just across the street. The magnificent finished building, topped by a gold-plated dome that was the first New York landmark seen from ships coming in from Europe, had to gall Dana every day until he died, seven years later at age seventy-eight.

The dome atop the new World Building contained Pulitzer's huge, semicircular office, providing a commanding view from Governor's Island and Brooklyn to the upper East River and Long Island. Tragically, Pulitzer could not see the spectacular view from his office, and his jangled nerves would not permit him to work there. By the time the building was opened in 1890, amid great fanfare that included the mayor and governor and a host of other celebrities, Pulitzer was too ill to attend the ceremonies.

Dr. George Washington Hosmer, a physician who treated Pulitzer and kept a diary during his travels with the patient, described him as a hopeless invalid:

> He was very ill—in a state so feeble that he could scarcely get around on foot. He passed days on a sofa....It

was a physical strain for him to cross the room and sit at the table.... Physical collapse had assumed the form of nervous prostration.

Making the prognosis even bleaker was the fate of his estranged brother. Albert Pulitzer, who had bitterly opposed Joseph's invasion of the New York newspaper market, was now in Vienna, running his *Journal* in absentia, and showing symptoms of the insanity that would eventually lead to his suicide. Albert was suffering extreme insomnia and compulsive eating that had bloated him to gross proportions.

But doomed as he appeared to be, Joseph Pulitzer produced another work of genius, courage, and sheer will, perhaps as astonishing as his rise to wealth and power. He conceived something that none of the world's most famous doctors had come up with: a way he could live with his debilitating illness while clinging to control of his newspapers. His solution was in ways bizarre, but it worked for more than twenty years.

Foremost, Pulitzer eliminated noise from his life. He spent his final two decades in the quietest resorts of Europe, in the hushed, womb-like stateroom of his private yacht, and in a heavily soundproofed room called "the Vault," part of a solid granite "Tower of Silence" that he had specially constructed at Chatwold, his vacation estate in Bar Harbor, Maine. The Vault's windows were triple-glazed, and the double walls were stuffed with insulation. There were three doors in the short hallway to the main house, with the hallway floor resting on ball bearings to retard vibration.

By 1890, Joseph and Kate had five living children—Ralph, eleven, Lucille, nine, Joseph II, six, Edith, four, and Constance, one—but Pulitzer lived mostly apart from them for the rest of his life.

He also developed an elaborate, craftily manipulative system for maintaining control of his papers, no matter how sick he felt or where on earth he might be. Essential to this system was a retinue of male companions who traveled with him to read correspondence, newspapers, and literature aloud to him and to take dictation for his prolific outpouring of cables and letters to employees and family members in New York and St. Louis.

To protect the confidentiality of all this long-distance communication, the increasingly paranoid invalid devised his secret code. Some of it had a certain logic: the morning *World* was "Senior" and the newer evening paper was "Junior." Some of the code was comically descriptive: Theodore Roosevelt was "Glutinous" and Woodrow Wilson was "Melon." And some of it was just quirky: the rival *New York Times* was "Geography" and the Democratic Party was "Gosling." Pulitzer himself committed all 20,000 code words to memory, while his colleagues used a 250-page key to the code.

Pulitzer made heavy use of corporate espionage during his exile. Since he couldn't oversee his employees, he secretly assigned employees to take notes on each other. Just about every executive of any importance was being spied on by another executive, all of them passing their surreptitious reports along to the publisher in his yacht, "Vault," or European spa.

To a lesser extent, Pulitzer also had employees spy on the competition. More than once he planted spies at rival papers by assigning his people to defect and go to work for competitors while staying on the Pulitzer payroll.

Although Pulitzer could no longer direct day-to-day news coverage in the *World,* he could still set news policy, make hiring decisions, dictate editorial page positions, and tinker with the product. Some of his most innovative content changes came after his breakdown.

He introduced the "invented" news story, most notably the hiring of reporter Nellie Bly to try to outdo the eighty-day journey around the world by Jules Verne's fictional Phileas Fogg. Bly's race against time, reported in colorful daily dispatches in the *World,* was outrageously artificial "journalism," but the stunt riveted readers in New York and throughout the nation for the seventy-two days it took her to circumnavigate the globe.

He inaugurated the newspaper "funnies" by hiring R. F. Outcault to draw the escapades of a slum urchin called "The Yellow Kid." The comic was such a hit with readers that Pulitzer's breezy style of newspapering soon become popularly known as "the yellow press" and "yellow journalism"—labels the *World* promoted for a few years, until the terms began evolving into pejorative synonyms for sensationalism.

Beside comics, Pulitzer brought together many other elements that became familiar features of American daily newspapers: sports sections, women's pages, bigger headlines, illustrations, and promotional stunts and contests.

As his competitors copied him, trying to keep up, the nature of the American newspaper quickly changed, creating what was eventually called the modern American metropolitan daily and the "New Journalism"—long before the so-called New Journalism of the late sixties and early seventies.

One of his competitors copied him so successfully that it led to a circulation war—and eventually to a real shooting war. The rival was code-word "Gush," William Randolph Hearst. The brash Californian, sixteen years younger than Pulitzer, had successfully purchased and operated the *San Francisco Examiner* with his deceased father's mining fortune and decided to invade New York in 1895 the same way Pulitzer had done twelve years earlier. Ironically, the failing paper that Hearst bought in New York was the *Journal,* given up by Pulitzer's increasingly deranged brother, Albert.

Hearst went into battle against the *World* as no other rival had ever dared. He successfully imitated Pulitzer's news strategy and carried it even farther, appealing to the working class with simple language and plenty of lurid sensationalism, entertainment, and crusading stories. And Hearst undercut Pulitzer's newsstand prices while pumping millions of dollars into the *Journal* at a loss, confident he would get it back when the advertisers started to switch to his papers. He also raided Pulitzer's staff with unheard-of salary offers, once hiring away the entire editorial crew of the *Sunday World,* including Outcault, the "Yellow Kid" cartoonist. So Pulitzer upped the ante and hired the whole bunch back. They stayed one day before Hearst offered even higher pay, and they all jumped ship again—for good this time, except for one secretary who remained loyal to Pulitzer.

The *Journal's* circulation began soaring. It quickly eclipsed the waning establishment papers—the *Herald, Sun, Tribune,* and *Times*—and began approaching the *World's* figures, which had stagnated.

Pulitzer counterattacked. He hired a new cartoonist to replace Outcault, and both papers ran competing "Yellow Kid" funnies. Pulitzer also cut his morning paper's newsstand price

in half, matching Hearst's one-cent paper, assuming this bargain price would strip readers away from the *Journal* and kill it
off. The tactic backfired. It did not affect either paper's
circulation significantly, but *World* advertisers defected en
masse because Pulitzer had disastrously raised ad rates to
compensate for halving his newsstand price.

The resulting loss of revenue appalled Pulitzer. He reacted
by unleashing his papers in frenzied combat with Hearst's
Journal. From 1896 through 1898, New York newspaper readers
witnessed the sleaziest circulation war in U.S. history. In their
tug-of-war for street sales, both publishers exhorted their
staffs into a repugnant display of inaccurate, slanted, exaggerated, and fabricated news.

Most disgraceful was their coverage of Cuba's uprising
against Spanish rule. Both publishers leaped on the story,
sending boatloads of correspondents to the Caribbean to
churn out sensational reports aimed at winning the newspaper
war on the streets of New York. The journalistic frenzy that
ensued produced millions of words of error and pure fiction.
As each paper raced to outdo the other with scare headlines,
rumor stories, and false reports, their shameless jingoism
stirred up intense public outrage against Spain. The na-
tionalistic fervor sweeping America was good for newspaper
sales, so the war correspondents were ordered to produce more
of that kind of coverage, and they obliged with numerous
accounts—mostly unfounded—of alleged Spanish treachery
and atrocities against Cubans. Both papers screamed editorially for U.S. military intervention to liberate Cuba.

Spain, for its part, was in no position to fight the United
States and clearly did not want war. Madrid was offering a form
of self-government to Cuba when the U.S. battleship *Maine*
exploded mysteriously in Havana harbor on Feb. 15, 1898,
killing 260 of its 360 officers and men. Both the *World* and
Journal seized on the disaster as cause for immediate war with
Spain, which certainly had no interest in blowing up an
American battleship. But for weeks, both Pulitzer and Hearst
sought to surpass each other with their editorial cries for war.
Pulitzer himself published a signed editorial on April 10, 1898,
calling for an immediate attack on Spanish colonies. "It would
hardly be a war," he wrote, "but it would be magnificent."

President McKinley knew Spain wanted peace talks, and he ignored Pulitzer's demand. But nine days later, both the Senate and the House passed a war resolution. Pulitzer's editorial was the match that lit the fuse, and he got his war.

The Spanish-American War lasted four months and was as pathetic as the journalism that incited it. About five thousand U.S. servicemen died, but fewer than four hundred of those deaths were in combat. The rest were caused by disease. No official count was made of Spanish casualties, but that death toll was estimated to be considerably higher. The war's financial cost to the United States was $250 million—more than $4 billion in 1990 dollars. The United States gained the Spanish possessions of Puerto Rico, Guam, and the Philippines, and earned a reputation for imperialism that continues to haunt the nation today.

It isn't difficult to understand the shameful journalistic performance of Hearst, an ambitious, shallow opportunist who lacked many meaningful personal convictions. Pulitzer, by contrast, was an idealist who earnestly believed—despite his history of excesses—in newspaper accuracy and fairness. His rapid descent into irresponsible journalism is harder to understand.

Part of the explanation certainly lay in his fragile health and mental condition. Hearst launched his all-out war against the *World* during a period when Pulitzer was particularly vulnerable, worrying about his daughter Lucille. He had already lost baby Katherine to pneumonia. As the Cuban crisis raged, Lucille was seriously ill. She, more than any of his other children, including another son, Herbert, born in 1895, had inherited her father's all-consuming energy, intellect, and drive for achievement. Without doubt, Lucy was Pulitzer's favorite. But in the final days of 1897, shortly after her seventeenth birthday, she was stricken by typhoid. Pulitzer, who was with her at Chatwold when she died, was shattered.

Other likely explanations for Pulitzer's darkest moments as a publisher probably had root in his contradictory nature. True, he valued responsible journalism, but he also valued profit. He had always succeeded in reconciling the two when they conflicted—until Hearst attacked. Then profit prevailed, and

Pulitzer spent three years violating most of the journalistic principles he had espoused for years.

The Pulitzer-Hearst sideshow continued throughout the brief war. By its end, many educated Americans had become weary and disgusted with "yellow journalism." So had Pulitzer. He ordered his flagship paper, the morning *World*, to stop that kind of sensationalism.

To a degree, Pulitzer can be credited for regaining his sense of responsibility. However, the profit motive may have lurked somewhere behind his directive. Even though the frothy war coverage had whipped his circulation to an all-time high, the *World* was losing money for the first time ever. The war coverage proved terribly expensive, the one-cent newsstand price was too low, and above all, many advertisers had fled to the more responsible newspapers, perceiving their readers as the audience with retail buying power.

In effect, Pulitzer abandoned all-out "yellow journalism" when he discovered it didn't pay. And even though his morning *World* quickly returned to respectability and won back its advertisers, the evening *World* continued to peddle sensationalism to the city's working class.

On balance, Pulitzer probably did more good than bad for his country. His tireless crusading against corrupt politics and shoddy business practices did much to promote clean government and social reform. More than anyone, he was responsible for the antitrust law that curbed the license which laissez-faire American business had fostered. Among his other major contributions was the *World*'s 1905 exposé of a great insurance scandal that led to a series of New York laws putting insurance companies under rigid controls.

Pulitzer's most courageous triumph, though, came in 1909 when the *World* reported a scam involving the disposition of $40 million that the United States had paid to the French Panama Canal Company. The federal government secured indictments against Pulitzer for criminally libeling President Theodore Roosevelt, the financier J. P. Morgan, the statesman Elihu Root, and several others. Pulitzer refused to be muzzled, however, and kept his papers on the story. Later, after the courts had struck down the indictments one by one, Pulitzer was credited with winning a crucial victory for freedom of the press.

Pulitzer's loyal editor, John Cockerill, once called him "the greatest journalist the world has ever known." That is debatable, but it is safe perhaps to view Pulitzer as the most important journalist in American history. For better or worse, he did more than any other individual to influence the nature of modern newspapers.

He was a giant and he had giant-size expectations of others. Not surprisingly, no one could match those standards and avoid ultimately disappointing him—no president or politician, no editor or reporter, and certainly not his children. Perhaps Lucille, the brightest of the brood, could have won his confidence had she survived, but Pulitzer viewed his two older sons, Ralph and Joseph II, as weaklings and treated them cruelly. Meanwhile, the youngest son, Herbert, received extraordinary affection and pampering in the father's irrational belief that the boy—whom Pulitzer never lived to see reach manhood—had the talent to take over the publishing dynasty someday. The old man was deceiving himself, of course. He had faith in little Herbert only because the child hadn't grown up enough to form any ideas that might counter his father's and thus disappoint him.

Herbert was only fourteen in 1911 when Joseph Pulitzer died aboard his 269-foot yacht, *Liberty,* moored at Charleston. Although Herbert had never worked in the family business and had never even shown any interest in it, Joseph Pulitzer willed to the boy 60 percent of the income from the newspaper company stock, which he had placed in a trust. Ralph received 20 percent and Joseph II, the black sheep of the family, received 10 percent. The remainder went to company executives. Pulitzer left no stock to his two surviving daughters. Reflecting the male chauvinism of his era, he feared fortune hunters might marry the young women to gain control of the stock.

Joseph II went to St. Louis to run the *Post-Dispatch.* Despite his father's low opinion of him, he worked hard and did a creditable job. With assistance from superb editors, he helped guide the paper's growth into one of the nation's most respected, influential, and profitable newspapers.

Ralph, meanwhile, tried his best to run the *World,* but it quickly went downhill without his reclusive father's driving force behind it. Herbert, who had supposedly inherited his father's brains, was no help whatsoever. When he graduated from Harvard in 1919, he was clearly less interested in journalism than in a life of idle wealth and self-indulgence. He spent most of the next ten years partying and traveling abroad. Finally, in 1928, he moved into an office in the World Building's dome, saying he was ready to devote himself to the business. By then, however, it was rapidly losing money. Herbert made a half-hearted attempt at being a publisher, but three years later he and his brothers gave it up, selling all three *World* papers to Scripps-Howard for $5 million. The new owners killed the morning and Sunday *Worlds* and perpetuated only the lower-quality evening paper as part of the newly combined *World-Telegram.* It eventually died, too.

Herbert's principal contribution to the Pulitzer saga was in siring Herbert Pulitzer Jr., who grew up to become a Palm Beach playboy involved in a sensational sex and drug scandal that captured national headlines throughout 1982. Herbert Junior's suit for divorce from his wife, Roxanne Pulitzer, spawned a nasty outpouring of charges and counter-charges of adultery, group sex, lesbianism, and cocaine addiction. The nation's news media gorged on the story, which offered such lurid accusations as Roxanne Pulitzer allegedly sleeping with a sex-toy trumpet.

The attention lavished on the Pulitzer divorce trial may have been frivolous, but it wasn't a total waste. It did much to make the American public more aware of the history of Joseph Pulitzer and his prizes. And the story resulted in a tabloid headline classic: STRUMPET WITH A TRUMPET!

It was not the kind of attention Joseph Pulitzer would have wanted. But, in the greatest irony of all, it was exactly the kind of story that had made him rich.

6

Claire Spiegel: Heartbreak Hospital

A DIFFERENT KIND OF STORY, one that would have moved Joseph Pulitzer in an earlier era, was forming in Claire Spiegel's mind as she helplessly watched the boy on the hospital gurney. Only five, he writhed in agony and cried out in Spanish for his mother, who was not there. A steam-heat radiator had erupted on him at the south-central Los Angeles home where he apparently had been left unsupervised, along with some other children. The boy's chest was severely scalded. So were his genitals and hands. But he was among the luckier new arrivals that night at "Killer King." He would survive the visit.

"Killer King" was the nickname many Los Angelenos—especially officers of the law—still used in early 1988 for Martin Luther King Jr.–Drew Medical Center. The hulking institution on South Wilmington Avenue, in the heart of Watts, looks more drab than dangerous, but "killer" was the reputation the hospital labored under at the time. Any paramedic could recite the unwritten rule of the Los Angeles Police

Department: When a cop gets shot in this part of town, you don't take him to King.

In medical circles, the county-operated teaching facility was known as "a bad hospital" that was "doing bad things to patients," Claire Spiegel recalls.

That begins to explain why Claire, the *Los Angeles Times*'s health-care reporter, was there that night in the hospital's emergency room, trying to comfort the scalded Hispanic boy.

No relative was with him. No doctor or nurse, either. Claire used what little Spanish she knew to try to soothe the boy. And as he whimpered, outrage welled within her. The harried emergency room staff seemed to be ignoring him. She struggled to keep a grip on her professional objectivity.

"I'm a reporter," she kept telling herself. "I'm here only to observe. I will *not* get involved."

More time passed. Still no attention for the boy. Finally, his suffering shattered her resolve. To hell with objectivity, she told herself, and she stormed over to a couple of interns.

"Look at this little guy here," she demanded. "He can't speak English, and his mother's not here. Can't you please give him some attention?"

In the rebuke that followed, Claire was informed that the emergency department was understaffed, undersupervised, and overwhelmed that night trying to save people with far more ghastly injuries, including a woman who had been shot in the face and a child who had been torn apart by a pit bull.

Stunned, Claire went back to the gurney. She stayed by the burned boy's side for the next two hours as she watched, increasingly appalled by the chaos around her. James Haughton, she realized, had been right.

Dr. James Haughton III was King hospital's new medical director. Claire was there that night become he had practically begged her to come and observe. He had called her after seeing Claire's *Times* coverage of a crisis brewing among Los Angeles hospitals: Some of the big private hospitals were threatening to close their emergency rooms because they were ridiculously overloaded.

"This would have thrown the whole health-care system into chaos," Claire says. "It's bad enough as it is now, with a lot of emergency rooms open, but if the big ones started closing it could trigger a domino effect, and you'd have a situation where the public hospitals, which are already stretched beyond capacity, would have to absorb a lot of the load the private sector had been shouldering."

King was among those worried public hospitals. So Haughton, medical chief at the hospital for less than six months, called Claire at the paper and spoke bluntly.

"If all these private hospitals do close their emergency rooms, we won't be able to cope. We already are doing bad things to patients," he told her. "We've got only one ultra-sound machine. We have brain microscopes that fall apart during surgery. Our equipment is from the 1950s. This is a terrible place to practice medicine."

Claire quoted him in a story that ran on the front page. And afterward she could not stop thinking about his invitation: "We can't do our job now," he'd told her. "Come on down here and look at us."

At first, she resisted the idea. What was the point, anyhow? She had already put the guy on record reporting this information on the front page of the *Los Angeles Times*. She didn't have any trouble believing he was telling the truth. So what would she accomplish by visiting King?

"But," she recalls, "I started thinking, how can I possibly let something like that go? When you have a medical director who calls you, rather than the supervisors whom he is supposed to report to, and he says he doesn't think he has any other way of getting attention and he says this hospital is really the pits, it's incumbent on you to take a look at it."

Maybe it would result in a feature story, she thought. Or maybe no story at all. But at least she wouldn't be guilty of ignoring the man's plea.

So she accepted Haughton's offer—with a few conditions: She wanted unrestricted, unescorted access to the emergency room, which is normally off limits to reporters. She wanted to observe the place at night, when the action was hottest. And she wanted advance clearance to bring in a photographer, if she so decided.

"No problem," Haughton replied.

Soon afterward, on a lovely spring night in May, Claire read a bedtime story to sleepy little Allison, tucked her in for the night, and said goodbye to her husband, Brad. She got into her Volvo 240 SL in the driveway of their beautiful beach house, then drove south down palm-lined Grandview Avenue, past many more handsome homes, and turned east onto Manhattan Beach Boulevard, drove east along its little boutiques and cafes, and headed out toward the freeway that would take her to hell.

To reach the hospital from Manhattan Beach, you have to drive through the most dangerous part of Los Angeles. Even in daylight, south-central L.A. is a place where people can get killed just standing on a street corner. Drive-by shootings have become commonplace—to the point that they're not particularly newsworthy anymore. King hospital has had to install metal detectors on the wards, out of fear that rival gang members will slip in and finish off a killing that they muffed on the street. Nurses at King would advise Claire that the best way to get out of this neighborhood at night is to avoid stopping at any red lights, because any woman alone in a car like her new Volvo is going to get picked off if she stops.

Claire was no ingenue. And she wasn't afraid that night. She pulled into the hospital parking lot shortly before midnight, found the best-lighted spot, locked the Volvo, and sprinted from the car to the hospital entrance.

Four years on the mean streets of New York had prepared her for this.

Or so she thought.

"I really sort of pride myself on being a thick-skinned reporter," she says. "I mean, I've seen a lot of things. And I've learned that you can pull a curtain between you and what you're reporting."

She had been around hospital trauma centers, so she knew this wasn't going to be a pleasant experience. But this tough pro—seasoned by years of reporting on grisly crimes and accidents, and other kinds of human suffering—was unprepared for what she was about to see in the emergency room at Martin Luther King Jr.–Drew Medical Center.

The carnage—the parade of bleeding victims of knifings, shootings, beatings, and maulings—wasn't what turned Claire Spiegel inside out. It wasn't the chaos, either. Even the best trauma centers can seem chaotic. What shocked Claire was the center's dispirited, leaderless, and ultimately insufficient response to this tide of suffering.

"The thing that impressed me the most was that the interns and the residents were saying, 'We don't have anybody teaching us here. You know, where is the attending physician who's supposed to be in charge, who's supposed to be training us right now? He's asleep in the faculty lounge.' "

They were right. Claire found him there at 2 A.M. and woke him up by knocking. He came to the door stretching and yawning. "Come back later," he told her, declining an interview.

"It was evident," she says, "that there was virtually no supervision of the interns and residents. And that they were faced with incredibly complex, difficult medical situations. The numbers were just overwhelming."

As Claire watched that night, paramedics hauled in an eleven-year-old boy with a shotgun wound to the head and his eighteen-year-old friend, whose arm was partially blown off by another blast. Several other gruesome cases came along before the night ended, and she saw a man go unattended for hours after his leg had been mangled in a power mower. It was the soft cries of the scalded boy, however, that pushed Claire over the edge.

"His suffering was so painful, and my heart just went out. I really felt like it was my own little girl there on the gurney."

In the same way Jim Dwyer had been deeply affected by the near-collision of the A trains, Claire personalized the suffering she saw at King.

And her observations confirmed what Haughton had argued: The hospital was indeed operating with insufficient resources. "But I noticed there was a tremendous lack of commitment, as well, on the part of the attending physicians," she says.

Claire knew there was a story here, one even more substantial than the piece the hospital's medical director was seeking. By dawn, she had made up her mind to pursue it.

Quite correctly, Claire had observed that something was terribly wrong at King. Over the next year, she would uncover a pattern of bungled hospital care described by one expert as "atrocities of medical malpractice."

As the sun began to rise that next morning and Claire drove

away from Watts, being careful not to stop completely at the lights, she could not have guessed where her investigation would lead. Nor could she have seen that it would put her on a collision course with Jim Dwyer for a Pulitzer Prize.

And certainly she could not have known that her pursuit of the story would have an adverse impact on her personal life, causing pain for herself and for her own little girl.

* * *

Joseph Pulitzer's once-proud World Building had become a seedy Manhattan warehouse, with demolition just three years away, when Claire Spiegel was born in July of 1952 in Berkeley, California. Nothing about her early life suggested she would become, like Jim Dwyer, the kind of street-smart, crusading reporter that Pulitzer so admired.

The daughter of a San Francisco tax attorney and a school-teacher, Claire had an idyllic childhood. Her life consisted of ballet and tennis lessons and private all-girls schools on week-days and Congregational Church services on Sundays.

Unlike Jim Dwyer's ancestors, Claire's had been in the New World for six generations before she was born. They were working-class immigrants—German and Irish farmers, miners, and factory workers—who eventually produced a Spiegel who obtained a college education and became a civil engineer in Topeka, Kansas. That engineer had a bright son who won a scholarship to Yale, survived combat wounds as a Marine on Okinawa during World War II, and came home to start a successful law practice in California. That was Hart Spiegel, Claire's father. Her mother, Genevieve, a former Idaho farm girl with a teaching degree, married him during the war, in Hawaii where she served as a WAC.

The young teacher and her lawyer husband settled after the war in Berkeley and began living the postwar American dream, giving their children advantages that were unimagin-able to Spiegels just a few generations removed.

"As a girl, I was a little bookworm," Claire recalls. "I studied a whole lot. I really liked school. I also liked books and I liked reading."

All three of the Spiegel children were high achievers. Her younger sister, Jennifer, grew up to become vice president of marketing for The Sharper Image merchandising company. Her older brother, John, became a lawyer like their father.

John, always a large influence in Claire's life, was a tennis star at Stanford—the university's top player for a while, "and a little bit of it rubbed off" on her, she says. She competed on her high school tennis team and later would keep up with the sport throughout her adult career.

But what was her career to be? As a bookish, serious-minded teenager, she thought about that a lot. And her answer started taking shape at the same time her social consciousness took root, during her high school years when her hometown was rocked by the Free Speech Movement at the University of California at Berkeley. Claire could easily observe the campus upheaval. She attended the exclusive Anna Head School for Girls, which at that time was directly across the street from People's Park. She saw a lot of the student demonstrations and violence. More than once, on her way home after classes, her school bus drove through clouds of tear gas.

Claire became fascinated with the ideas, rhetoric, and human conflict that filled the air and the newspapers and the dinner-table conversations during that period. The turmoil jolted her out of her girlhood cocoon and made her become, if not radicalized, at least more idealistic. She realized she wanted a career that would somehow improve people's understanding of others.

At seventeen, Claire leaped at an opportunity to become a foreign exchange student. She went to Indonesia for three months "and became enamored of the very, very different culture of a third-world country."

By the time she returned to California, she knew what she wanted to do with her life. Or at least she thought she knew. "I wanted to study the headhunters in Borneo," she says. "I wanted to go off and read the hieroglyphics on the temple wall."

She planned to become an anthropologist and travel the world. Soon thereafter she enrolled at Stanford, following her brother there. But John Spiegel thought Claire was making a poor choice, she says.

"He sort of set me straight. He convinced me it sounded great on paper [to become an anthropologist], but in reality it would be a very lonely life and I ought to reconsider my career and make sure that I didn't end up working as a teller in a bank like a lot of people he knew. So I started thinking about other sorts of careers. And I knew I didn't want to be a lawyer or a doctor. There were enough lawyers in my family already, and I don't like blood."

Eventually, she figured out a way she could see the world and observe the human condition "without leading as lonely a life as an anthropologist would have to lead." She would become a foreign correspondent.

With that critical life-path decision, Claire changed her major to journalism and started working on Stanford's student newspaper. There, just like Jim Dwyer a continent away, she discovered what any successful journalist discovers: The work made her happy.

"I found out that journalism gives you a license to ask all kinds of questions and hobnob with all sorts of different kinds of people," she says. "And it gives you a unique insight on the world, whether it's the world abroad or your own community."

She apologizes if that sounds a little like the hype students hear on Journalism Career Day. But that's how she felt about her new field, and she applied herself to it with the same bookish seriousness she had always shown.

An outstanding student, Claire won two highly prized summer internships during her college years—in 1973 at the *Idaho Statesman* in Boise and in 1974 at the *Boston Globe*. Claire received a bachelor's degree at Stanford and went off to seek her master's degree at the Graduate School of Journalism Joseph Pulitzer had endowed at Columbia (four years before Jim Dwyer, who was just starting his undergraduate work at Fordham at this point). Columbia's journalism school was still enjoying substantial prestige in the mid-1970s. In Claire's view, the program deserved its reputation.

"Columbia was my introduction to New York, and it was a great way to go," she says. "I'd hate to have to move from California and go straight to covering Brooklyn. You wouldn't even know how to find the subways.

"Columbia is a tremendous laboratory for young journalists. You get a real feel for the city," roaming it, as the program required students to do, practicing the reporter's craft. "So my work experience was a sort of natural outgrowth of my having interned there [at Columbia] the prior year."

One of her instructors at Columbia was Dick Oliver, who at that time was city editor of the *New York Daily News*. She climbed high on the learning curve through his tutelage, which included a lot of guidance on her master's thesis. It was an in-depth article on controversial plans to import liquefied natural gas into New York, store it on Staten Island, and ship it up the East River. Her instructor's newspaper bought the piece from her on a free-lance basis and published it in its Sunday magazine.

With that foot planted nicely in the doorway, Claire followed through and was hired as a reporter at the *Daily News* in the summer of 1975. At the time, the tabloid was the nation's third-largest metropolitan daily, with circulation exceeding one million.

"I started out working on the zoned section, in Brooklyn, which was—and still is—a big slum," she says. "So there was just lots of good nuts-and-bolts reporting there for me—stories about housing projects, mob murders, fires, subway crimes."

Claire soaked in the street journalism of Brooklyn for eight months before the paper brought her downtown to cover the same kind of news in Manhattan. Then she was transferred up to Albany, New York's capital, to help cover the statehouse for several months.

By the time the *Daily News* brought Claire Spiegel back to the newsroom in Manhattan, she was becoming seasoned, tough, and respectably skilled at her job. The editors handed her some investigative work. Years later, she remains proud of her exposé of a federal bankruptcy judge's political patronage. The judge had appointed a friend as a receiver for a company, and the friend had appointed the judge's brother's bookkeeping firm to do all the accounting—a rather chummy relationship—and Claire found out that checks were being written to addresses that were nonexistent, such as alleys in Tennessee.

The story caused a giant stir, "like throwing a baseball into a bee's hive," as Claire remembers it. There was the predictable public outcry, posturing by politicians, and subsequent push for bankruptcy court reforms.

It was a heady time for young Claire. The work exhilarated her. Looking back, she realizes she was fortunate to be at the *Daily News* while it was perhaps at its best. "This," she recalls, "was before Rupert Murdoch bought the rival *Post* and the two tabloids began trying to out-yellow each other."

Claire was in love with her job at the *Daily News,* and she was in love with New York. Unfortunately for both the paper and New York, she was also in love with a man. Brad Brian was a student at Harvard Law School. Claire met him through a mutual friend and quickly discovered she and Brad had much in common. He, too, was interested in corporate law, just like her father and brother. And Brad, too, was from the Bay Area—born and raised in South San Francisco. He had attended U.C.-Berkeley while she was at Stanford. They had to move twenty-five hundred miles away to link up.

"We wanted to get married, and he didn't want to practice law in New York. He wanted Los Angeles," she recalls. "I loved New York and didn't want to leave it. And, of course, I thought I was giving up the best job in the world and moving out to the sticks," which is how many New Yorkers tend to view the West Coast.

"Now I think in retrospect it was the smartest thing I ever did, because the *Daily News* has since experienced a lot of difficulties and a lot of labor strife."

Claire is perhaps too kind to her former employer. The *Daily News* has since descended into a garish street-fight for survival against the racy *Post* and the newer tabloid competitor, *New York Newsday.* The circulation war has been compounded by a vicious contract dispute at the *Daily News,* which began the 1990s seeking concessions from its labor unions to reverse what it claims is more than $100 million in losses over the past decade. The paper entered 1991 mired in a bitter strike by nine of its ten unions.

So instead of staying around to become a bit player in that sad drama, Claire went west, following Brad back to "the sticks." They were married in August 1978 in San Francisco, and settled in Los Angeles, where Brad joined the U.S. Attorney's Office and Claire found work as a county government reporter at the *Los Angeles Times.*

Claire admits she still felt a little blue about leaving the excitement of New York. Looking back, though, she now realizes she was lucky she decided to let her career follow Brad's. In L.A., she was joining the staff of a very good newspaper that was just then completing the transition to becoming a great one. Over the next twelve years, the *New York Daily News* would collect just one Pulitzer Prize (for work by columnist Jimmy Breslin, who would soon defect to *New York Newsday*). During the same period, Claire's new employer would collect eight Pulitzers.

She couldn't possibly have guessed that one of those eight prizes might have her name on it.

* * *

Manhattan Beach resembles nothing like its namesake. Just thirteen miles from downtown Los Angeles, the California beach community was named after the New York City borough in 1912, because city founder Stewart Merrill was luckier than co-founder George Peck. Merrill, a native New Yorker, wanted to incorporate the little resort town as "Manhattan Beach." Peck, a Midwesterner, favored "Shore Acres." A coin toss resolved their friendly dispute.

Since then, Manhattan Beach has grown up to be an arty bedroom community with a low-key, resort-like atmosphere. The town has a clean, accessible municipal beach, several good restaurants, two fine coffee houses, dozens of expensive stores such as Chez Rebecca's, which sells silk flowers, and about thirty-five thousand residents, mostly well-to-do Los Angeles commuters.

One of those commuters, Claire Spiegel, found herself driving against the flow of evening traffic in early 1988, returning to a part of Los Angeles devoid of stores selling silk flowers. After her eye-opening night in the emergency room at Martin Luther King Jr.–Drew Medical Center, she returned the next night, and the next, and the next, bringing a *Times* photographer along. She spent an entire week of all-nighters at the Watts hospital.

The additional nights of observation helped to confirm the judgments Claire had formed during her first night at King. Besides witnessing the hospital's problems, she interviewed numerous staff people—doctors and nurses speaking to her at considerable personal risk—who were chagrined at the poor level of care.

The following week, Claire briefed Craig Turner, the *Time's* metropolitan editor, about the King story. She received his blessings to invest more time on it while doing her best to continue covering the health-care beat.

Her next step, identical to Jim Dwyer's after he determined he had a story worth investigating, called for document collection.

"I was persona non grata immediately at the hospital, as soon as I started asking for records in writing," she says. "I think they initially thought I was just going to do a one-week story about, gee, how harried things are in the emergency room."

Haughton, the medical director, continued to be quite forthright with Claire, even though he could see she was onto more of a story than he had bargained for. But his boss, the hospital administrator, circled the wagons. Claire succeeded in getting mounds of reports and documents through her official requests, but a lot of it was irrelevant. Most of her requests for truly helpful information, on treatment of patients at King, were turned down on grounds of confidentiality. Initially, after this rejection, she hoped to find some of that information in medical malpractice claims that had been filed against the county. But she discovered there were few such claims, quite clearly because many of the low-income people who were treated at King "didn't have cases that a lawyer would take."

However, she did find a few malpractice claims, only to have county officials refuse to turn over the documents, insisting they weren't public records.

"We had to sue them," Claire recalls. "We won in Superior Court, and they appealed. We won in the Court of Appeals. They appealed to the California Supreme Court, and it agreed to hear the case. This was like six months after I'd requested these claims. And finally, the county said, 'Okay, we'll give them to you.' At this point, though, the records weren't nearly as useful to me as they would have been earlier."

That is because she had spent those six months amassing the same kind of patient records using a quite different approach. She became the hospital flower shop's best customer.

"If you're carrying flowers, you look a whole lot different

than if you're carrying a notebook, right? So I carried flowers around and visited patients and tried to get them to sign forms releasing their medical records to me."

The tactic worked spectacularly well.

"I never got any flak from any patient. They were just so glad to feel that somebody cared about them. Sometimes they just wanted company. Once I found patients and explained myself to them, I think they trusted me. I think that they felt that I was not out to do them any harm. And I wasn't."

In this manner Claire obtained records for nearly fifty patients at King. She also obtained records on several deceased King patients by tracking down their survivors and getting their signatures on forms permitting release of the files.

"A lot of these relatives were scattered all over. They didn't speak English, and I had to go back to south-central L.A. at night because that's when they tended to be home," she says. "Sometimes it was tricky, trying to get past the guard dogs, accompanied by somebody who spoke Spanish and who'd explain what I was doing."

To Claire's great relief, the people she visited opened up immediately, once they understood what she was doing. Generally, they were astonished, and pleased, that some "white lady with flowers" cared about their departed.

As she collected patient records, Claire began running them past medical experts who had agreed to review them, off the record. Later, after they had seen what she had turned up, several of these medical professionals *asked* her to quote them with full attribution. The experts were appalled. Claire showed them records of dismaying medical bungling:

An eighteen-year-old shooting victim whose throat was accidentally slit by trauma doctors at King.

A thirty-seven-year-old woman who died after routine surgery in which her colon was accidentally cut and improperly repaired.

A woman whose spleen was mistakenly removed.

A woman who was declared brain-dead after languishing for several critical hours at King because no neurosurgeon was available to perform surgery that almost certainly would have saved her.

Claire's list went on and on.

Meanwhile, in addition to the poor medical care, Claire found that senior doctors at King were "playing hooky," not giving the county hospital the service they were being paid to provide. Many had extensive private practices that they had not disclosed, as required, by county regulations. Some doctors were breaking the law by cheating on their time sheets.

"So I had to spend a lot of time not only tracking patients, but also tracking doctors," Claire says.

For example, she and a *Times* photographer spent a day in separate cars tailing a doctor whose absenteeism was a notorious sore point among King interns. Claire and the photographer parked near the physician's home early one morning and followed him discreetly throughout the day. He spent less than four hours at the medical center, leaving shortly after noon and not returning. Instead, he ran errands and visited other hospitals, where he treated private patients. Later, he put down a full eight hours on his King payroll card.

She documented several instances of doctors who were scheduled to appear as attending (supervising) physicians in the King emergency room but routinely skipped out, working instead in their very busy private practices.

She also turned up an attending physician who was sending residents of the hospital to a private medical center to perform abortions for a fee. Since this was questionable use of residents' time, she went to his office at King to ask him about it.

She says, "I went without an appointment, because I felt that if I made one, he would not talk to me, and I felt that I owed him the opportunity to respond to what I was going to report. The receptionist said he wasn't in the office and she didn't know when he would be back. So I just sat and waited. Much later, he finally came out of his office."

The doctor, a huge man, glowered down at Claire.

"I don't want to talk to you. I don't want to have anything to do with you," he told her.

"Well, sir," Claire shot back. "It is my responsibility as a journalist to tell you what I intend to write about you."

He turned on his heel and headed for the door, as Claire jumped up and followed. She clicked on her tape recorder, trying at least to make a record of her attempt to give the doctor a fair chance to respond to her allegations about his use of hospital residents.

He marched briskly down a hallway with Claire in pursuit, all the while informing him—as she spoke into the tape recorder—that she was making a record of his refusal to talk.

"As we got to the stairwell," she recalls, "he grabbed my wrist, took the tape recorder out of my hand, and started running down the stairs—with the tape recorder on. So I ran clattering down the stairs after him."

She chased him all the way to the hospital's head office, where the fugitive doctor placed the tape recorder on the startled administrator's desk.

The doctor's performance never made it into Claire's stories on King hospital, but she still has the tape. It's a classic. You can hear the CLACK-CLACK-CLACK-CLACK of her heels as she chases him down the stairs, yelling "You give me back my tape recorder," and you can hear the doctor barging into the administrator's office, saying "This woman has been trying to tape-record me!"

Claire was never completely detached from her daily reporting duties during the year and a half she pursued the King story. "During this whole period, I was covering a beat as well as trying to report this story, and I had daily obligations. There were a number of times when I thought, gee, it'd be a lot easier to just put this baby to rest quickly. You know, get the story in the paper and scale it way down and not tackle it in the manner that I ultimately chose to."

Resisting that temptation added considerable stress to her life. So did her situation at home.

By mid-1989, Claire had spent over a year working long and varied hours on the hospital investigation and on her regular reporting duties. But her absences from home had not created any marital difficulty. Brad worked similarly long hours in his thriving law practice. There was no time for either spouse to feel neglected while both labored so hard. And Claire was getting strong support from Brad, who vividly recalls that period:

"She would drive across town in the middle of the night, calling people at all hours, tailing people. But I wasn't that worried about her. She has always picked stories like that. Hey, this is a woman who once crashed a Hell's Angels wedding to get a story."

Instead of clashing, their busy careers complement each other, he says. "It's a fabulous mix. She has helped me immensely on my writing, and I think I've helped her on her organizational skills."

Claire had also become pregnant again by mid-1989, but she and the unborn baby were perfectly fine. That was not amplifying her stress.

The problem was Allison, who by that time had turned three.

"We went through a period of terrible separation anxiety," Claire says. "She was just so upset about my going to work and my being away from her that she didn't want to go to nursery school. Every morning she woke up and said, 'Is this the weekend?' And while I was doing this story, I kept asking myself, 'Is this worth it? I mean, am I ruining my little child here? If she needs me home, I can afford to stay home. I don't have to work. So what am I doing this for?'"

The answer, of course, is that Claire loved being a reporter. So she stayed with it, dreading each workday morning's inevitable crisis: Allison's tears and pitiful screaming as Mom had to drop her off at nursery school.

The problem was compounded when Allison's nanny developed an eye problem and said she could no longer work.

"It was traumatic," Claire says. "She'd been like Allison's surrogate mother for three years. Losing a nanny is the next worse thing to a divorce. It was like having your husband die and having to remarry immediately, with no courting. You don't even have time to adjust to the grief of her leaving, and then you have to interview all these other people and make up your mind about them in like three days."

With all the pressure she was under at work, Claire had little time to advertise and find a new nanny. Her job of screening applicants turned out to be less than thorough.

"Here I am, this ace investigative reporter, and I ended up picking this lady who turned out to be a real lulu."

Claire soon discovered, to her everlasting chagrin, that her new nanny's principal reference—her employer for the past four years, who gave a glowing recommendation—was actually the nanny's boyfriend.

The young woman was abruptly fired, and the difficult search for a new nanny resumed. To Claire's great delight, she hired a young woman who was "fantastic, gifted with children, and taking child-development courses on the side."

But Claire's concern about Allison took a new twist, Claire says. "Here was this child who everybody had always said was the most precocious, intelligent, sweet, fantastic little girl—who was now stuttering."

At first, Claire was devastated.

"Allison was feeling stress. She couldn't separate from me. She was having these anxiety attacks, saying 'I can't get my words out, Mommy,' and this sort of stuff."

Claire read everything she could find on stuttering. She consulted child psychologists. And she learned that the problem isn't uncommon in children, and almost all get over it by the age of eight or nine. Finally, she relaxed.

August 1989 proved a hectic time for Claire as she crunched her eighteen months of investigative work into a three-part series. It began on the *Times* front page on September 3, 1989. Her lead—the opening paragraphs—was graphic and gory:

> An 18-year-old girl was rushed to the hospital in December after a bullet fired from a passing car tore through her neck, pierced her jawbone, lacerated her tongue and blinded her in one eye.
>
> But when she arrived at Martin Luther King Jr.–Drew Medical Center in Watts, her ordeal was not over. In surgery, trauma doctors mistakenly slit her throat.
>
> Both jugular veins were cut, causing a massive hemorrhage in what was described by one physician who later reviewed the case as a "botched" attempt to open a small airway for her to breathe.

Claire's story went on for one hundred column inches, a litany of documented medical malpractice at the hospital. She tied it down by quoting an impressive array of medical experts—she used no unnamed sources—who had reviewed the patient records that she had worked so hard to obtain.

The following day, the second installment of her series documented the failure of senior physicians to perform the supervisory work they were being paid to do at the hospital.

And on the third day, her series concluded with an examination of financial and mismanagement problems at the Charles R. Drew University of Medicine and Science, across the street from King hospital.

Noel Greenwood, the *Times* senior editor who helped with the editing of Claire's series, says it brought almost immediate results. The day after the final installment was published, the Los Angeles County Board of Supervisors ordered an investigation. Then the hospital administrator was fired. That was followed quickly by state and federal inquiries. The feds found care so inadequate at King that they threatened to cut off $60 million in funding, which probably would have closed the hospital's doors.

Under that threat, the county took immediate steps to improve patient care, administrative policy, financing, hiring, and equipment. As a result, federal officials lifted their threat to revoke funding. They cited a "dramatic turnaround" in patient care.

What might sound like a reporter's fairy-tale ending, however, was actually an extremely stressful period for Claire. Immediately after her series ran, she and the newspaper took heavy flak from the black community, which raised charges of racism. The Friends of the Hospital called a news conference to blast the white woman from the white newspaper for doing a racially biased hatchet job on a hospital that is essentially black-operated.

Editors at the *Times* rejected those charges and stood by Claire and her reporting.

"I've worked with Claire for many years, and she is a premier investigative reporter," says Greenwood, the senior editor. "She has persistence, curiosity, doggedness, nonwillingness to take no for an answer, and the ability to understand what is worth pursuing and what isn't. She is very professional and responds well to editing. She works nonstop, which is a hallmark of any first-line investigative reporter, and she is very careful, very accurate."

Greenwood and other *Times* editors found it easy to back her up. Nonetheless, it was difficult for Claire—by now nearly eight months pregnant—to attend that hostile news conference and deal with other personal attacks on her and the paper.

At one such meeting, one of the speakers pointed directly at Claire and hollered: "And there's the reporter who wrote it!"

She recalls, "Here I am surrounded by all these angry people, and I thought, 'Thank God I'm pregnant. They won't hang a pregnant woman—I hope.'"

Beneath the joking, Claire was afraid she'd have a premature baby as a result of the strain and exhaustion she was feeling.

"It was just a very, very stressful period for me. I kept thinking I was going to go into preterm labor right on the spot."

But on December 6, 1989, Claire amazed herself. She gave birth to a perfectly healthy baby girl, Leslie—thirteen days late.

Early in Claire's maternity leave, she acted on the advice of a child psychologist who recommended a change in nursery schools for Allison. Perhaps because of that successful change, and probably in part because of Claire's presence at home, the little girl, by then four, soon began overcoming her stuttering.

For the *Los Angeles Times* and Claire Spiegel, her maternity leave was a crossroads. Editors at the paper began putting together an exhibit of her work to submit for a Pulitzer Prize. And Claire, a reporter who had almost single-handedly forced a hospital to take better care of its patients, began thinking seriously of quitting her job.

7

Looking Back at the Prizes for Journalism

LIKE JIM DWYER'S SUBWAY COLUMNS, Claire Spiegel's hospital exposé was another outstanding example of the kind of journalism Joseph Pulitzer appreciated most—with two minor exceptions. He would have demanded more brevity than the *Los Angeles Times* is accustomed to, and he would have insisted on more sensational headlines than editors put on Claire's stories. Otherwise, the hospital series was exactly what Pulitzer had in mind when he dreamed up his prizes as the twentieth century began.

Over the decades since then, the competition has generally fulfilled his vision, while adding some dimensions Pulitzer could not have predicted. His prizes have been a reliable barometer of American attitudes, especially in journalism, and they have been a lightning rod for controversy, particularly in arts and letters.

Pulitzer was brooding in his soundproofed "Vault" at his Maine estate when he conceived the prizes in 1902 at the age of fifty-five—nine years before his death and fifteen years after

101

his health had collapsed. Almost totally blind by that point, he summoned a secretary and dictated a rough plan to establish the prizes as part of a $2 million endowment to start a Graduate School of Journalism at Columbia University. A sense of his own mortality probably helped motivate him. Without a doubt, though, the previous year's announcement of Alfred Nobel's first big prizes also weighed heavily in his thinking. Pulitzer much admired the Swedish inventor of dynamite and modeled his own awards after the Nobel Prizes.

But Pulitzer had some quirks. He tried to limit his recipients to Americans, while Nobel disregarded nationality. Pulitzer bequeathed less money for the prizes—$500,000 to Nobel's $9 million. Pulitzer was mostly interested in journalism and literature, while Nobel was more focused on science. And Pulitzer wanted to honor timely work, published "during the year," while Nobel Prizes usually honor winners for the body of their work over several years.

Pulitzer's will outlined nine prizes—four in journalism (public service, reporting, editorial writing, and press history), three in literature (novel, biography, and American history), one in drama, and one for the best annual essay on "the future, development and improvement" of his Graduate School of Journalism. Not surprisingly, no one ever entered the essay competition, which soon vanished. So did the journalism prize for "best history of the services rendered to the public by the American press during the preceding year."

All of the prizes originally were to be for "the best" in each category. Later, as the prizes aroused heated controversy, that wording was changed to "a distinguished" or "a distinguished example of."

Pulitzer's will did not ask for poetry or music prizes, which were added after his death, along with ten more journalism prize categories, including photography, editorial cartooning, commentary, criticism, and several types of news reporting.

Requirements for Pulitzer's original four journalism awards were fairly straightforward and timeless. But his directions for the arts and letters prizes shackled the competition with rules perpetuating high-flown American morality circa 1902.

For example, Thomas Wolfe's classic novel, *Look Homeward, Angel,* was denied the 1930 prize despite vigorous and immediate critical acclaim. Instead, the prize went to Oliver LaFarge's forgettable *Laughing Boy,* after judges agreed Wolfe's book failed to meet moralistic requirements in Pulitzer's will. It directed that the winning novel "shall best represent the whole atmosphere of American life and the highest standard of American manners and manhood." Visionary though he was, Pulitzer failed to consider that his mid-Victorian values would become passé as America's Puritan society matured and entered a literary renaissance.

His will also required, for example, that the drama prize be awarded "for the original American play performed in New York which shall best represent the educational value and power of the stage in raising the standard of good morals, good taste and good manners." And his will specified that the biography prize must honor books "teaching patriotic and unselfish service to the people."

In endowing his prizes, Pulitzer made another major mistake in his choice of those empowered to fix such problems as outdated rules. He placed shared control of the prizes in the hands of Columbia University's trustees and a powerful "Advisory Board" composed of heads of newspapers. Over the decades, this conservative, change-resistant coalition of publishers and academic administrators would form a genteel bureaucracy capable of misjudgment on a magnificent scale.

Like Nobel, Pulitzer directed that his prizes be inaugurated after his death—specifically, after at least three years of operation of his journalism school, which was to open the year after his demise. He died in 1911, the school opened in 1912, and the first Pulitzer Prizes were handed out in 1917 for work done the previous year.

Although Pulitzer dictated many basic requirements of the prizes, he left it up to the university trustees and the Advisory Board to work up a specific plan for making the awards. One of their first acts was to devise the complicated, multilayered judging system that still exists today. The trustees and board members also lost no time in tampering with the wording of Pulitzer's rules. For instance, his stipulation that a winning novel must "best represent the whole atmosphere of American life" was changed to "wholesome atmosphere."

That moralistic bit of editing was rammed through by

Nicholas Murray Butler, the priggish Columbia University president who dominated the Advisory Board for its first thirty-three years. Following Butler's stuffy leadership and Pulitzer's outdated rules, the power structure behind the Pulitzer Prizes duplicated the folly of the *Laughing Boy* decision many times over the years.

Much of that embarrassment is recorded in an indispensable, three-volume history of the prizes written by Columbia journalism professor John Hohenberg. Unfortunately, his work has the ring of a company history, witch it is. Hohenberg, far from being a neutral observer, wrote his books during the twenty-six years he served as administrator of the Pulitzer Prizes and secretary of the Advisory Board.

Hohenberg carefully avoids offering any analysis, objective or otherwise, about the value of the Pulitzer Prizes in arts and letters. And his basic conclusion about the journalism awards is that despite their flaws they will endure, continuing to "do honor to the profession they represent." He is correct, but the reverse also is true: Outstanding work by journalists will continue to do honor to the Pulitzer Prizes and, by extension, to Columbia University and to the late Joseph Pulitzer. In truth, these awards shower less glory on the recipients than on the givers, who reap an incalculable public relations harvest and, in the benefactor's case, immortality.

* * *

The Pulitzer Prizes in journalism have always been dominated by the exposé—news stories revealing information that certain parties, most often the government, do not want disclosed. Of the 580 journalism prizes awarded between 1917 and 1990, nearly 40 percent fit that definition.

Another 40 percent of the prizes have honored a mix of war, crime, civil liberties, race relations, politics, disaster, and international reporting. The remaining prizes have involved a variety of specialized subjects such as those covered by Jim Dwyer, Claire Spiegel, and Tamar Stieber.

Throughout the seventy-five-year history of the Pulitzer competition, it has served as an accurate mirror of mainstream American society and the press that serves it.

In earlier times, for example, when unabashed nationalism was in vogue, the prizes reflected it. The 1919 public service

award went to the *Milwaukee Journal* for its "strong and courageous campaign for Americanism in a constituency where
foreign elements made such a policy hazardous from a business point of view." And the 1932 Pulitzer for news reporting
was awarded to five staff members at the *Detroit Free Press* for
their flowery account of an American Legion parade.

When the nation's conscience was stricken by activities of the
Ku Klux Klan, the prizes mirrored that, too. Numerous
Southern newspapers won Pulitzers for courageous reporting
and editorializing about the Klan over a thirty-year period
beginning in 1922.

In an era when science reporting was lightly regarded, that
also showed up in the prizes. In 1941, for example, the prize
board brushed aside a Pulitzer jury recommendation for an
award to William L. Laurence, a science reporter for the *New
York Times*. Instead, the board gave the reporting prize to a
celebrity journalist, *New York World-Telegram* columnist Westbrook Pegler, for articles on a labor scandal. And what did the
obscure Mr. Laurence report that was deemed to be less
worthy? His exclusive story, rejected for a prize by the
unimpressed Pulitzer board, disclosed that Columbia University scientists on May 5, 1940, had split the atom—two years
after the Germans and two years before the world's first
controlled atomic chain reaction at the University of Chicago's
Stagg Field.

When America went to war and the nation rallied around its
military effort, so did the press, and so did the Pulitzer Prizes.
During World War II, twenty-four Pulitzers were awarded for
reporting, photography, and editorial cartoons dealing with
the war effort. The nation's total commitment showed in the
prizes, which included a 1941 "group award" to all American
news reporters in the war zones. The Pulitzer Board also
handed out three special citations during the war—one to the
New York Times for the "public educational value of its foreign
news report," another to the director of the Office of Censorship "for the creation and administration of the newspaper and
radio codes," and a third to "the cartographers of the American press whose maps of the war fronts have helped notably to
clarify and increase public information on the progress of the
armies and navies engaged."

After the war, the Pulitzer Prizes accurately reflected the newspaper industry's performance—or nonperformance, as it were—during the anti-Communist witch hunt of the late 1940s and early 1950s. Almost all of the newspapers that really counted—the establishment papers—were silent. They failed to take a stand against Senator Joe McCarthy and his fellow Red-baiters and black-listers when it really mattered.

Edwin R. Bayley, a *Milwaukee Journal* reporter during the Red Scare, covered the Wisconsin senator's rise to power and later wrote about it after becoming dean of journalism at the University of California at Berkeley. Bayley's 1981 book, *Joe McCarthy and the Press*, documents in scrupulous detail how America's mainstream news media failed to expose McCarthy as the dangerous demagogue that he was. The book paints an unflattering portrait of a press that became cowardly silent in 1950, when McCarthy burst into national headlines by claiming to have a list of 205 Communists working in the U.S. government—a claim that coincided with the publication of *Red Channels*, a book by three former FBI agents that listed 151 writers and artists who purportedly had helped advance "Communist objectives." The media's timidity lasted until 1954, when broadcaster Edward R. Murrow found the courage to stand up to McCarthy on television. Murrow's high-impact "See It Now" program was followed by six weeks of the televised daily Army-McCarthy hearings, which exposed the senator for what he was and effectively ruined him.

At that point, it was suddenly safe and fashionable for the proper press to begin attacking the rapidly self-destructing senator. But to what end? McCarthy's four-year witch hunt had already done its damage, wrecking scores of lives and careers.

Throughout those four years, however, a small group of journalists worked bravely to alert the public about McCarthy and his threat to civil liberties. Besides I. F. Stone and columnists Drew Pearson and Elmer Davis, this cadre included reporters and editorial writers and cartoonists at the *Washington Post*, the Madison Wisconsin *Capital Times*, the *Sheboygan* (Wis.) *Press*, the *Milwaukee Journal*, the *Raleigh News & Observer*, the *Tampa Tribune*, the *Syracuse Post-Standard*, the *St. Louis Post-Dispatch*, and others. All wound up on McCarthy's list of "left-wing newspapers."

In his book, Bayley says the *Washington Post,* which was fighting for financial survival during that period, "deserves at least as much credit for its long struggle against McCarthy as for its Watergate triumph."

Unfortunately, during the four years that McCarthy was riding high, none of those who stood up against him were honored with Pulitzer Prizes.

Robert Christopher, the prize administrator, denied that assertion. In a written response to the author, Christopher referred to *The Pulitzer Prizes* by former administrator John Hohenberg:

> In fact, on Page 191 of the book, John notes that in 1948 the National Reporting Prize went to Bert Andrews of the old [New York] *Herald-Trib* for revealing that the State Department had fired an employee as a security risk without any semblance of due process and that in 1950 the same award went to Ed Guthman of *The Seattle Times* for clearing a professor of charges that he had attended a Communist training school. Finally, in 1954, Herblock won the cartooning award for a portfolio that included a drawing of McCarthy as a rotten apple.

Christopher's defense misses the point, however. Neither of the prizewinning stories by Bert Andrews or Ed Guthman had a word about Joseph McCarthy. And the 1954 prize for "Herblock" (editorial cartoonist Herbert L. Block of the *Washington Post*) came shortly *after* the "See It Now" telecast in which Edward R. Murrow helped end McCarthy's career. Nobody at the *Post* or at any of the other few nonintimidated papers received a Pulitzer for journalism involving McCarthy between his "I have a list" speech in 1950 and his "See It Now" comeuppance in 1954.

The records of Pulitzer jury and board deliberations during those four years would be interesting for whatever light they might shed on journalistic prize-giving during McCarthy's heyday. However, Christopher and his assistant, Bud Kliment, said the Pulitzer Prize records for 1950–1955 were inexplicably missing.

None of McCarthy's "left-wing newspapers" received

Pulitzer Prizes for editorials during that period. Records at two of those papers, however, show that their anti-McCarthy editorials had been entered in the competition: Alan Barth's long-running crusade against McCarthyism at the *Washington Post* and Irving Dilliard's harsh criticism of McCarthy at the *St. Louis Post-Dispatch.*

The lack of recognition for Dilliard and other *Post-Dispatch* editorial writers is especially interesting. They maintained their anti-McCarthy position throughout 1950–54 with great difficulty, under almost constant pressure from the publisher, Joseph Pulitzer II, to ease off on the senator, according to Bayley's book, *Joe McCarthy and the Press.*

Bayley wrote, "Pulitzer's memoranda to Dilliard over the next four years were a succession of notes that pleaded, wheedled or demanded that the editor be kinder to McCarthy and the Republicans." He quoted from one such memo from Pulitzer, admonishing Dilliard in April of 1954 as the Army-McCarthy hearings got under way: "Please, please, please lay off the McCarthy hearings. To me—and I believe to the great majority—they are the most terrific bore."

A subsequent memo from Pulitzer to Dilliard banned any reference to "McCarthy" or "McCarthyism" on the editorial page without Pulitzer's specific approval.

Between 1950 and 1954, the chairman of the Pulitzer Prize Board was none other than Joseph Pulitzer II. Thanks to him and his colleagues on the board, the handful of journalists and newspapers that *did* stand up to Senator McCarthy remain underappreciated.

The Pulitzer Prize administration has the power to remedy that failing. Belatedly but apologetically, the board could issue the special citations that should have been awarded nearly forty years ago.

After all, in 1987, the board voted such a citation for Joseph Pulitzer Jr., son of the man who ordered his editorial writers to "lay off McCarthy."

The Vietnam War provided yet another national crisis in which American journalism was challenged to show some courage. This time, certain segments of the press—and, at the same time, the Pulitzer Prizes—fared better.

During the fighting in Vietnam there were no Pulitzer Prize

"group awards" to war correspondents and no special citations to government censors. Instead, there was a string of prizes for unvarnished war reporting—much of it unflattering to U.S. military leaders and policy makers—by Peter Arnett and Malcolm Browne of the Associated Press, David Halberstam of the *New York Times,* and William Tuohy of the *Los Angeles Times.* Among the Saigon press corps, they represented a minority of reporters who refused to accept the Pentagon's specious claims of success. The foursome risked their careers and in some cases their physical survival to report how the war was really being conducted.

On the homefront, editorial writers John Knight of the Knight Newspapers and Robert Lasch of the *St. Louis Post-Dispatch* took unpopular stands against the war and received Pulitzer Prizes for their efforts. So did editorial cartoonists Don Wright of the *Miami News,* Patrick Oliphant of the *Denver Post,* and Paul Conrad of the *Los Angeles Times.*

Seven wire-service staffers won Pulitzers for Vietnam combat photography that jarred the American conscience. Among them were three U.S. citizens, Horst Faas, Edward Adams, and Dave Kennerly; two Japanese, Toshio Sakai and Kyoichi Sawada; one German, Slava Veder; and a Vietnamese, Huynh Cong Ut. Along with AP's Peter Arnett, a New Zealander who later went to work for Cable News Network, this group comprises the few non-Americans ever to win Pulitzers.

Of all the prize-winning Vietnam reporting, none was more inspirational than the work of Seymour Hersh, at that time an unknown, unemployed reporter who did his story without leaving U.S. soil.

The thirty-two-year-old Chicagoan was unemployed early in 1969 after working as a press agent for Eugene McCarthy's ill-fated presidential campaign. Richard Nixon had just taken office, the Vietnam War was raging, and American university campuses were being rocked by antiwar protests. Hersh was job-hunting at the time, without much success, when he picked up a story tip that was almost too sensational to believe. His source, a Pentagon employee he had met a few years earlier when he worked for the Associated Press, told Hersh about a rumored incident in which U.S. troops supposedly slaughtered Vietnamese civilians in a village in Viet Cong territory.

The story sounded flimsy to Hersh. Atrocities like that were the work of war criminals, not well-disciplined American soldiers. But Hersh respected and trusted his Pentagon source, who thought there was some truth in the appalling rumor.

Hersh's conscience and his journalistic instincts demanded that he look into it. But that wasn't going to be easy. He had little money, no job, no credentials, no resources of a news organization.

He had heard, however, of a small foundation, the Philip Stern Family Fund in Washington, D.C., that was willing to support investigative reporting with modest contributions. He appealed to the Stern Fund and won a $2,000 grant to pursue the story.

That isn't much money for a big-time newspaper investigation. For Hersh, though, the bankroll was all he needed to track down members of the Army unit his source said was supposedly involved. He located and interviewed several soldiers from a platoon of the Eleventh Brigade of the Americal Division. They described in a sickening account the shooting deaths of more than a hundred Vietnamese civilians on March 16, 1968, about six miles northeast of Quang Ngai in a tiny hamlet called My Lai. The GIs also told Hersh of the role of the platoon leader, a seasoned combat veteran named Lt. William Calley.

When he tried to locate Calley, Hersh discovered that the Army was conducting its own hushed-up inquiry of the massacre and that Calley was being detained at Fort Benning, Georgia, and facing court martial.

Hersh had his story—a gut-wrenching blockbuster. But how was he going to get it published? He sensed, correctly, that the establishment press was highly unlikely to be willing to print such a story from an obscure free-lancer.

His neighbor and confidante, twenty-four-year-old David Obst, had an idea. They could try offering the My Lai story to the nation's newspapers through their own news syndicate. That would provide the imprimatur that a free-lancer lacks and would give the story greater potential circulation.

Working feverishly, Hersh and Obst formed "Dispatch News Service." Its "office" was a room in Obst's home. There was only one reporter: Seymour Hersh.

But the series of articles ignited an inferno of press attention. Thirty-six newspapers ran the story, beginning late in 1969. Hersh's stories, quoting members of Calley's platoon, chronicled the savage murder of civilian men, women, and children by American troops at My Lai. His series not only stunned the nation; he jolted the entire fourth estate, which somehow—despite resources that dwarfed Hersh's little bedroom news service—had missed the story.

The 1970 Pulitzer Prize for international reporting went to "Seymour M. Hersh of Dispatch News Service." The voting by both the prize jury and the board was unanimous. It was one of the rare occasions when a Pulitzer Prize in reporting has been awarded to anyone not working for the mainstream press.

Soon, however, Hersh was. His prize propelled him onto the staff of the *New York Times,* where he firmly solidified his reputation as a top-drawer investigative reporter. He went on to disclose the U.S. secret bombing of Cambodia before 1970 and the secret files kept on at least ten thousand American citizens by the CIA. In 1979, he left the *Times* to pursue a free-lance writing career.

Score one for the Pulitzer Prize administration: It honored a piece of remarkable journalism that did not originate within the establishment that controls the prizes. Unfortunately, however, that is an all-too-rare occurrence, as exemplified by the case of I. F. Stone.

No other journalist of the twentieth century embodied the muckraking spirit and intellect of Joseph Pulitzer more faithfully than Stone. "Izzy," as his admirers called him, was a brilliant scholar, a combative investigative reporter, and the father of the modern alternative newspaper. He launched *I. F. Stone's Weekly* in 1953 after the mainstream press blackballed him for his outspoken attacks on McCarthyism. For the next nineteen years, his weekly crusaded like Pulitzer's fiery *World,* charging official Washington—and especially the Pentagon—with misleading the press and the people.

In his publication, he relied primarily on documents, using them to attack racism, McCarthyism, the nuclear arms race, U.S. military involvement in Vietnam, human rights abuses, and many other issues he regarded as assaults on democracy. Stone was briefly a member of the Socialist Party, but like

Joseph Pulitzer, he was a successful capitalist. Stone's newsletter, profitable throughout its existence, had more than 70,000 paid subscribers when he ended publication in 1971.

His tenacity produced a number of important exclusive reports. Most notable, perhaps, was his disclosure in 1957 that the Atomic Energy Commission's first underground atomic test was detected not only two hundred miles away, as the government said, but twenty-six hundred miles away. The government's statement suggested that a test ban would allow the Soviet Union to cheat without fear of discovery—an assertion that Stone proved was grossly misleading.

The longtime Washington journalist deserved a 1958 Pulitzer Prize for that piece of investigative work. Some of his other reporting was equally strong. But he died on June 18, 1989, at the age of eighty-one, without ever having won a Pulitzer.

It's a safe bet that Stone could not have cared less. He was an iconoclast, an independent, and a radical who called himself "a new Lefty before there was a new Left." The Pulitzer Prizes have always been an institution of the establishment press, and Stone was always a gadfly. He was barred from the National Press Club, for example, because he took a black judge to lunch there in 1941 during his battle to get it to admit nonwhites.

Born Isidor Feinstein, the son of Jewish immigrants from Russia, Stone produced a huge outcry among his own readers when he criticized Israel. He visited the country many times and wrote two books eloquently favorable to Zionism and Israel's fight for independence. But after the Arab-Israeli war of 1967, he urged Israelis to compensate Arab refugees for their losses and to cede the occupied territories to them to create an Arab Palestine federated with Israel, with Jerusalem the joint capital.

Opinions like that made even his own followers squirm, but that was I. F. Stone. At a memorial service for him on a sweltering July day in Manhattan, one of the speakers, Random House associate publisher Peter Osnos, noted that many in the audience of six hundred were too hot and declared, "I'm sorry about the air conditioning, but Izzy would have preferred that we all be just a little bit uncomfortable."

That sounds like Joseph Pulitzer's definition of a great

journalist. So does Stone's obituary in the *New York Times,* which called him "the muckraking pamphleteer who tirelessly crusaded for peace and civil liberties and against official evasion and wrongdoing."

So how could a journalist such as Stone die, after so many years of distinguished work, without receiving American journalism's highest honor?

Robert Christopher, the prize administrator and secretary to the board, doesn't know the answer but guesses that Stone wasn't eligible because his publication was a "newsletter," not a newspaper. And the rules allow consideration only of "material appearing in a United States newspaper published daily, Sunday or at least once a week."

A more cynical guess would be that *I. F. Stone's Weekly* never won a Pulitzer because it was a left-leaning, alternative newspaper, and the prize competition has never been generous to what was once called America's "underground" press. The glaring truth is that in seventy-five years of Pulitzer Prizes, none has ever been awarded to work done at an alternative (nonestablishment) newspaper, even though it can be shown that some of the nation's most vigorous reporting is being accomplished at that level. (The *Village Voice* has won two Pulitzers, in 1981 for feature writing by Teresa Carpenter and in 1986 for editorial cartooning by Jules Feiffer. Some might argue that the two prizes prove, if there remains any doubt, that the *Voice* has grown up to become an establishment paper.)

There also were opportunities to honor Stone's many books. Most notable, perhaps, was *The Hidden History of the Korean War,* which made a strong case using documents that the United States provoked the war—a charge so explosive in 1952 that only the tiny *Monthly Review Press* had the courage to publish it. (Little, Brown reissued the book in 1988.)

However, there apparently is no record in the Columbia University archives that Stone ever sought a Pulitzer Prize or was nominated for one. Neither fact, if accurate, would be adequate to explain the lack of recognition. The Pulitzer Board has the power to give a prize to anyone, regardless of whether the person's work was entered in the competition. From time to time over the years, the board has done exactly that. The board is also empowered to grant special Pulitzer Prize citations, such as the 1958 award to the late Walter Lippmann of the *New York Herald Tribune*, the 1976 award to former prize administrator John Hohenberg, and the 1984 award to author Theodore Seuss Geisel (known as Dr. Seuss).

Nine months after Stone died, the Pulitzer Prize Board met at Columbia to deliberate on the 1990 prizes. The occasion was an excellent opportunity for the righting of an old wrong. Sadly, though, in two full days of discussion, there was not a word about a posthumous citation.

There will be more chances for the board to redeem itself. Every April, when the prizes are announced at Columbia, I. F. Stone's thousands of admirers can hope that the power structure, just once, will be willing to salute a pesky gadfly who represented to many what journalism ought to be.

If Dr. Seuss deserves a Pulitzer, why not Izzy Stone?

The prize administration has been known to make amends for past slights. In Neil Sheehan's case, it took two decades.

In 1971, when Sheehan was the *New York Times*'s Pentagon correspondent, he obtained a top-secret Defense Department record of U.S. involvement in Vietnam, Laos, and Cambodia from World War II through 1968. The bulky report made clear that the administration of President Lyndon Johnson had engaged in a policy of deceit, misrepresentation, and intrigue about U.S. involvement in Southeast Asia. After the *Times* began publishing these documents, which filled forty-seven book-length volumes totaling more than 2.5 million words, the Nixon administration went to federal court and won a temporary order halting publication. It was the first time in U.S. history that the government had attempted, without a declaration of war, to place prior restraint on publication.

When the *Times* was forced to halt publication, the *Washington Post* obtained some of the documents and also began printing them, which made the *Post* a second defendant in the government's attack. Several other papers, notably the *Boston Globe*, also printed pieces of the Pentagon Papers, but the *Times* and the *Post* were the government's primary targets.

The newspapers fought all the way to the United States Supreme Court, which handed the press a major First Amendment victory. Fifteen days after being ordered to cease printing the records, the *Times* resumed publishing the Pentagon Papers.

That following spring at Columbia University, the Pulitzer Prize jury for public service voted unanimously to recommend that the 1972 gold medal go to Sheehan and the *New York Times* for publication of the documents. The Advisory Board concurred in another unanimous vote, although it dropped Sheehan's name from the award because Joseph Pulitzer's will directed that the gold medal go to newspapers, not to individuals.

In 1972, the Pulitzer Prize judging was still a trilevel system: Jury recommendations had to be accepted by the Advisory Board, whose recommendations were passed along for final approval and public announcement by Columbia University's twenty-two-member Board of Trustees. And when the trustees received the recommendation for a prize to the *New York Times* for publishing the Pentagon Papers, an antimedia volcano erupted. Several of the trustees, many of them prominent lawyers, objected to honoring a newspaper for publishing secret government reports—an act which Vice President Spiro Agnew had assailed as illegal. The same objection was being leveled at a second journalism prize recommended that year, for columnist Jack Anderson's investigative reporting on the Indo-Pakistan War, in which he had also used secret documents.

Two trustees abstained from the debate over the controversial prizes. One was a federal judge, Fredrick van Pelt Bryan, who absented himself because the Pentagon Papers case had been in the federal courts. The other trustee was Arthur Ochs Sulzberger, publisher of the *Times* and the man who ultimately decided to print the Pentagon Papers.

In a special meeting, the remaining trustees voted twice to reject the prizes for the *Times* and columnist Anderson. And after each vote, Columbia president William McGill—a member of the Pulitzer Advisory Board—insisted on reconsideration. He coaxed the trustees into an alternative method of distancing themselves from the prizes. They issued approval with a carefully worded statement of "reservations," announcing that "had the selections been those of the trustees alone, certain of the recipients would not have been chosen"—a clear reference to the *Times* and Jack Anderson.

The strained relationship between the Advisory Board and the trustees continued until 1975, when the trustees finally delegated their powers to Columbia's president and withdrew altogether from the prize process. The board then became the final arbiter and changed its name to the Pulitzer Prize Board.

Score another point for members of the board. Had the university trustees prevailed and rejected the award for publication of the Pentagon Papers, the resulting stain on the Pulitzer Prizes might have destroyed them.

But dropping Sheehan's name from the prize citation was grossly unfair—another example of the board's resistance to changing Joseph Pulitzer's turn-of-the-century rules. For Sheehan, it was the second time he had come close and then been denied a Pulitzer. Many of his colleagues thought he had been ill-treated in 1964 when the prize for international reporting was shared by Malcolm Browne of the Associated Press and David Halberstam of the *New York Times*. They were honored for their accurate dispatches from Vietnam—in the face of harassment from the U.S. military—on American involvement in the Diem regime.

Sheehan, at the time a Saigon correspondent for United Press International, performed as honestly and bravely as Browne and Halberstam, his colleagues thought, and should have shared in their prize. Unfortunately, when Diem was ousted in a coup, Sheehan was in Japan and thus missed the final episode of a story he had been reporting with brilliance. On the basis of that unfortunate timing in the otherwise outstanding exhibit of his work submitted by UPI for the prize, the Pulitzer judges passed him over.

Sheehan finally received a measure of justice twenty-five years after that arbitrary bit of judging. His book, *A Bright Shining Lie: John Paul Vann and America in Vietnam*, received the Pulitzer Prize for general nonfiction in 1989.

Technically, America's two most celebrated reporters never received Pulitzer Prizes, for the same reason Sheehan was not honored individually for the Pentagon Papers. Watergate reporting by Bob Woodward and Carl Bernstein won a Pulitzer in 1973, but because it was the "public service" prize, the gold medal went to their paper, the *Washington Post,* not to them.

Most people would also be surprised to learn that the two

Watergate sleuths' exploits—celebrated in books and on the screen—almost failed to win any Pulitzer at all.

Throughout the latter half of 1972, the *Post* and its Woodward-Bernstein team worked almost alone in investigating the June 17 break-in at Democratic National Headquarters in the Watergate complex in Washington, D.C. Few other news media showed any serious interest in the Watergate story while the *Post* hammered away at it, exposing a link between the White House and the five masked men who were arrested at Watergate in the middle of the night with extensive wire-tapping equipment. Woodward and Bernstein exposed evidence of a cover-up campaign reaching all the way to the White House, and they uncovered a widespread campaign of political "dirty tricks" against the Democrats, financed by secretly contributed Republican money.

As the Nixon administration railed at the *Post's* coverage, branding it as shoddy journalism, most of the rest of the nation's news media remained safely, noncourageously hands-off. The story was treated so lightly outside Washington, in fact, that it posed no re-election obstacles for President Nixon and his vice president, Spiro Agnew, who won by a thunderous landslide in November of 1972.

The *Washington Post,* meanwhile, continued its lonely crusade, pounding away at the blossoming scandal in news columns and on the editorial pages. When 1973 arrived, a total of seven conspirators were convicted or pleaded guilty in the Watergate break-in, and the *Post* submitted the work by Woodward and Bernstein for a Pulitzer Prize.

In early March of that year, a Pulitzer jury at Columbia University listed the *Washington Post* as only its third choice for the gold medal for public service, behind *Chicago Tribune* and *New York Times* entries for reporting unrelated to Watergate.

John Hohenberg, in his history of the Pulitzer Prizes, quotes an unnamed member of that prize jury, explaining why the *Post* had not been recommended for the gold medal. "Watergate," the juror said, "is only a pimple on the elephant's ass."

That echoed the view of editors across the heartland of America. The *Post* was widely considered to be a left-leaning, insulated, almost anarchist paper operating out of control. Its gutsy publisher, Katharine Graham, must have felt fright-eningly alone—until two weeks later, when the story blew wide open. One of the Watergate burglary defendants, James Mc-Cord, wrote a letter to federal judge John Sirica disclosing the cover-up. Then Sirica handed stiff sentences to McCord and the other conspirators while implying he would be lenient if they cooperated. McCord then implicated former attorney general John Mitchell along with John Dean, counsel to the president, and Jeb Stuart Magruder, former deputy campaign director of CREEP (the Committee to Re-Elect the President). Then Dean implicated Nixon's two highest aides in the White House, H. R. Haldeman and John Ehrlichman.

The cover-up was unraveling in spectacular fashion as the Pulitzer Prize Advisory Board met at Columbia on April 12 to pick the 1973 winners. In a unanimous vote, board members overruled the jury's recommendation and gave the public service gold medal to the *Washington Post.*

By then, the Watergate story was moving to its historic conclusion, Richard Nixon's August 9, 1974, resignation in disgrace. His own tape recordings of private White House conversations proved that he had ordered the Watergate cover-up, but he never admitted it. One month later, he received an unconditional pardon from his successor, Gerald Ford, whom voters removed from the presidency at their first opportunity, in 1976.

Score yet another point for the people behind the prizes. They came within a whisker of failing to honor a piece of journalism that few publishers since Joseph Pulitzer would have had the courage to pursue. But just as events vindicated the *Washington Post,* its Pulitzer vindicated the prize-givers.

The Watergate work by Woodward and Bernstein made them celebrity journalists. The retelling of their exploits in print and on the screen made them millionaires. They received almost every major American award in journalism, except for a share of the *Post's* Pulitzer Prize. More recently, the Pulitzer Board has found simple ways of getting around that arbitrary rule that the public service gold medal must go to a newspaper, not to individuals. But the creativity has come too late to remedy the insult to Woodward and Bernstein.

The prizes not only reflect press courage, as exemplified by the *Post*'s performance on Watergate. They also reflect press cowardice, as represented by the same paper's handling of the Janet Cooke scandal.

That sad episode surrounding a news story labeled "Jimmy's World" probably did more than any heroic journalistic achievement to familiarize the American public with the Pulitzer Prizes. The public's low-level awareness suddenly rocketed skyward in April of 1981 when Americans learned that a Pulitzer Prize had been awarded for a news story that turned out to be a hoax. Most shocking of all was that the newspaper that had won the prize with a fraudulent story was the *Washington Post,* the almost legendary journal of Watergate fame.

News of the *Post*'s disgrace filled newspapers and magazines and television broadcasts for weeks. Never in its history, despite almost annual minor tempests, had the Pulitzer Prize competition received such attention. Interestingly, only the newspaper and not the prizes suffered a bruised reputation. The firestorm of publicity served instead to enhance the Pulitzers' familiarity and esteem in the American consciousness. And that heightened status happened as a result of the nation's media either missing or choosing to ignore the fact that the Pulitzer Prize administration did not distinguish itself in its response to the fakery.

"Jimmy's World" was the sensational account of an eight-year-old drug addict in a District of Columbia ghetto. *Washington Post* reporter Janet Cooke wrote the piece, which included her vivid eyewitness description of the boy's mother allowing her lover to inject Jimmy with heroin. Publication of the story caused an uproar. Washington mayor Marion Barry ordered police to find the boy. When a wide search failed to locate him, Barry denounced the story as a fabrication.

But *Post* editors stood by Cooke and her story. A few months later, they submitted it to the Pulitzer competition. It won the prize for feature writing.

As news about Cooke and the other 1981 winners went out on the news wires, the hoax began to unravel. First, *Post* executive editor Benjamin Bradlee received a phone call from Vassar College, reporting that Cooke had not graduated from Vassar as she had claimed in the biography submitted to

Pulitzer judges. Meanwhile, another *Post* editor learned that Cooke had not received a master's degree from the University of Toledo, as she also had claimed. Under questioning by her editors, Cooke admitted she had exaggerated her credentials. And eleven hours later, after more grilling and a fruitless search for "Jimmy's" house, she admitted that the boy did not exist and that she had made up most of the story.

Cooke resigned and went into seclusion. The *Post* promptly returned the award and published a lengthy and self-serving explanation to readers, placing virtually 100 percent of the blame for the hoax on Janet Cooke.

Around the nation, many editors knew better than that and considered the *Posts'* handling of the whole affair to be inexcusable. The twenty-six-year-old reporter had committed a grievous journalistic sin for which she should have been fired. But the paper's editors shared much of the blame:

- For hiring a reporter and publishing her stories without checking the veracity of her credentials.

- For failing to insist that Cooke confidentially reveal her source, "Jimmy's" mother, to an editor prior to publication.

- For submitting her work for a Pulitzer Prize even though many people on the *Post's* staff, including editors, had growing doubts about the story's authenticity.

- And above all else, for failing to show appropriate humanity by instantly insisting on action to locate "Jimmy" and seek help for him as soon as they learned of his plight. The editors evidently believed that the mortally endangered child existed. Yet they did nothing to find "Jimmy" until motivated by a need to react to a public outcry.

At least four *Post* editors, including celebrity journalist Bob Woodward, who had been promoted to management after his Watergate achievements, had direct responsibility for the aforementioned failings. Not one editor, however, received even a reprimand. Janet Cooke was allowed to take the fall entirely by herself.

That, however, is not the point here. The Pulitzer Prize administration *also* allowed Janet Cooke to take full blame. Where was the Pulitzer Board's outrage at a newspaper that let its lust for prizes cause it to submit a story whose authenticity was doubted by the very editors who submitted it? The *Washington Post* had set up the Pulitzer Prize Board to look foolish, and it certainly did—especially after film critic Judith Crist and other members of the features jury revealed they had *not* listed the "Jimmy's World" story among their recommendations. The board, without even consulting Crist's hardworking jury, pulled the Janet Cooke story out of the "local general reporting" category and gave it the feature-writing prize.

When Crist read it, she was outraged. "It was such an obvious piece of crap," she told a *New York* magazine writer.

So board members were embarrassed as the hoax made national headlines. Perhaps that is why they kept a low profile and tried to stay out of the story. Or perhaps they took no action because they did not want to add to the pain of their friends at the *Post,* especially the charismatic Bradlee, who was their colleague on the board throughout most of the 1970s.

For whatever reason, the board avoided any punitive action against the *Washington Post* for submitting a prize entry that some of its own editors knew was under a cloud of suspicion. A braver, less chummy board would have disqualified the *Post* from future competition—an "NCAA suspension," if you like—for at least a year. At the very least, a formal and public letter of rebuke would have been an appropriate expression of indignation.

"The Pulitzer," as Thomas Griffith of *Time* magazine once wrote, "is a nice club."

8

Seventy-five Years of Arts, Letters, and Music Awards

AN ARGUMENT CAN BE MADE that Joseph Pulitzer's journalism prizes never would have become famous if he hadn't tacked on the separate awards in arts and letters. These first national prizes for books and plays captured the public attention right from the start. And that happened primarily as a result of headline-grabbing controversy.

America's literary awakening in the early twentieth century had the bad fortune to occur during the thirty-three years when Nicholas Murray Butler was president of Columbia University and the guiding force on the Pulitzer Prize Board. His Puritan tastes resulted in years of controversial awards—particularly for novels and plays—that do not accurately represent the best or even "distinguished examples" of American writing.

The aforementioned *Laughing Boy* decision provides a good example. *Laughing Boy* is Oliver LaFarge's sweet, tragic tale of a Native American love affair, in which the Indians live up to many of the stereotypes assigned to them by white Americans and speak in the stilted, wooden dialogue reserved for Indians in older Western movies and television shows. The novel is not an American classic, or even a particularly good book.

In 1930, the year *Laughing Boy* won the Pulitzer Prize, the board rejected not only Thomas Wolfe's *Look Homeward, Angel*, but also William Faulkner's *The Sound and the Fury* and Ernest Hemingway's *A Farewell to Arms*, all three of which are now considered classics.

Hemingway also failed to receive Pulitzer Prizes for *The Sun Also Rises* and *For Whom the Bell Tolls*. The latter was recommended in 1941 by a prize jury, but the Pulitzer Board rejected it and gave no award after university president Butler angrily denounced the book as "offensive and lascivious." Even though the "wholesome" requirement had been dropped from the prize rules for fiction ten years earlier, Butler announced his disgust with Hemingway for writing about such subjects as a man spending time with a woman in a sleeping bag.

President Butler also failed to see the appeal of Faulkner, whose best novels were denied the Pulitzer Prize. Besides *The Sound and the Fury*, these included *As I Lay Dying* (which lost in 1931 to *Years of Grace* by Margaret Ayer Barnes), *Light in August* (which lost in 1933 to *The Store* by T. S. Stribling), and *Absalom, Absalom!* (which lost in 1937 to *Gone with the Wind* by Margaret Mitchell).

After Butler retired in 1945 at the age of eighty-three, the Pulitzer Board played catch-up. Hemingway received a 1953 prize for *The Old Man and the Sea,* one of his lesser works. And Faulkner received a pair of late-career prizes for less-than-worthy novels: *A Fable* in 1955 and *The Reivers* in 1963.

By then, irreversible damage had been done to the prizes. Not only had the best works of Hemingway and Faulkner been slighted, but several of the era's greatest writers were ignored altogether. Besides Thomas Wolfe, these included F. Scott Fitzgerald, Theodore Dreiser, and Flannery O'Connor.

Meanwhile, the prizes were given instead to such baffling choices as *The Able McLaughlins* by Margaret Wilson, *Lamb in His Bosom* by Caroline Miller, and *Journey in the Dark* by Martin Flavin.

A few times, the Pulitzer judges' decisions on novels were

widely acclaimed, such as the 1940 award to *The Grapes of Wrath* by John Steinbeck and the 1947 prize to *All the King's Men* by Robert Penn Warren. Overall, though, there were far more controversial choices, such as the 1936 Pulitzer for *Honey in the Horn* by Harold L. Davis, chosen over Thomas Wolfe's *Of Time and the River* and John Steinbeck's *Tortilla Flat.*

Another mild controversy occurred in 1947 when the Pulitzer Board, in a bit of sentimental, behind-the-scenes manipulation, voted to change the name of the "novel" prize to "fiction." That was done solely to permit the board to award the 1948 prize to James Michener's *South Pacific,* which wasn't a novel but a collection of romantic short stories about World War II.

Shortly afterward, in 1950, the book publishing industry began sponsoring the National Book Awards—in part a reaction to unhappiness with Pulitzer Prize decisions in American literary circles. Among writers and publishers, the National Book Awards generally have been held in higher esteem, but the Pulitzers are far better known to the public as a result of all the press attention they enjoy.

Both competitions rely on qualified critics, writers, and educators as judges. The difference is that the powerful board of news executives makes final judgments on the Pulitzer Prizes, and these journalists occasionally stir outrage by failing to listen to their expert juries. Two notable examples:

—A prize jury recommended Thomas Pynchon's *Gravity's Rainbow* for the 1974 Pulitzer, but the board found the critically acclaimed novel to be confusing and decided to make no award that year. In doing so, board members ignored the fact that it had been an especially strong year in American fiction, and they also passed up new books by Kurt Vonnegut, Joyce Carol Oates, John Cheever, Bernard Malamud, Philip Roth, Gore Vidal, I. B. Singer, Thornton Wilder, Thomas Berger, Stanley Elkin, Arthur Cohen, Thomas McGuane, and John Gardner.

—The same thing happened again in 1977, when a jury recommended Norman Maclean's brilliant trio of stories, *A River Runs Through It,* for the fiction prize. *Publishers Weekly* hailed the retired University of Chicago professor's book, set in his home state of Montana, as "a stunning debut." But the

Pulitzer Board decided the book was unworthy and made no fiction award that year. Maclean, who was seventy-four at the time, took the rejection gracefully and suggested that the Pulitzer Board, heavily weighted with Easterners, objected to his book because "the stories have trees in them."

From time to time, the Pulitzer administration has been accused of racism. These charges rise from the fact that two of America's most acclaimed black writers, Richard Wright and James Baldwin, died without receiving Pulitzer Prizes. In 1988, forty-eight black authors signed a letter, published in the *New York Review of Books,* complaining that Baldwin had been unfairly denied both the Pulitzer Prize and the National Book Award. The letter also expressed outrage that black author Toni Morrison had failed to receive the 1988 National Book Award or the National Book Critics Circle Award for her novel *Beloved.* A few weeks after the letter appeared, *Beloved* received the Pulitzer.

Then some accused the Pulitzer Board of caving in to pressure. Sometimes, obviously, the board can't win.

But once in a while, the prize-givers have made a wonderful decision, heralded by all and resulting in a little magic.

Such is the bittersweet and bizarre story of John Kennedy Toole. His Pulitzer Prize and accompanying fame came too late to change his life. Instead, the prize changed his mother's life.

Toole won a posthumous Pulitzer in 1981 for his critically acclaimed novel *A Confederacy of Dunces.* He was a twenty-four-year-old army man serving in Puerto Rico in 1962 when he began to write the book, a picaresque farce set in New Orleans. He finished the work in 1963. Sometime thereafter he entered into a lengthy and still mysterious correspondence with an editor at Simon and Schuster. Exactly what transpired between them has never been clear, but after Toole had made a number of revisions, the manuscript was rejected in 1965 or 1966. Toole did not make any further serious efforts to publish the novel.

After his army discharge, the aspiring writer, who had a master's degree from Columbia University, taught at Dominican College in New Orleans. In December of 1968, he stopped teaching. Three months later he was found in his car, asphyxiated by carbon monoxide fumes.

After her son's suicide, Thelma Toole began a crusade to get his novel published. For almost a decade she labored at the task unrewarded. Her single copy of the manuscript, a smudged carbon, returned from each publisher increasingly battered. At least eight houses refused it. Her break came in 1976 when she read that novelist Walker Percy was teaching that year at Loyola University in New Orleans.

Percy was sitting in his office one day in 1976 when the seventy-four-year-old woman, using a walker, hobbled in, followed by a chauffeur carrying a tattered manuscript. She introduced herself as a widowed, retired schoolteacher and pleaded with him to help find a publisher for her deceased son's novel. She assured him it was "a masterpiece."

To get rid of her, Percy agreed to take a look at it, confident that he'd have to read only four or five pages before returning it. But at the end of five pages, he could not stop. He found it "a fantastic novel, a major achievement, a huge comic-satiric-tragic one-of-a-kind rendering of life in New Orleans." Percy decided to help her. His own publisher rejected the book on grounds that a first novel without an author alive to help promote it had little chance of success in today's marketplace. But Louisiana State University Press, about to embark on a publishing program of "worthy noncommercial fiction," agreed to bring it out.

In May of 1980, *A Confederacy of Dunces* appeared. Despite having an academic publisher, the book began to catch on as an underground sleeper, even something of a cult book. Rave reviews appeared in the national press. And then it won a Pulitzer.

Thelma Toole accepted her son's prize on his behalf. As a result of the Pulitzer, her poignant story made headlines across the nation and helped push the book onto best-seller lists. She made a small fortune off his novel before her death in 1984.

The much-maligned Pulitzer judges deserve some credit on this prize—not for providing an upbeat ending to a tragic story, but for picking an outstanding book while adding a dash of justice to the literary universe.

The drama prizes, like those in fiction, have always attracted controversy. For many years, Joseph Pulitzer's "uplift" requirements, along with Columbia president Butler's prudish values, shackled the awards for plays just as they did the novel prizes. Unhappiness over Pulitzer decisions gave birth to other national drama prizes in the same way it spawned the National Book Awards.

The Glass Menagerie by Tennessee Williams stands high on many critics' short list of the best American plays. In fact, William Henry of *Time*, chairman of the 1990 drama jury, ranks *The Glass Menagerie* as one of the nation's top four plays of all time. However, it lost in 1945 to the insipid *Harvey* by Mary Chase. Two years later, the outraged American theater industry began its own Antoinette Perry (Tony) Awards.

That was actually the second time the Pulitzer Prizes begot a new drama award. In 1935, *The Children's Hour* by Lillian Hellman was rejected for the drama prize because Columbia President Butler and some Pulitzer Board members were offended by the play's theme of lesbianism. The winner that year was *The Old Maid* by Zoë Akins. Broadway theater critics were so outraged they created their own New York Drama Critics Circle Awards.

Hellman never did receive a Pulitzer. Even her best-known play, *The Little Foxes*, was rejected in 1939 in favor of *Abe Lincoln in Illinois* by Robert E. Sherwood.

The Pulitzer judges deserve credit for recognizing Eugene O'Neill as perhaps America's greatest playwright. O'Neill won four Pulitzers—a total equaled only by Robert Frost in the poetry category. However, O'Neill was not always honored with Pulitzers for his best work. Three of his better plays were rejected: *Mourning Becomes Electra* lost in 1932 to *Of Thee I Sing*, a musical; *Desire Under the Elms* lost in 1925 to *They Knew What They Wanted* by Sidney Howard; and *The Iceman Cometh* lost in 1947 when the Pulitzer Board decided there was no play worthy of a prize.

Overall, though, the Pulitzer drama judging has undoubtedly achieved greater success than the fiction judging in reflecting the best writing for the American stage. Examples include prizes in 1938 for *Our Town* by Thornton Wilder, in 1948 for *A Streetcar Named Desire* by Tennessee Williams, in 1949 for *Death of a Salesman* by Arthur Miller, in 1955 for *Cat on a Hot Tin Roof* by Tennessee Williams, and in 1957 for *Long Day's Journey into Night* by Eugene O'Neill.

Occasionally disturbing decisions continued, however. In 1958, for example, the drama prize went to Ketti Frings for her plodding *Look Homeward, Angel.* The play was an adaptation of Thomas Wolfe's classic novel, rejected for the fiction prize in 1930. Book critics could only roll their eyes.

Controversy roared in 1963 when the Pulitzer drama jury's recommended prize for Edward Albee's *Who's Afraid of Virginia Woolf?* was rejected because the Pulitzer Board considered the play to be insufficiently "uplifting." As a result of the turmoil that followed, the board agreed that all members henceforth would abstain from passing judgment on any book they had not read or any play they had not seen—an unintended admission of irresponsibility that left critics fuming. The board also voted to delete the "uplift" provision from the rules—but too late to benefit Albee's play. He received a catch-up prize in 1967 for *A Delicate Balance.*

Occasionally, the Pulitzer judges win a measure of revenge on their scoffing critics. That happened after the 1988 drama prize to *Driving Miss Daisy* by Alfred Uhry. His play about a crotchety Jewish widow and her friendship with a patient black chauffeur had received generally lukewarm reviews. The motion picture version of the play, however, was the surprise hit of 1990, harvesting huge financial returns and four Oscars, including best picture.

Prizes and box-office receipts proves nothing about artistic merit, of course. But Pulitzer judges could take satisfaction in showing the critics who was in better touch with public tastes.

Pulitzer Prize decisions in the other book categories— history, biography, poetry, and general nonfiction—have generated hardly any controversy compared to the high-profile fiction and drama awards. The notable exceptions have come in the biography competition.

In 1957, the biography jury had selected two outstanding books as finalists: *Harlan Fiske Stone: Pillar of the Law* by Alpheus T. Mason and *Roosevelt: The Lion and the Fox* by James MacGregor Burns. However, the Pulitzer Board rejected both nominations and gave the prize to *Profiles in Courage* by a young senator from Massachusetts named John F. Kennedy.

As rumors circulated that Kennedy associate Theodore Sorensen had actually written the book, the Pulitzer office received demands that the senator's prize be revoked. John Hohenberg, Columbia's prize administrator at the time, looked into the complaints and satisfied himself that Kennedy had indeed written the book during a long convalescence after surgery in 1954 to relieve a back injury. The prize stood.

Lost in the gossip over the authenticity of Kennedy's authorship was the manner in which he won the prize. His book, basically a recycling of other biographers' work on such figures as John Quincy Adams and Daniel Webster, was a carefully calculated political treatise that helped position him for his run at the White House. Kennedy's close friend at the *New York Times*, Arthur Krock, who served on the Pulitzer Board from 1940 through 1954, vigorously lobbied his former colleagues on the board to overrule its biography jury and go with the Kennedy book.

The biography prize made headlines again in 1962 when the Pulitzer Board, by unanimous vote, awarded it to *Citizen Hearst* by W. A. Swanberg, virtuoso biographer of media giants. However, Columbia trustees still had final say in those days, and they rejected the award to Swanberg, declaring that the book failed to meet Joseph Pulitzer's mandate to honor only biographies "teaching patriotic and unselfish services to the people, illustrated by an eminent example." The rules were subsequently changed to omit that musty requirement, and Swanberg finally won a Pulitzer eleven years later for a solid but less worthy biography, *Luce and His Empire.*

John Hohenberg, in his official history of the prizes, wrote that even William Randolph Hearst Jr., who had been displeased by Swanberg's highly unflattering biography of his father, thought the Columbia trustees' rejection was unfair. Others, however, reported that Hearst had privately strong-armed the trustees, threatening unspecified retribution against the university if it honored the book. Those charges have never been substantiated, but the rejection of the Hearst biography stands out as the only time the Columbia trustees ever overruled the Pulitzer Board.

Very little emotion has surrounded the poetry and music prizes over the years. That seems only fair, since Joseph Pulitzer did not ask for awards in those categories.

Pulitzer was not particularly interested in poetry. His will made no mention of it. That, however, did not keep the custodians of his prizes from adding a category for verse. They did this in 1922 at the suggestion of the Poetry Society of America.

In the decades that followed, the poetry prize remained one of the least controversial Pulitzers, probably because the American public, like Joseph Pulitzer, is not particularly enamored of poetry.

Nevertheless, the early-day prize judges managed to commit acts of omission that belong in any Pulitzer Prize Hall of Shame. No awards were ever made to T. S. Eliot or Ezra Pound.

In his official history of the prizes, John Hohenberg wrote that there was "no indication in the record that either Eliot or Pound was ever considered, leading to the conclusion that their work was believed by the jurors to be outside the scope of the Plan of Award." Translation: The two expatriates, though born and educated in the United States, chose to live in Europe. Therefore, they weren't "American" writers as required by the rules.

Hohenberg's theory about the jurors' thinking is probably correct. But the professor should have added that the jurors, in that case, were wrong. Both poets wrote most of their best verse while living in the United States. In fact, Eliot's best-known poem, "The Love Song of J. Alfred Prufrock," was written while he was an undergraduate at Harvard University, at least a decade before he became a naturalized British subject.

A more honest guess about the Pulitzer jurors is that they simply did not like these two men or their work. Eliot was a little strange, and his poems were complex and often hard for some people to understand. Pound was a fascist, and his verse was a bit complicated, also, for the Poetry Society of America.

For whatever reason, two of the greatest poets ever produced by the United States never received the Pulitzer Prize.

In fairness, though, it should be noted that prizes *were* awarded over the years for the poetry of Edwin Arlington Robinson, Edna St. Vincent Millay, Stephen Vincent Benet, Archibald MacLeish, W. H. Auden, Carl Sandburg, Theodore Roethke, Wallace Stevens, Robert Penn Warren, and, of course, four-time laureate Robert Frost.

Unlike poetry, music was one of Joseph Pulitzer's passions. He particularly loved the compositions of Beethoven, Wagner, and Liszt. The publisher's will bequeathed $500,000 to the New York Philharmonic Society—an amount equal to his bequest for the Pulitzer Prizes.

But the man's will did not ask for a prize in music. It called only for a scholarship for a music student. In 1943, long after Joseph's death, the Pulitzer Board rather cavalierly converted the scholarship to a prize. That rather dubious decision was made with little discussion and for reasons that have never been made clear.

Pulitzer's intent is obvious in his will: He wanted to honor and encourage *American* arts and letters. The winners had to be Americans. The subject matter had to be American. As much as he loved the music of his native Europe, he would have wanted a Pulitzer Prize in music to honor indigenous *American* music.

Instead, in the nearly half-century of dubious Pulitzer Prizes in music, they have mostly honored American imitations of European music forms. So instead of celebrating the blues of W. C. Handy, a black man, or the blues-inspired compositions of George Gershwin and Leonard Bernstein, both white men, the Pulitzer Prizes have almost invariably honored white-European works with titles such as "Symphony Concertante" and "Meditations on Ecclesiastes." Here are the rules for the music prize as written by board members in 1943:

> For distinguished musical composition by an American in any of the larger forms, including chamber, orchestral, choral, opera, song, dance, or other forms of musical theatre, which has had its first performance in the United States during the year....

"Larger forms?" The Prize Board could hardly have chosen more offensive words to communicate its message: No Afro-American composers need apply. What makes these rules especially jarring is the fact that the most original, enduring and influential music ever created on U.S. soil has African American roots. However, with only one minor exception, music of black origin has been ignored for the Pulitzer.

That's why it was refreshing in 1965 when the Pulitzer music jury recommended a special award for jazz great Duke Ellington, the band leader whose arrangement of "Take the A Train" immortalized the subway that ended up creating events that thrust *New York Newsday* columnist Jim Dwyer into being nominated for a Pulitzer Prize in journalism.

The Ellington recommendation was a milestone. No other black composer of truly American music had ever been put forth for a Pulitzer Prize. The three jurors—Ronald Eyer of *Newsday*, Winthrop Sargeant of the *New Yorker*, and Thomas B. Sherman of the *St. Louis Post-Dispatch*—broke new ground with the following recommendation to the board, written by Ewen:

> My fellow jurors and I have come to the unanimous decision that no major musical composition by an American composer performed for the first time in this country during the past season...was worthy of a Pulitzer Prize award....therefore, we respectfully suggest that an appropriate citation of some sort be given to the American composer, pianist and conductor, Edward K. "Duke" Ellington, who has made many notable contributions to American music over a period of 30 years or more with compositions of high artistic quality couched mainly in the idiom of jazz....

When word of the jury recommendation was leaked to the press, jazz fans everywhere had reason to celebrate. Joseph Pulitzer might have preferred Wagner to Ellington, but more Americans probably agree with Mark Twain, who once remarked that "Wagner's music is actually better than it sounds."

Unfortunately, the Pulitzer Board denied the award for Duke Ellington. His music did not meet the criteria outlined by the rules.

How do composers such as Ellington, Gershwin, and Bernstein die without receiving the Pulitzer Prizes that go instead to the likes of the not-so-immortal Leo Sowerby, Virgil Thomson, and Leslie Bassett?

A strong argument can be made that Ellington should have received more than a special citation. He should have received the Pulitzer Prize itself, and long before 1965.

Gershwin should have won a share of the 1932 drama prize that was awarded to the musical *Of Thee I Sing*. The prize was given to the authors of the book, George S. Kaufman and Morrie Ryskind, and the lyricist, Ira Gershwin, George's brother. George Gershwin was slighted a second time, in 1936, when his *Porgy and Bess* was overlooked for the drama prize, which went to Robert E. Sherwood's *Idiot's Delight*.

Bernstein should have won in 1958 for his bluesy, enduring score for *West Side Story*, or for his earlier *Candide*, or for *On the Town* or his later *Kaddish*.

For every Ellington, Gershwin, and Bernstein, there are scores more who could be added to the list of great American composers who have been overlooked for the Pulitzer Prize.

How can this happen? Robert Christopher, administrator of the prizes, seems a little awkward when he tries to explain what kind of music the award seeks to honor.

"It ain't popular music," he says. "It is for contemporary composers—piano concertos, suites and, you know, serious and formidable music."

Anyone who tracks down and listens to some of this material, such as the aptly titled 1979 winner, "Aftertones of Infinity," has to agree with Christopher's use of the word "formidable."

He points out that the rules are specific, limiting the prize to "larger forms" of American music. And therein lies the key to this particular award's embarrassing history: misguided rules written and perpetuated by mostly middle-aged white men who have never composed a note of music.

At best, this prize is silly and pretentious. At worst, it represents institutional racism.

One solution available to the Pulitzer Board would be to award a raft of belated special citations, such as the posthumous prize voted in 1976 for ragtime composer Scott Joplin, the only black ever honored with a Pulitzer for music. But putting together such a list would be a daunting, thankless, Pulitzer for music and ultimately useless task. A better move by the board would be elimination of the music prize. Joseph Pulitzer never asked for it. And America could probably live without an award that by definition excludes music that reflects the nation's genius.

A footnote should be added, though, in defense of the Pulitzers in arts and letters and music. Prize-giving, by nature, is a dangerously subjective task. No institution has ever given prizes without making mistakes that come back to haunt. This includes the greatest competition of all, the Nobel Prizes, which in literature alone have failed to honor such giants as James Joyce, Marcel Proust, Franz Kafka, Thomas Hardy, Joseph Conrad, Henry James, and D. H. Lawrence.

Despite the many glaring oversights of the Pulitzer Prizes over the years, only two writers have ever protested by refusing the honor. Playwright William Saroyan, who won the 1940 drama prize for *The Time of Your Life,* rejected it on grounds that acceptance would compromise his work. He described the Pulitzer Prize track record as "consecration of the mediocre" and said he wanted no part of it.

In 1926, when novelist Sinclair Lewis won the fiction prize for *Arrowsmith,* he was still miffed at the Pulitzer Board's rejection of *Main Street* in 1920. The jury that had recommended Lewis's novel resigned in protest when the board found the book insufficiently "wholesome" and gave the prize instead to Edith Wharton's *Age of Innocence.* In refusing to accept the prize for *Arrowsmith,* Lewis condemned all awards as "dangerous" and wrote the following in a letter to the board: "The seekers for prizes tend to labor not for inherent excellencies but for alien rewards; they tend to write this, or timorously to avoid writing that, in order to tickle the prejudices of a haphazard committee."

Prizes, Lewis said, were another "compulsion put upon writers to become safe, polite, obedient and sterile." Those who give out the prizes, he said, were becoming "a supreme court, a college of cardinals, so rooted and so sacred that to challenge them will be to commit blasphemy."

"Only by regularly refusing the Pulitzer Prize can novelists keep such power from being permanently set up over them," he wrote.

Depending on one's point of view, Lewis's words were either admirable or self-righteous. Only four years later, he apparently forgot his own pronouncement and accepted the 1930 Nobel Prize for literature.

Joseph Pulitzer, who changed the nature of the American newspaper in the 1880s and created the modern metropolitan daily, posed for this photograph before the age of forty, when his health broke down and he began losing his sight. (Courtesy Associated Press)

Pulitzer endowed the Columbia University Graduate School of Journalism, which opened in 1912, and established the Pulitzer Prizes awarded annually at the school since 1917. (Courtesy Columbia University)

The Pulitzer Prize jury for the specialized reporting category meets in the World Room. Clockwise from left, the jurors are David Hall, David Witke, Al Johnson, Walt Bogdanich and Leonard Downie Jr., the jury chairman. (Courtesy Joe Pineiro, Columbia University)

The Pulitzer Price Board poses in the World Room. Standing, from left: David Laventhol, James Risser, Peter Kann, Sissela Bok, Robert Maynard, Meg Greenfield, Michael Gartner, Russell Baker, James Hoge, Walter Rugaber and Geneva Overholser. Seated, from left: Charlotte Saikowski, Joan Konner, Eugene Roberts, Michael Sovern, Robert Christopher and Claude Sitton. Not present: Burl Osborne. (Courtesy Joe Pineiro, Columbia University)

Jim Dwyer, columnist for *New York Newsday*, became a Pulitzer Prize finalist after discovering and exposing a link between subway accidents and worker fatigue. (Courtesy *New York Newsday*)

Los Angeles Times reporter Claire Spiegel became a Pulitzer finalist for stories disclosing mismanagement and medical malpractice at a public hospital. (Courtesy *Los Angeles Times*)

Tamar Stieber of the *Albuquerque Journal* was nominated for a Pulitzer for disclosures linking a rare blood disorder to an over-the-counter drug, L-Tryptophan. (Courtesy *Albuquerque Journal*)

After being tipped off that his reporting had won the Pulitzer gold medal, Gilbert Gaul of the *Philadelphia Inquirer* brought his son, Gregory, nine, to the newsroom on prize day to hear the announcement. (Courtesy United Press International)

Betty Gray of the *Washington* (N.C.) *Daily News* raises a toast on Pulitzer Prize Day after hearing that reporting by her and Mike Voss won a share of the gold medal, along with the *Philadelphia Inquirer*. (Courtesy Associated Press)

A view of both sides of the Pulitzer Prize gold medal for meritorious public service. The medal is awarded to newspapers, not to individuals, and is widely considered to be the most prestigious Pulitzer of all. (Courtesy Columbia University)

This photo by Michael Macor of the *Tribune* of Oakland, showing rescue efforts after the 1989 earthquake that flattened a freeway structure, was among 20 *Tribune* earthquake pictures that won the Pulitzer Prize for spot news photography. (Courtesy Associated Press)

Champagne fills the air as the *Tribune*'s photo staff celebrates upon receiving word on Pulitzer Prize Day that their earthquake coverage has won the coveted award. (Courtesy Associated Press)

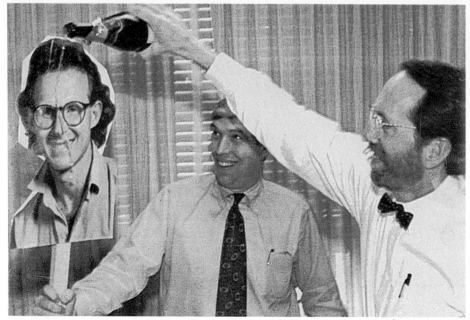

Randy Miller, deputy managing editor of the *Detroit Free Press*, pours champagne as photo director Mike Smith holds a cut-out photo of David Turnley, moments after Turnley–away on assignment in South Africa–was named winner of the Pulitzer Prize in feature photography. (Courtesy United Press International)

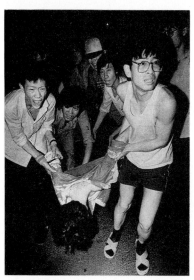

Chinese students carry a fallen comrade from Tianamen Square in this photo from David Turnley's prize-winning portfolio. It had been entered in the spot news category, but the Pulitzer Board declared it the "feature photography" winner so Oakland's *Tribune* could receive the spot news prize. (Courtesy Associated Press)

A Romanian vents years of grief at the hands of the regime of Nicolae Ceausescu, two days after his overthrow, in this photo from David Turnley's portfolio. (Courtesy *Detroit Free Press*)

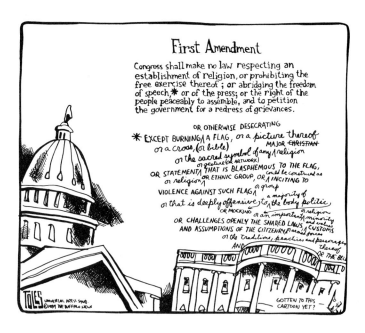

Tom Toles of the *Buffalo News* won the Pulitzer for his editorial cartoons, as exemplified by the work at right. (Courtesy Columbia University)

Seattle Times staffers celebrate their Pulitzer Prize for coverage of the *Exxon Valdez* oil spill. From left: Bill Dietrich, Mary Ann Gwinn, David Boardman and Eric Nalder. (Courtesy Associated Press)

Sheryl WuDunn and Nicholas Kristof, a *New York Times* husband and wife team, receive a congratulatory call after winning the Pulitzer for international reporting for their China coverage. (Courtesy Reuter)

Oscar Hijuelos, winner of the Pulitzer Prize for fiction. (Courtesy Columbia University)

Stanley Karnow, winner of the Pulitzer Prize for history. (Courtesy Columbia University)

Playwright August Wilson, author of *The Piano Lesson*, on stage after learning he had won his second Pulitzer Prize for drama. (Courtesy United Press International)

Charles Simic's verse won the Pulitzer Prize for poetry. (Courtesy Columbia University)

Mel Powell, winner of the Pulitzer Prize for music. (Courtesy Columbia University)

Michael Williamson and Dale Maharidge, winners in general nonfiction. (Courtesy Columbia University)

9

Tamar Stieber: Tracking the "Mystery Virus"

A T FIRST, THE WOMAN was hesitant and a little indig-
nant. Her medical problems were personal, she
said, and she didn't feel like discussing them, especially over
the phone with a reporter she had never met.

Tamar Stieber persisted, though, promising she wouldn't
use the woman's name. Eventually, after much coaxing, the
woman reluctantly began answering a few questions. Yes, she
had been suffering from intense, excruciating muscle and joint
pain. No, it wasn't a virus. Her doctor had diagnosed it as
eosinophilia, an unusual blood disorder. And yes, the cause
remained unknown.

Then Tamar sprang her big question.

"I heard you've been taking L-Tryptophan. Is that correct?"

The woman became hostile. Yes, she had been taking the
dietary supplement L-Tryptophan for relief of premenstrual
syndrome. But that wasn't being blamed for her illness. And it
certainly wasn't anybody else's damn business.

Tamar persisted: "What brand of L-Tryptophan are you taking?"

At that, the woman angrily hung up. Strike One.

Tamar Stieber sighed and gently placed her phone back in its cradle. Nice job of winning the confidence of a news source, she said to herself. Way to go.

For a few moments, Tamar gazed out the window of the *Albuquerque Journal*'s bureau office in downtown Santa Fe and considered her place in the universe: Here it was, late afternoon on November 2, 1989, and she definitely did not need another strikeout. Her personal life was in disarray, she felt, and her young career as a newspaper reporter wasn't going anywhere, as far as she could tell. She was still upset over a couple of errors she had made in her reporting recently. Her self-confidence—never in generous supply—was ebbing precariously low. Maybe she was not well suited for journalism, she thought. Maybe she had picked the wrong profession. Maybe she should quit.

She looked down at her scribblings from the aborted telephone interview. She had jotted a few quotes from the ailing woman on a note handed to her a half-hour earlier by Tim Coder, managing editor of the *Journal*'s Santa Fe bureau. There, in Coder's writing, were the scrawled words, MYSTERY VIRUS.

Coder had made the note that afternoon while running a meeting in the bureau's conference room. He and a handful of reporters and stringers had been planning the bureau's annual Christmas tabloid, an obligatory advertising supplement. Coder mentioned that the food editor who was supposed to be there was out sick, and suddenly he found himself swapping flu stories with the staffers. One of the stringers, Santa Fe freelance writer Louis Weisberg, offered that he knew a woman whose flu-like aches and pains had been so severe that she had been hospitalized. What was most interesting, Weisberg said, was that the woman's physician discovered it wasn't influenza but some sort of rare illness and that a second northern New Mexico woman also was hospitalized with the same symptoms. Their doctors, he said, were trying to find a link.

After the meeting, Coder approached Tamar Stieber, who was working at her desk. He liked this thirty-four-year-old beginner. She was green, but smart and creative. Coder especially valued her enthusiasm. She wanted to please. And she had natural journalistic instincts. You could hand her the flimsiest news tip, and if a story was buried there, she would find it.

"This looks promising," he said, handing her the note. "See Louis Weisberg first, then let's go after it."

Despite her inexperience, Tamar was the logical staffer to be handed the story. She was the Santa Fe bureau's "medical reporter." That means she wrote about health-care issues when she wasn't covering city hall, county government, the arts, special projects, or the police beat. That's life in the eight-reporter bureau, responsible for news in all of northern New Mexico and the state capital city. Every staff member must wear several hats.

So Tamar looked up the stringer, Louis Weisberg, and asked him to repeat his story tip. In doing so, he added something: Both of the women with the strange illness had been taking some sort of dietary supplement for insomnia and premenstrual syndrome, and their doctors were baffled over whether this was the common link.

Tamar's curiosity was suddenly aroused. "L-Tryptophan?" she asked.

"Yeah," Weisberg said. He thought that was it. L-Tryptophan.

Now her mind was racing. Tamar had some experience of her own with the over-the-counter drug. She had taken it for a full year—just for insomnia, not premenstrual syndrome. For years, the pills—a synthetic version of an amino acid called tryptophan—had been widely recommended as a "natural," nonprescription remedy for those problems, as well as for muscle tension and stress. Tamar had used the drug throughout 1976. It significantly relieved her sleeplessness, and she experienced no ill effects.

After getting the ill woman's name and phone number from Weisberg, Tamar was brimming with energy when she called her up. This, she realized, could be an intriguing story.

But the woman's unexpected hostility—and her abrupt end to the conversation—left Tamar slightly shaken and discouraged. As she stared out the newsroom window, she asked herself, "Am I good enough for this work?" Then her eyes fell on Coder's note. She didn't want to let Tim down. He was a good boss. Also, she realized, she was intrigued by the possibility, remote as it seemed, that at least one woman—and maybe two—had been harmed by a common drug that she herself had taken.

Looking at her notes, she noticed that the hostile woman, before hanging up on her, had provided the name of her physician. Tamar telephoned the doctor, who confirmed she had a patient suffering from eosinophilia myalgia syndrome, a relatively rare blood disorder—not a virus—involving extremely high counts of white blood cells called eosinophils. Besides intense muscle and joint pain, the symptoms could include body rash, extreme weakness, and even difficulty chewing. She said the condition usually occurs as a result of bronchial asthma, allergies, drug reactions, or parasitic infections.

The doctor also confirmed that her patient had been taking L-Tryptophan. However, she stressed that the clinic had been using the drug safely for years and that it was too early to determine whether L-Tryptophan had anything to do with the symptoms of her patient or of a second hospitalized woman.

Tamar obtained the name of the second woman's doctor in nearby Los Alamos. She telephoned him and received an identical response: Eosinophilia, yes. L-Tryptophan, yes. Link, uncertain. The second doctor, however, mentioned he knew of a *third* doctor, in Taos, who was treating a woman critically ill with eosinophilia. And yes, the doctor said, that woman also had been using L-Tryptophan, a coincidence he called "suspicious" but certainly no reason to jump to conclusions.

This news hit Tamar like a thunderbolt. Three women, all between the ages of thirty-seven and forty-three, with the same rare disease within a thirty-mile radius. And all three of them taking L-Tryptophan.

That didn't prove anything, of course. But Tamar became alarmed. Shouldn't the public at least be informed of the situation? Shouldn't other doctors and clinics be advised about the three worrisome cases?

Dr. Mai Ting was the director of the Santa Fe medical center where the first woman was being treated. Dr. Ting bristled when Tamar posed those questions.

"It's not just myself," Dr. Ting said. "I've spoken to other doctors in this town and in Albuquerque who feel the link between tryptophan and this particular situation is a red herring. A lot of people take tryptophan and nobody else has [reacted]."

Dr. Ting angrily threatened a lawsuit against Tamar and the paper if she published Dr. Ting's name, the doctor's name, or any reference to the clinic in connection with the sick women.

Next, Tamar telephoned Dr. Ron Voorhees, medical investigator for the New Mexico Office of Epidemiology. He acknowledged that his office was investigating the cases but said L-Tryptophan was just one possible cause under consideration.

"There could be an infection," he said. "It could be a substance in a medication; it could be a food allergy, or it could be totally unrelated. All I really know is that three people have the condition around the same time."

Dr. Voorhees warned Tamar it would be "unethical" for the *Journal* to publish speculation about L-Tryptophan's possible connection to the three cases. He said that would amount to an unwarranted "scare story."

Tamar decided then to take her questions all the way to the federal government. She called the Centers for Disease Control in Atlanta, but no doctors there were familiar with the New Mexico cases or willing to discuss them. So she tried the federal Food and Drug Administration, which referred her to District Director Gerald Vince. He said L-Tryptophan did not need FDA approval and thus was not an FDA concern.

"L-Tryptophan is an amino acid commonly used as a food supplement," he said. "There is no safety concern."

No safety concern? The words rang in Tamar's head that night as she went to bed—on the floor of a friend's home. After six months, she still hadn't found an apartment she could afford in the tight and expensive Santa Fe housing market.

No safety concern? Man, she thought: What a story, and what a day. A phone receiver had been slammed in her ear. She had been threatened with a lawsuit. She had been warned against a "scare story." And she had been blithely assured there was "no safety concern."

Tamar had trouble going to sleep that night. Ironically, she recalled, back in the seventies she took heavy doses of L-Tryptophan for stress like this. In some ways, that was a lifetime ago.

Before beginning her newspaper career, she was married and divorced, worked as a waitress and at various other low-paying jobs, lived in London for a few years "doing Lord knows what," and found herself constantly "going back to school and quitting, and going back to school and quitting."

Her journey down the Santa Fe Trail was long and arduous. Finally, here she was, still in her first year as a daily newspaper reporter and already wondering whether it was all a mistake.

That night, as she struggled to go to sleep, questions kept spinning in her mind, each one growing more cosmic than the last:

What is making those three women so sick? Does L-Tryptophan have any connection?

What do I tell my editor tomorrow? Can I handle this story? Am I suited for this kind of work?

When will I find myself?

Who am I?

* * *

Tamar Stieber was born in Brooklyn in 1956, one year before Jim Dwyer began life a few miles away in Manhattan. Her father, Alfred Stieber, born in Vienna, was shipped off to America in his early twenties, just in time to avoid the Czechoslovakian concentration camp where both of his parents died at the hands of the Nazis. Tamar's mother, Freidele Spector, was born in New York shortly after her parents fled Czarist Russia to escape anti-Jewish pogroms.

Freidele became a child star of sorts on New York's Borscht Belt, dancing and singing before the age of five. By the time she was a young woman, the Depression had arrived and she had changed her name to Florence. She was singing in a night club when she met Alfred, working then as a waiter. They eloped, moved to Brooklyn, and started chasing the American dream. Florence became a teacher, and Alfred, who shortened his name to Fred, hopped from job to job, mostly selling insurance and real estate.

Tamar was the youngest of three daughters born to the Stiebers. By the time she was four, the family had moved to West Nyack, a small town in Rockland County, north of the city.

"It was a middle-class white development, very suburban and mostly Jewish, but not completely," she recalls. "We were a lower-middle-class family trying to reach the middle. I never went to a private school. We couldn't afford it. Many a night's dinner would be potatoes and eggs—mashed potatoes and fried eggs and onions, all mooshed up together. A big, special dinner would be chuck steaks. We were always outsiders in Rockland County, and I never understood it as a child. Actually, I don't understand it now. But that's just the way it was. And that's where I grew of age."

She remembers herself as "a wild child" during her teenage years—not so much rebellious as curious, "experimenting with all sorts of different things" in the heyday of flower power.

"I think I was always the son my father never had. There was very little my parents wouldn't let me do. I had no curfews at all, very few rules as an adolescent. If I didn't come home, I just had to call and let them know that I was alive."

Tamar played at being a flower child—a "hippie-ette," as she puts it now.

When she was fifteen, her parents separated for a while. Tamar left home and moved in with a friend. Always a good student, she continued going to the public schools. And when she wasn't studying, she was often hitchhiking all over the region, especially into Manhattan, where she loved to explore the galleries and museums. Only halfway through her fifteenth year, she took a part-time job at the New York City Library, taking the bus home at night or hitchhiking if she missed the public transportation.

Inevitably, the hitchhiking led to an assault—a man who picked her up attacked her. "I fought him off," she says. The petite, freckled brunette is decidedly tough, but just five-foot-one. She would later study aikido. And give up hitchhiking.

"I was always a loner, a little bit of the outsider, even in high school," she says. "I was sort of on the periphery of some of the cliques but never part of any of them."

When she turned sixteen, Tamar bought a used car with her library earnings and started driving herself to a different public high school. But she hated it there, too. Even the so-called accelerated classes for college-bound students bored her. With hardly any effort, she received straight A's. The lack of challenge proved stifling.

She dropped out and enrolled in Rockland Community

College's two-year program for gifted high school students. The second year of the program was at a school in Britain. "That's when my life really changed," she says.

She entered West London College at the age of nineteen. The ideas and the people and the challenges she encountered there exhilarated her. She stayed on for two additional years with financial help from a New York State Regents' Scholarship. Then she spent an additional year overseas, traveling throughout Europe and the Middle East, supporting herself by waiting tables.

In 1977, she returned to New York and enrolled at Columbia University. But *not* in Joseph Pulitzer's Graduate School of Journalism. As an undergraduate, she was still ineligible. More significantly, she had no interest then in a journalism degree. She decided to major in linguistics and Romance languages.

Tamar enjoyed her Columbia studies, "but life once again got in the way," she says.

This time, it was romance.

"I was living then at the 92nd Street Y, where I got locked out of my room one night. I came down looking for somebody to let me in, and there was my future husband, who was the security guard. He, too, was a Columbia student—going to class by day, working as the security guard at night. We spent many nights staying up together, talking. And we fell in love."

Soon, she was living with the young man, who wanted to be a writer. Tamar dropped out of Columbia and went to work in a bookstore so he could quit his night job and pursue his writing.

"So, in 1979, we got married. He was a Catholic, but an agnostic Catholic. And I was an agnostic Jew. That's why we decided to get married in the United Nations Chapel. It really represented our world view—the ethical culture of Judeo-Christianity without the theism. And the wedding was very nice, except that my mother hired the photographer, and I'm sure she must have called on the sly and made a special arrangement, because all his pictures showed only the Jewish tradition—and none of the Christian."

That might have been an ill omen, she now realizes. The newlyweds quickly discovered they had huge differences. Within a year, the marriage was under stress. They agreed they needed to make a change. A big one.

"In 1980 we decided it was time to get out of New York. So we had an apartment sale and got rid of most of our things, and then moved to San Francisco with no friends and no jobs, no place to live, and no money."

Tamar's mother strongly advised against the risky move. "Don't go! You'll end up divorced," she told her headstrong daughter.

"And damned if it wasn't true," Tamar says today. "A year later we split up. Best thing that ever happened."

At the time, she was working as a clerk in the San Francisco Public Library. She couldn't survive on that meager income, so she went looking for higher-paying work and ended up as a secretary in the city's Associated Press bureau.

The newsroom atmosphere appealed to Tamar. She liked the bright people, the tension, the feeling of being out on the edge of current events. Over the next two years, she often told her AP co-workers she'd like to become a reporter. Few people took the twenty-seven-year-old secretary seriously. One who did, though, was news editor Bill Schiffmann.

If you want to do this, he told her, you really should go back to school and get your degree. So Tamar took Schiffmann's advice. She quit and enrolled at U.C.-Berkeley, paying her own way by working at three different jobs and scrounging together some grants, scholarships and loans. Finally, in 1985, at the age of twenty-nine, Tamar Stieber received her undergraduate degree, with high honors—Phi Beta Kappa.

But this was not a bachelor's degree in journalism, or literature, or political science, or anything else that is typical of graduates aiming for newspaper careers. Her degree was in film theory. Tamar's focus had somehow shifted from journalism during her Berkeley days. Then she entered the university's graduate program with intentions of working toward a doctoral degree in comparative literature.

"But money got in the way again, and I had to stop," she says.

So she took another full-time job, this time as the office manager for a clinic that performed abortions and cosmetic surgery. Like so many of her previous jobs, this one took her nowhere, although the $500 a week she was paid there was more than she'd ever made—even later when she finally found her way into news reporting.

That would not happen until Tamar was thirty-one years old, frustrated and worried about her future. The key moment arrived one day while she was skimming the help-wanted ads in the *San Francisco Chronicle*. She spotted a reporter position to be filled at the twice-weekly *Sonoma Index-Tribune*. To her delight, she was granted an interview. To her dismay, she didn't get the job.

But Tamar learned that the little paper would soon have an additional opening. When it occurred a few months later, she pushed hard for the job. This time, the paper hired her. For a whopping $335 a week.

Tamar gratefully accepted the $8,000 pay cut and began working determinedly on her new career. Over the next fourteen months she lived in poverty while breaking in at the little Sonoma weekly, covering a lot of fires and auto accidents, school board meetings, and dog-licensing hearings. Though chronically broke, she loved the work. To herself she said, "This is it!" And she began fantasizing about working her way up to the *New York Times*, the nation's greatest paper, in the biggest city, which just happened to be her hometown.

Finally, Tamar heard about a better opportunity: a reporting job at a bona fide daily newspaper, the *Vallejo Times-Herald*. It was tiny (26,000 circulation), and the pay wasn't much better ($385 a week), but what the heck, she thought quite correctly, you don't go from Sonoma straight to the *New York Times*.

She got the Vallejo job and worked there for six months, covering more crime news and government meetings, until she spotted another opportunity to move up: a $484-a-week entry-level reporting job in the *Albuquerque Journal's* Santa Fe bureau. This, she thought, sounded promising. She had heard good things about Santa Fe: beautiful setting, charming town, good climate, great livability, an excellent place to take up jogging. And Santa Fe *had* to be a better news town than Vallejo, she thought. Best of all, $484 a week would be a raise of over 25 percent.

She applied—along with nearly one hundred other reporters from around the nation, most of them with more experience. On the basis of her "clips"—examples of her reporting at Sonoma and Vallejo—both Tim Coder, the Santa Fe bureau managing editor, and Howard Houghton, the city editor, decided to fly her out to New Mexico to get acquainted.

"In those first interviews, I remember being impressed by her smarts," says Rod Deckert, deputy managing editor. "She's a very savvy woman. And she said all the right things about being aggressive and wanting to do investigative stories if she came across them. She had aspirations that were fairly lofty, as I recall. She said she wanted to move up to a national paper sometime, maybe as a foreign correspondent. And that she had started late. And I got the sense that she wanted to make up for lost time."

Although her experience was limited, Deckert says, there was something about Tamar Stieber that made *Journal* editors want to take a chance on her. The paper did just that, and Tamar made her biggest career step ever, moving up to a medium-size metropolitan paper with well over 100,000 circulation. For the first time in her life, a company paid her moving expenses, which were actually quite low because much of what she owned could be squeezed into her car.

In May 1989, she started over again in Santa Fe, one of the oldest U.S. settlements, some sixty miles northeast of Albuquerque. Tamar would be captivated by Santa Fe's Old World flavor—the quaint adobe houses with tiled roofs and shady patios, the Indian and Spanish shops still lining the narrow, winding streets, the rich abundance of artists and artisans, and the relaxed feeling of a tourist town. Here, she would continue to cover police news and public meetings, and even an occasional medical story, one of which would have the power to change her life.

*   *   *

At daybreak on Friday, November 3, 1989, after her long night of self-doubt and troubled sleep, Tamar knew what her eosinophilia story needed: more reporting.

She went to the newsroom early and started making phone calls. Who, she wanted to know, was the nation's foremost expert on eosinophilia? A dozen or so calls to state and federal health officials produced a solid consensus. She should talk to Dr. Gerald Gleich, head of the immunology department at the Mayo Medical School, Clinic, and Foundation in Rochester, Minnesota.

"Calling the Mayo Clinic is a little like dealing with a federal bureaucracy," Tamar says. "You don't just dial up and get your

Mayo doctor on the line. There are layers of receptionists and public relations people you have to go through first."

She spent nearly eight hours trying to get Dr. Gleich on the phone. Luckily for her, he was at Mayo that day, but his schedule was jammed. Late in the afternoon, Santa Fe time, Dr. Gleich returned her call. He really didn't have time to talk, he told her, but he felt obligated. His daughter, he explained, was a reporter, too.

By the time the conversation ended, Tamar was jubilant. Dr. Gleich practically gift-wrapped the story for her. He called the triple occurrence of eosinophilia "pretty big league" and said he suspected the L-Tryptophan.

"Lightning can strike, but it doesn't strike twice," Dr. Gleich told her. "It could be a red herring, but a red herring in three people? I'm not willing to buy that. I'm trained to look for unexpected associations. Once is chance, twice is kind of interesting, but three and I say full speed ahead for an investigation."

Tamar whooped as she hung up the phone and headed for Tim Coder's office.

"What the hell is L-Tryptophan?" he asked.

Somewhat breathlessly, Tamar summarized everything she had learned in the past two days of digging. Coder instantly became excited. By then it was early evening.

Coder called the Albuquerque newsroom and alerted his boss, Deckert, the deputy managing editor, that the Santa Fe bureau had a hot, sensitive story and was being pressured by the local and state medical community against running it. Coder said the story was solid and he wanted to run it on the cover of his zoned Santa Fe section (inside the paper), but first he thought Deckert should have a look at it.

Deckert called up the story on his computer terminal, read it, and called Coder back. Sorry, Deckert said, but Coder couldn't have the story for the Santa Fe section. The story belonged "out front"—on page one.

First, though, Deckert had a few questions for Tamar. And he wanted his boss, assistant editor Kent Walz, to have a chance to look at it. After all, if this bombshell was going to cause heavy flak, Walz would catch most of it.

Walz was then shown the story. Great, he said. Let's go with it—after we plug a hole or two. Walz was most concerned that no attempt had been made to solicit response from any manufacturers of L-Tryptophan.

Tamar and her editors agreed. Walz had a good point. Frankly, nobody so far had thought of contacting the drug's makers. Basic fairness dictated that they be given a chance to comment. But now it was Friday evening. There would be no way to reach the pharmaceutical companies until Monday.

So the *Journal* sat on Tamar's story over the weekend. She was relieved, actually, because she wanted more time to polish it so it wouldn't sound alarmist. And she was fairly confident the story was safe from competing media for at least a couple more days.

Tamar spent Monday, November 6, contacting L-Tryptophan manufacturers and rewriting her story. As she expected, she did not obtain any useful new information from the drug companies. All denied that their product could be responsible for the three cases of eosinophilia. One company official suggested that doctors needed to take a closer look at the sick women's diets. Another company spokesman said that if any link to L-Tryptophan were found, the fillers or binders in the capsules would more likely be the villain than the drug itself.

Tamar's story, twenty-five column inches long, ran the following morning, Tuesday, November 7, on the *Journal's* front page. The story was displayed just below the fold, more than halfway down the page, beneath a conservatively worded forty-two-point headline that spanned six columns.

The story itself had been rewritten more times than Tamar can remember. At least six different editors took turns agonizing over it, raising questions, and suggesting changes throughout the final hours before publication. And Tamar was given a chance to review the final edited version. It was letter-perfect when she signed off on it.

Unfortunately, one typographical error crept into her work after she finally let it go. The *Journal's* city desk, in putting a byline on the most important story Tamar Stieber had ever written, misspelled her name. It came out "Steiber."

In the hours that followed, though, Tamar hardly had time to feel upset about the typo. Her story let loose a chain reaction nobody at the newspaper could have predicted.

Coder, Deckert, and Walz had braced for an outpouring of

wrath from the hypersensitive medical community that had warned against any "scare stories." There was a deluge, all right, but not the one the editors expected. Tamar's story touched off a flurry of additional reports of New Mexico cases of eosinophilia—among patients using L-Tryptophan.

In the next issue of the *Albuquerque Journal*, on Wednesday morning, November 8, Tamar Stieber's byline had moved to the top of the page—right beneath a sixty-point banner: NINE MORE CASES OF OBSCURE SYNDROME REPORTED. As a result of the previous day's story, state health officials were hearing from physicians all over New Mexico. The flood of new reports prompted Dr. Millicent Eidson, the state's environmental epidemiologist, to ask for a voluntary sales ban on L-Tryptophan. In an emergency news release, she also urged:

• That anyone taking L-Tryptophan immediately halt usage until health officials investigate the problem.

• That any such patients immediately contact their physician if they were experiencing severe muscle pain.

• And that all physicians with eosinophilic patients immediately contact the Office of Epidemiology.

The next day, November 9, seven investigators from the Food and Drug Administration fanned out across New Mexico, from Los Alamos to Las Cruces, collecting L-Tryptophan belonging to stricken patients. Meanwhile, in her third consecutive front-page story, Tamar reported four more identical cases. And this time, one of the victims, a thirty-eight-year-old Albuquerque woman, Judy Kody Paulsen, went public. She had been stunned to read Tamar's story in the previous day's *Journal* while on a flight to the Mayo Clinic to seek help for her eosinophilia. Paulsen called Tamar from the Salt Lake City airport to describe her ordeal and how she had been taking heavy doses of L-Tryptophan for the past eighteen months with no idea whatsoever that the drug had been linked to eosinophilia. None of *her* doctors had made the connection.

The interview with Paulsen was a gut-grabber. The Associated Press picked it up and moved it on its national wire to newspapers all across the United States.

That's when all hell broke loose.

Eosinophilia victims, many of whom had been taking L-Tryptophan, began popping up in other states. First Missouri. Then Arizona. Then Oregon and Mississippi.

By Friday, November 10, the total of such cases was up to twenty-one.

By Saturday, November 11, additional cases had turned up in Texas, California, Virginia, and Minnesota. The case total climbed to thirty-one.

By Sunday, November 12, the total had soared to fifty-five. Now Tamar's story was national news. The Centers for Disease Control in Atlanta jumped into the investigation, and the FDA warned U.S. consumers to temporarily stop using L-Tryptophan.

At this point, Tamar was worn out. She had been putting in grinding hours on the story for over a week. What she needed was a day off, or at least a couple good nights of sleep. She was literally living out of her car, which was loaded with her clothes and parked outside whatever house she happened to be sleeping in temporarily. During November, while working the L-Tryptophan story, she would sleep in four different homes— on floors, sofas, and even on a tiny kiddie bed.

That wasn't the only personal problem she had on her mind. Her automobile insurance company was making a move to cancel her policy as a result of a rash of speeding tickets she had received—some of them while rushing to news events. "I admit it. I love to drive, and sometimes I get lost in thought and exceed the speed limit," she says.

She also was feeling depressed over her recent estrangement from one of her two older sisters. Tamar and Sharon Stieber, who was two years older, had argued bitterly several weeks earlier, and neither had spoken to the other since.

"We had a very bad fall-out," Tamar says. "Whatever precipitated it isn't that important, but it was incredibly bad."

Guilt, anger, remorse, love—all those emotions and others had been roiling within her for weeks. Every day, even during the eruption of the L-Tryptophan story, Tamar found herself thinking about Sharon and brooding over the apparent impossibility of patching things up.

At the end of her first week on the story, Tamar finally was faced with an opportunity for a full night's rest. However, she couldn't sleep. Her nerves were stretched too tight. She tried meditation, music, exercise, and television. Nothing worked. So she bought a bottle of California red wine, hoping to sedate herself. She vividly remembers what happened:

"I'm not much of a drinker to begin with, and in Santa Fe, at seven thousand feet elevation, you have to be careful with alcohol. But I drank three-quarters of that bottle. It worked, I guess. I went right to sleep. But I had one hell of a hangover the next day."

The Santa Fe bureau editors, Coder and Houghton, could see they had an exhausted reporter, and they tried to get Tamar to ease off. She vigorously objected, though, when they suggested that somebody else could take over the story for a day or so.

After the story had burst into national headlines, Tamar thought she sensed subtle hints from Albuquerque that perhaps the story was so big now that it ought to be handed off to one of the seasoned veterans—most likely the full-time medical reporter. No editor came right out and made such a remark, she says, and she admits now her paranoia might have been fueled by fatigue. But she nevertheless felt sufficiently worried that she forewarned her bosses there was no way she would let go of the story.

"Sometimes, in the Santa Fe bureau, we had to fight to keep a story," she says. "There's a little bit of a feeling that we're the weak stepsister, the underdog, the second-class citizens, compared to the main newsroom in Albuquerque. We're still considered the renegade group. We sit in hot tubs, snort cocaine, and drink Perrier. At least that's how Santa Fe is looked at, like the Marin County of New Mexico.

"In Albuquerque, the atmosphere is very, very corporate. The newsroom walls have nothing on them. People are allowed only certain things on their desks. And nobody yells across the newsroom. What I love about our bureau is that people get involved in your story, if they have something to add. There aren't that many ego problems. There's a lot of sharing. I think that makes for better stories, much better stories, and I love that. I don't believe it happens as much in Albuquerque. It's very quiet, very staid there. It ain't that way in Santa Fe."

So Tamar kept a tight grip on the story. And she worked the next sixteen days straight with no more than four hours sleep a night.

Her editors say they can understand why Tamar might have been concerned about losing the story to a more experienced hand, but they are unanimous in insisting there was never any talk of such a move. In fact, Walz, the assistant editor, says he would have opposed it. He didn't know Tamar or her work very well when the story first broke, but within a few days she had his full confidence.

"She was delightful, a great sense of humor, very pleasant to work with," he says. "And I guess if I had to pull one word out of the air to describe her, it would be persistence. She just keeps going. She's not intimidated easily and she's not inclined to take no for an answer if she has reason to believe there's a different answer."

The story continued to mushroom. By November 14, the total number of eosinophilia cases had soared to 81 in eighteen states. In New Mexico alone, the total was up to 30. That figure forced state health officials—some of the same ones who had accused Tamar of pushing a "scare story" a few days earlier—to ban the sale or display of L-Tryptophan. Violators would face a $100 fine and up to six months in jail.

Four days later, on November 18—just sixteen days after Tim Coder had handed Tamar the MYSTERY VIRUS note—the story hit front pages across the nation. The catalyst was the FDA, which issued a national recall of all products in which L-Tryptophan was a major component. By then, the total number of reported eosinophilia cases had skyrocketed to 287 in thirty-seven states and the District of Columbia. One of the cases had resulted in the death of an Oregon woman who had been using L-Tryptophan.

Within five months, the total number of cases reported across the United States would exceed 1,500. Of these, 63 would end in death. Most of the victims were women who had been taking the dietary supplement.

Early in December, one month after she began the big story, life began to smooth out for Tamar Stieber. The L-Tryptophan issue calmed down in New Mexico and was now virtually taken over by national media. She finally found an affordable apartment, the tiny adobe unit for $325 a month, and her car insurance policy was renewed, to her great relief. The falling-out with her sister Sharon continued unabated, but Tamar was no longer losing sleep or sedating herself with wine.

In appreciation for her outstanding work, the *Journal's* publisher, Thompson Lang, rewarded Tamar with a company-paid vacation trip to Key West aboard his private jet. She took the trip but says, at the risk of sounding ungrateful, that she didn't particularly enjoy it because it somehow felt wrong:

"Prizes like that are okay for travel agents and realtors, but not for reporters. We don't do stories to win prizes."

When Tamar returned to Santa Fe, she was met by another surprise. *Journal* editors had submitted her L-Tryptophan reporting for a Pulitzer Prize. The entry was accompanied by a formal letter signed by *Journal* editor Gerald J. Crawford (but actually written by an underling, Rod Deckert). The letter, outlining Tamar's work on the eosinophilia outbreak, concluded:

> An important part of the puzzle remains unsolved—medical investigators still don't know how or why L-Tryptophan triggers the ailment. But one thing is clear. Without Tamar Stieber's stories, hundreds of people suffering from this life-threatening ailment would have continued to take the very supplement doctors now believe caused their problem, and many others would have unknowingly exposed themselves to the risk.

One of the attractions of journalism is that news creates whirlwinds that sometimes sweep reporters along in life-changing ways. In such a fateful fashion, Tamar was suddenly being whisked unknowingly into head-to-head conflict with Jim Dwyer and Claire Spiegel for a 1990 Pulitzer Prize.

Meanwhile, at about that time, a wind more literal in nature was blowing Tamar's way. Somewhere out on the arid plain between Santa Fe and Albuquerque, a sudden winter gust caused a dead amaranth plant to snap off at the stem and roll with the wind, becoming what is known as a tumbleweed. Like a great, light ball, it would travel for weeks and months, scattering its seeds over the plain, until a night in April when another sudden gust would toss the ghostly weed onto Interstate 25 and into the headlights of a speeding car driven by Tamar Stieber.

10

Ladies and Gentlemen of the Jury

6:30 A.M.—March 5, 1990

MANHATTAN'S TEMPERATURE HOVERS just above freezing, cold enough to put mittens on the newsstand vendors on Broadway and Amsterdam Avenue but warm enough to melt the tiny, ash-like flakes of snow as they drift onto the stacks of freshly inked tabloids.

Bundled-up employees are beginning to arrive at Columbia University, and some of them stop outside the campus gates to patronize the newsstands. If the dealers do well on this dank, late-winter morning, they can thank the nation's leading Catholic. Yesterday, during Mass at St. Patrick's Cathedral on Fifth Avenue, Cardinal John O'Connor handed the tabloids a fairly sexy Monday morning story. He ripped into rock music from the pulpit, linking heavy metal to Satanism and claiming it had led to some recent exorcisms. Hence this morning's front page screamers:

O'CONNOR: ROCK MUSIC IS THE DEVIL'S TOOL (*Newsday*)

CARDINAL VS. THE DEVIL (*Daily News*)
SATAN'S SONGS (*Post*)

The cardinal is a treasure for New York newspapers; he almost always says these sorts of things on Sundays, the lightest news day of the week.

Meanwhile, nearby in the journalism school built with wealth accumulated from headlines like those being peddled outside, a custodian opens the big doors to the World Room, admitting a pair of food-service workers.

7:05 A.M.

In the gloom of the unlit room, the caterers begin setting up coffee makers and cups, and plates of breakfast pastries, more than enough to handle the sixty-five guests who will soon arrive. They are the men and women of the Pulitzer Prize journalism juries—mostly American newspaper editors and reporters, with a sprinkling of educators and free-lance journalists. All have been invited here at their own expense (usually borne by their employers) to toil for two or three days as glorified screening committees. For their efforts they will receive all the sweet rolls they can eat, two free lunches, and the right to boast of having judged the Pulitzer Prizes. And brag, they will—many of them—because being a juror ranks high on the relative prestige chart of Pulitzer Prize involvement:

1. Pulitzer Prize Board chairman
2. Pulitzer Prize Board member
3. Pulitzer Prize winner
4. Pulitzer Prize juror
5. Pulitzer Prize finalist (nominee)
6. Pulitzer Prize winner's editor
7. Pulitzer Prize entrant

This arbitrary and arguable guide works like the Richter scale: Each level of respect is ten times greater than the one below it. "Entrant," at the bottom, carries so little prestige nowadays that many job-seeking former entrants try to pass themselves off instead as "once nominated for a Pulitzer Prize," when in fact they were merely entered. And anybody can enter the Pulitzer competition by filling out a form and paying a $20 fee. Even if the pope submits a reporter's work for the prize, that doesn't make the reporter a "nominee." The only true nominees are the relatively few picked as finalists by the jurors who will begin showing up this day in the World Room.

7:15 A.M.

The caterers begin to set out several large pitchers of juice— orange for the health-conscious, tomato for those with hang-overs. Experience has shown a slight preference for the tomato juice, perhaps a reflection that Pulitzer jury duty also means a night or two on the town, maybe a Broadway show, dinner, a little club-hopping and, for some, a headache in the morning.

7:19 A.M.

Bud Kliment enters the room, looks around and seems satisfied with the caterers' activity. Kliment, a Columbia gradu-ate and free-lance writer, has been the assistant Pulitzer Prize administrator for the past three years. He is efficient, highly organized, and constantly mindful of what he might be doing to help his boss, Robert Christopher. Details and logistics are left to Kliment. Christopher handles the big stuff—serving as secretary to the board and dealing with the media.

Kliment flips a row of light switches, and eight chandeliers illuminate the results of several hours of work he accomplished yesterday, getting things ready. Six large tables in the room are heaped high with prize exhibits waiting to be judged. The mountains of entries represent several prize categories, as indicated by neatly printed signs on each table: public service, general news reporting, investigative reporting, explanatory journalism, specialized reporting, and feature writing. Ex-hibits for the other eight journalism categories—national and international reporting, commentary, criticism, editorial writ-ing, cartoons, and spot and feature photography—are scat-tered throughout the building.

Buried somewhere in those piles are scrapbooks displaying the work of Jim Dwyer, Claire Spiegel, and Tamar Stieber.

7:35 A.M.

A custodial worker enters the World Room and flicks on the lights behind the stained-glass image of the Statue of Liberty. When Joseph Pulitzer's World Building was torn down in 1955 to make way for a new approach to the Brooklyn Bridge, legendary *World* editor Herbert Bayard Swope was instrumental in getting the colorful window removed and reinstalled in the World Room. The room itself is not looking as spiffy as Swope might have preferred. The windows are dirty, the faded blue drapes need cleaning, the carpeting hasn't been vacuumed in a week or so, and one end of the room is stacked with dozens of empty cardboard boxes—receptacles for all those journalism prize exhibits.

However, the clutter will be gone and the cleaning will be done before April, when the Pulitzer Board shows up— another reflection of relative prestige.

7:48 A.M.

One of the food-service workers moves around the room with a box of glass ashtrays, placing a pair of them on every table. There will be no smoke-free zones in the World Room today, although many of the smokers—a clear minority—will step outside to light up.

Kliment is hurrying right behind the woman with the ashtrays. He places note pads, pencils, and copies of the prize rules on every table top—not an easy task, because he struggles to find space among the astonishingly big stacks of prize exhibits. Each table is piled with nearly two hundred entries. Almost all of them have been prepared in elaborate book form, with professional-looking bindings, covers, and mounting boards. The rules require "scrapbooks measuring no more than 12 x 17 inches, except in cases where a full newspaper page is required to make clear the full scope and impact of the material entered." Not surprisingly, many exhibits are full-page in size and an inch or more thick, weighing more than twenty pounds.

Altogether on this day, 1,770 entries are awaiting the juries' verdicts for the fourteen journalism prizes. That is roughly double the number of entries received slightly more than a decade ago. Part of the increase can be attributed to a recent loosening of the rules, permitting a single entry to be submitted in two different prize categories. But most of the increase, records show, results from a trend by prize-seeking newspapers to flood the competition with entries.

The prize administrator, Christopher, disagrees with that conclusion.

"I can't think of anybody that I would say deliberately floods the competition," he says. "Obviously, a paper like the *New York Times* is going to have a lot of entries. It's a big paper with a lot of top-flight people on it. I think they try to control themselves in how many entries they submit. So I wouldn't say anybody floods us."

However, a statistical look at the entries stacked this day on the tables at Columbia tells a different story:

- Five newspapers have submitted entries in all fourteen journalism categories. They are the *Los Angeles Times,* the *Washington Post,* the *Philadelphia Inquirer,* the *Chicago Tribune* and the *St. Louis Post-Dispatch.* Combined, these five papers have submitted a total of 178 entries that their editors evidently consider worthy of the Pulitzer Prize. Those 178 account for 10 percent of the total 1990 entries.

- One-third of the 1,770 entries came from just twenty papers.

- The *New York Times* has submitted thirty-five entries, spread over all but one of the fourteen prize categories.

- *Newsday* has submitted forty-one entries, more than any other paper, followed closely by the *Washington Post* with forty.

- The Associated Press has turned in forty entries and will come up empty-handed, helping to prove that the shotgun approach to prize-winning is not a sure thing.

- Knight-Ridder newspapers take this contest very seriously indeed. The chain's 180 entries account for slightly more than 10 percent of all submissions for 1990 Pulitzer Prizes in journalism. Exactly half of those 180 entries are from three papers: the *Detroit Free Press* with twenty-four entries, the *Miami Herald* with thirty-two, and the *Philadelphia Inquirer* with thirty-four. Ultimately, the flooding will pay off, along with the superior quality of the chain's entries, when Knight-Ridder papers win four—nearly one-third—of the 1990 prizes.

8:02 A.M.

The first juror arrives a little earlier than Kliment had expected. As Helen Thomas takes off her overcoat, he appears a bit flustered because he doesn't have the name tags ready.

Thomas, White House bureau chief for United Press International, graciously apologizes for being so early. Wearing a bright red suit that accents her blazing red hair, Thomas will stand out in other ways this day as well. Among the sixty-five jurors, she will be among only a brave few not powered-up in pinstripes or otherwise dark, conservative uniforms.

Jury work can be quite draining, Thomas says, so she came early hoping to relax for a while with coffee and the morning's *New York Times,* which has played Cardinal O'Connor's heavy-metal pronouncements inside the second section.

Thomas has been a juror several times and enjoys the role, even though she calls it "scut work for the Pulitzer Board." This year she will help judge "national reporting."

Each of the journalism juries has five members. Although there are fourteen journalism prizes, there are only thirteen juries; one of them screens both photo categories—"spot news" and "feature photography."

8:30 A.M.

More jurors begin trickling in, and Kliment is ready for them. He has positioned himself by the doors at a table covered with name tags, all neatly labeled and lined up alphabetically in perfect rows.

The first seven to arrive after Thomas are all men, dressed in suits, and they ignore her as she sits alone with her paper.

Of the sixty-five jurors scheduled to arrive this day, only ten are women. That's undeniably lopsided, but newspaper journalism has always been a heavily male-dominated field. Make that *white* male-dominated; only eight of the jurors are nonwhite.

Eight of the jurors are previous Pulitzer Prize winners.

Seven jurors—more than 10 percent of the total—are from Knight-Ridder newspapers.

No jurors are from weekly, minority, or alternative (non-establishment) papers.

As always, the jury members are predominantly Eastern. Of the sixty-five, only fifteen are from cities west of the Mississippi River.

9:00 A.M.

The trickle of arriving jurors has become a torrent. The muted, library-like hush that hung in the air only minutes ago becomes a roaring din as swarms of professional-looking people exchange greetings, introduce each other to old friends, and go for the jelly doughnuts.

Like delegates at any American business conference, the jurors tend to break into three subgroups: (1) small cliques of the boardroom heavy-hitters who know each other from all the national meetings they attend together; (2) larger coteries of the rising stars, working hard—some of them shmoozing feverishly—in hopes of someday joining the heavy-hitters; and (3) a smattering of true working journalists—reporters, photographers, and hands-on editors who seem a little uncomfortable with this scene and clearly would be more at ease back in the newsroom with their sleeves rolled up. However, they've been invited here because they once won a Pulitzer or came close to winning one or somehow came to the attention of the prize administration, and like it or not they're on their way to joining group No. 2.

The first group—the heavy-hitters—includes a number of buttoned-down top executives such as John Driscoll, editor of the *Boston Globe;* Andrew Barnes, editor, president, and CEO of the *St. Petersburg* (Fla.) *Times,* and John Seigenthaler, chairman, publisher, and CEO of the *Tennessean* at Nashville and editorial director of *USA Today.*

The second group—the rising stars—is by far the largest, filled with dozens of senior-level editors from cities as big as Chicago and as small as Billings, Montana.

The third group—the working journalists—includes recent Pulitzer Prize winners such as Andrew Schneider of the

Pittsburgh Press, Bill Dedman of the *Washington Post,* Charles Shepard of the *Charlotte* (N.C.) *Observer,* Manny Crisostomo of the *Detroit Free Press,* Thomas Friedman of the *New York Times,* and Jonathan Freedman, formerly with the *Tribune* of San Diego.

A few jurors do not fit neatly into any of the three groups. These are the celebrity journalists, the ones with national reputations extending beyond the newspaper industry: the venerable Helen Thomas of UPI, Pulitzer-winning columnist Dave Barry of the *Miami Herald,* and Leonard Downie Jr., managing editor of the *Washington Post* and heir-apparent to Watergate legend Ben Bradlee, the paper's executive editor.

The route to becoming a Pulitzer Prize juror is somewhat as mystical and serendipitous as being selected to join an elite, secret society.

It all begins with Christopher, the prize administrator, who keeps a confidential list of names of prospective jury appointees, relying heavily on suggestions from his bosses, the other seventeen members of the Pulitzer Board. Composed almost entirely of senior news executives, the powerful board operates as a sort of supreme court, accepting or rejecting the juries' choices. Almost every year, the board throws out the selections of at least one jury. That will happen again this year when three finalists selected for the editorial cartooning prize fail to satisfy the board.

Each November, at an annual business meeting, Christopher presents a formal list of jury candidates for board members to consider. The list always includes about half of the previous year's jurors, to provide continuity. Jurors rarely are invited to serve more than two consecutive years.

How do names get on this list? One sure way, of course, is to become good friends with a member of the board. A more practical way, however, is to win a Pulitzer Prize. That's how Schneider, Shepard, Dedman, Crisostomo, Friedman, and Freedman found themselves invited to Columbia this time around.

Christopher says more and more former Pulitzer winners are being invited to be jurors in the belief that they are the most qualified people available. One of the 1990 jurors, Andrew Schneider, a two-time Pulitzer winner, laughed when told about this formula and suggested that it sounds "a bit incestuous."

Others win jury invitations not through their prize-winning journalism but after years of carefully building professional reputations within the industry. This means joining the proper associations, attending the national meetings, getting elected to the right positions, and publishing articles in the trade press.

Christopher says he is constantly on the lookout for distinguished people who also happen to be female or nonwhite, or both. Each year he also tries to make sure the juries include a fair representation of people from Western states and from smaller newspapers.

9:15 A.M.

Christopher finally enters the World Room and begins mingling, mostly with the heavy-hitters. He knows many of them—some through his ten years overseeing the prizes and others through his years in magazine journalism.

Besides holding top jobs at *Time* and then *Newsweek*, Christopher later was managing editor of *GEO* magazine for two years. After it folded, he served on the editorial board of the *New York Daily News* before taking the adjunct teaching position at Columbia and the role as Pulitzer Prize administrator, and secretary to the board. In addition to his magazine-editing background, Christopher is an expert on Japanese economics and trade. He has published two books on the subjects and is working on a third. He is a well-connected, well-educated (Yale) man who can be alternately articulate and polished or folksy and profane, much like Joseph Pulitzer, according to historians. One has to guess that Pulitzer would have approved of Christopher as the man to run this show, despite his background in magazines rather than in newspapers. If anything, Christopher seems overqualified for the job and slightly uncomfortable in it, particularly when asked to defend Pulitzer Prize traditions, such as the secrecy, that appear to conflict with his personal values.

9:45 A.M.

Christopher moves to the head of the room, where he raps on a table to quiet the chatter. As the din subsides, he introduces himself, formally welcomes the jurors, and assures them that they are "essential to the successful function of the Pulitzer Prize system."

Then he outlines the basic responsibility of each jury: "to supply the board, on the forms that you've been given, with no more and no less than three nominations per category." He repeats that requirement and says it is "really, really rigid."

Christopher goes on to announce that each jury should list its three nominations "in alphabetical order, since it's not part of the jury's charge to make preferences." In other words, don't indicate your favorite for the Pulitzer Prize. That is the board's job.

In his final admonition to the jurors, Christopher turns especially solemn:

"Another point that I would like to stress is the *extreme* importance of preserving the confidentiality of these proceedings. Members of the prize board feel very strongly that leaks concerning jury nominations are an unfortunate thing. When they're inaccurate, they inevitably bring discredit on the leaker, and when they are accurate, they can raise false hopes and can cause disappointments. The board feels so strongly about this that over the past few years they've moved the date of the prize announcements as close to the jury meetings as they possibly can—much closer than used to be the case—in order to reduce the time available for leaking."

9:55 A.M.

After finishing up with some nuts-and-bolts announcements about plans for lunch and an evening wine and cheese reception, Christopher puts the sixty-five jurors to work with a final exhortation:

"Good hunting!"

With a noisy stir, the jurors begin finding their way to their stations: six juries in the World Room, the commentary jury in a room upstairs on the fourth floor, the editorial cartoon jury on the fifth floor, the photography jury on the seventh floor, and so forth.

Many of the men begin hanging up their suit coats, loosening their ties, and rolling up their sleeves. They can see this is going to be a demanding two days—or even three days, if they can't finish up by Tuesday night. They receive no pay or honorarium for their work, but almost all of them are performing it on company time, as a job-related responsibility.

No jurors are at Columbia this day for screening the Pulitzer Prize in arts and letters and music. Those juries operate apart from the journalism judging. And the book juries have already done their work for the year.

Each jury for the five different book awards has three members, each receiving a $1,000 stipend. They certainly earn it, if they actually read even half the books that are submitted. A total of 590 titles have been entered in the 1990 competition. That's a huge amount of reading: 181 books entered in general nonfiction, 123 in poetry, 115 in fiction, 92 in biography, and 79 in history.

Some of the book publishers flood the competition in the same way some newspapers do. In its quest for 1990 prizes, Alfred A. Knopf has entered fifty-eight books, every eligible title it published. That's almost 10 percent of the books submitted by all publishers combined.

Meanwhile, in the 1990 competition, others are playing the numbers game, too. William Morrow and W.W. Norton have each entered twenty-six books—like Knopf, submitting every eligible title in their catalogs. Harper & Row has entered twenty-two books; Farrar, Straus & Giroux, twenty; Little, Brown and Company, sixteen; Viking, fourteen; Random House, twelve; and Houghton Mifflin, Doubleday, and Harcourt Brace Jovanovich, eleven each. More than one hundred other publishers, mostly smaller houses and university presses, have entered ten or fewer books.

To enter a book, the publisher has to send a $20 fee and four copies (or four sets of galley proofs) to Columbia by December 31. The Pulitzer office mails three copies to the appropriate jurors and keeps one copy for the board, in case the book becomes a finalist. The jurors select three finalists (nominees) in each category. Then each jury's chairman must send a formal written report—listing nominees alphabetically with no preferences indicated—to the Pulitzer Prize office by early January.

That adds up to a total of fifteen books (three in each prize category) that are nominated for Pulitzers each year. The Pulitzer office then mails one copy of each nominated book to a board member who serves as chairman of a subcommittee responsible for that prize category. Interestingly, if any of the other seventeen board members want to read that book before final judging in April, it's up to them to obtain a copy—even if that means going out and buying it.

The $20 entry fee, adopted by the Pulitzer Board in 1983, set off a furor among writers' groups, who protested that the fees discriminate against smaller publishers. The board denied there is any bias in the book competition and said judges will consider any good book, even if it hasn't been submitted. Since that year, however, no such book has won a Pulitzer Prize.

For Knopf, its fifty-eight books add up to $1,160 in entry fees and far more than that in the value of complimentary copies for all the judges. But what's that compared to the extra royalties that might accrue if one of those fifty-eight should win the Pulitzer? Knopf editors obviously think the strategy works, and other houses are clearly following the same practice.

The Pulitzer is the one award that publishers think consistently helps sell books. Says Christopher: "Since we began to announce the two runners-up in each category in 1980, publishers have begun to cite the fact that the book was a Pulitzer nominee on the jacket copy."

The poetry category works almost exactly like the other four book categories. The rules limit the award to "a distinguished volume of verse by an American author," and book publishers submit most of the entries. The one major difference between poetry and the other categories is that most of the winning books are collections, so verse theoretically has multiple chances to win. Poems that failed to win a prize one year could be published in a new collection that might win in a future year.

It is left to the members of the Pulitzer book juries to read these hundreds of books—or, one suspects, to at least skim them—and winnow the 590 titles down to 15 for the board's consideration.

Jurors for the book awards are selected in much the same ethereal fashion as journalism jurors. Christopher keeps a confidential file of names and annually presents a list for the board's consideration. Of the fifteen book jurors for 1990, ten are college professors and the remaining five are writers, editors, and critics. Only five of the fifteen are from states west of the Mississippi. Only four are women.

The jury for general nonfiction provides a good microcosm. Its members are Raymond Sokolov, arts page editor for the *Wall Street Journal;* Timothy Ferris, a professor at the University of California at Berkeley; and author Joyce Carol Oates, a professor at Princeton University. Summary: Two out of the three are men, two out of the three are professors, and two out of the three are Easterners. One thing the three of them have in common, however, is that all were bleary-eyed after looking at the 181 books submitted for the prize in general nonfiction.

12:30 P.M.

The journalism jurors are a bit rummy now, too, as they break for lunch after their first assault on the mountains of entries.

In the World Room, a time-honored judging practice has given the hall a littered look: All six juries in the room have spent the morning weeding out the weaker exhibits and getting them literally "off the table," in juror jargon. So the floor under each work table is piled with entries no longer in the running. The sight is surprisingly depressing, signaling the end of so many reporters' dreams of Pulitzer glory.

The sixty-five jurors start putting on their coats and heading for a luncheon at Columbia's Faculty House on Morningside Drive. There, after a welcoming speech by Joan Konner, dean of the journalism school and a member of the Pulitzer Board, they are treated to a lunch of bland tortellini and "broccoli with something white on it," as juror Andrew Schneider describes the dish. His boss and fellow juror, *Pittsburgh Press* managing editor Madelyn Ross, remarks that it's the first time in years she has seen so many health-conscious people reaching for salt shakers.

Throughout lunch, jurors seem to carefully avoid any talk of their morning's toil. Later, when they're away from Columbia, many of them will generously trade inside information on the judging, but for now they strive to focus instead on other things. Unfortunately for the Faculty House cooks, the quality of their food provides a most convenient topic, even though this is one New York meal the jurors do not have to pay for. All the guests survive, of course, and return to the journalism building for a few more hours of winnowing.

5:25 P.M.

Rubbing their tired eyes, yawning and stretching, jurors in the World Room begin calling it quits for the day. A few have left already, heading for a "wine and cheese reception" that's scheduled to start soon in the lobby downstairs.

The impressive mounds of exhibits that were heaped on the tables at sunrise are gone, replaced by large piles on the floor below. After the first full day of screening, most of the 1,770 journalism entries are "off the table." That is the case throughout the building, in all the rooms where judging took place this day, and it is dramatically true in the World Room, where the carpet is now a sea of rejected journalism.

Relatively few exhibits remain on most table tops.

At the south end of the room, about ten exhibits of varying sizes remain on the table serving the jurors screening the 159 public service entries. The other 150 or so are stacked on the carpeting, under and around the table. One of the exhibits on the floor is from the *Los Angeles Times*—a series of stories by reporter Claire Spiegel, exposing mismanagement and medical malpractice at a public hospital in Watts. Another exhibit on the floor is from the *Albuquerque Journal*—stories by Tamar Stieber revealing the link between a rare blood disorder, eosinophilia, and the drug L-Tryptophan.

Both Claire and Tamar have been rejected for the public service Pulitzer Prize.

Nearby, at another jury's table, about a dozen exhibits remain on top and the other 120 or so are stacked on the floor. One of the floor stacks includes a scrapbook of columns by Jim Dwyer of *New York Newsday*, highlighted by a series exposing a link between subway accidents and worker fatigue. Jim has been rejected for the Pulitzer Prize in general reporting.

But Jim, Claire, and Tamar are not out of the competition. At all three papers, their respective editors were aware of a rule allowing an entry to be submitted in *two* different prize categories. Thus separate exhibits of the three reporters' work also were submitted in the category for specialized reporting.

At the north end of the World Room, about one hundred exhibits are stacked in melancholy piles beneath the jury table for specialized reporting. This prize is awarded for coverage of specialized subjects such as sports, business, science, education, or religion.

The scrapbooks for Jim, Claire, and Tamar are among about fifty exhibits still on this table. They have survived the first day of ruthless screening for the Pulitzer Prize.

Tomorrow will be a lot tougher.

5:45 P.M.

In the lobby downstairs, about seventy-five people engage in chitchat while sipping wine from plastic cups at the reception being put on by the Society of Professional Journalists.

The imbibers are predominantly Pulitzer jurors with a sprinkling of spouses, Columbia faculty, and students. The jurors are primarily from two groups—the rising stars and the working journalists. Very few of the heavy-hitters have bothered to stay for the little soiree.

Not enough wine is flowing to threaten anyone's self-control, but a juror from California manages to spill his chablis onto the green marble floor. A colleague quickly stoops to sop the puddle with cocktail napkins. He leaves them there on the floor, soaking up the wine, just inches from a bronze seal inscribed with Joseph Pulitzer's wish that the journalism building be erected in the memory of his beloved daughter Lucille, victim of typhoid at age seventeen.

As at lunch, gabbing jurors seem to work hard at keeping the conversation away from the day's business. Robert Christopher's dire warnings about confidentiality still reverberate, so talk turns to safer subjects. A favorite among out-of-towners, of course, is the New York theater—what shows are on, how to get tickets, what's hot, and what's not. Everybody here is a critic, and no two critics agree: *Les Misérables* ("moving," "beautiful music," "too goddam long"), *Cats* ("fantastic," "a piece of crap"), *The Phantom of the Opera* ("it's fun," "it sucks"), *The Heidi Chronicles* ("amusing," "so-so," "hey, it won a Pulitzer").

Mention of Wendy Wasserstein's 1989 winner inevitably steers the conversation toward the forbidden subject, Pulitzer judging. Comments by some of the journalism jury members reveal they know as little about the mysterious drama judging as the general public knows. An editor, for example, asks a colleague:

"When do the drama jurors meet?"

The answer, which his colleague doesn't know, is that the drama jurors *don't* formally meet. They confer by phone and occasionally at performances. In early March, the jury chairman sends a written report of their nominees, as in the book judging, to the Pulitzer Board.

Unlike the book jurors, however, the three drama jury members receive no stipends. But they are offered modest reimbursement for travel so they can see plays outside New York, according to Christopher. Two of the 1990 drama jurors—theater critics William A. Henry III of *Time* magazine and Linda Winer of *Newsday*—are from New York, and the third is drama critic Kevin Kelly of the *Boston Globe*.

The board long ago dropped Joseph Pulitzer's requirements that the winning play be performed in New York and that it "promote good morals, good taste and good manners." Today's rules specify that the play must be "by an American author, preferably original in its source and dealing with American life."

Drama is the only Pulitzer Prize category that requires no fee or formal entry. Says Christopher, "The presumption is that the drama jurors are familiar with all those plays that are eligible each year. It wouldn't make sense getting two hundred scripts when the jurors aren't going to read them anyway." Also, accepting an entry fee would seem to obligate the Pulitzer judges to actually view the play, and there's no way drama jurors are going to fly to Idaho to see some novice playwright's first production at the Pocatello Community Theatre. Frankly, they don't even want to read the manuscript until the play is produced in New York or in an important regional theater.

To be eligible, a play must be performed within a twelve-month period ending each March. That gives plays an advantage no other Pulitzer entries except poetry enjoy: additional chances to win. For example, *The Piano Lesson* by August Wilson was a finalist for the 1989 prize but failed to win. But since the play was still being performed in 1990, it continued to be eligible, and this time it will win.

Nearly a week ago, on March 1, drama juror Linda Winer visited William Henry, the chairman, in his office at *Time*, and they called up the third member, Kelly, on the phone in Boston. In a ninety-minute telephone conversation, they came up with their list of three finalists: *The Piano Lesson* (Henry's first choice), *And What of the Night?* by Maria Irene Fornes (favored by both Winer and Kelly), and *Love Letters* by A. R. Gurney (third choice of all three jurors).

Henry, who won the 1980 Pulitzer for criticism, then wrote a thousand-word report to the Pulitzer Board, outlining the jury's thoughts about the three nominated plays and why any one of the three would be worthy of the prize.

As part of their jobs as critics, all three jurors had viewed the plays at various regional theaters, which have become increasingly important in the Pulitzer process. Each had also seen a few additional plays—to judge rather than review—at the suggestion of fellow jury members. Kelly, for example, would not normally review a Cleveland production, but he traveled there to judge a play that Henry had seen and admired while on assignment for *Time*, which covers the theater nationally.

In most years, the drama jury is composed of two New Yorkers and a third member—usually a critic—from elsewhere. That formula has resulted in charges of regional bias.

"If a critic happens to be from Chicago, he's much more likely to be recommending work from Chicago," says Henry, who has been a juror twice. "In fact, if you look over the last five to ten years, you will find almost every year there is at least a finalist and sometimes a winner which owes its victory in part to the vagaries of who happens to be a juror and where that person happens to work."

A more equitable system, he says, would involve "a somewhat larger jury, probably five people, with three of them not based in New York but in different parts of the country."

The music jury has only three members, too, also serving without pay. A $2,000 stipend is paid, however, to a secretary who keeps track of the entries, which total 129 in the 1990 competition.

Juries in the music competition are almost always made up of composers, critics, and music educators. The 1990 jurors fit that mold perfectly: The chairman, Donald Martino, is a composer and music professor at Harvard University. The other two are David Hamilton, music critic for *The Nation*, and Roger Reynolds, composer and music professor at the University of California at San Diego. Both Martino and Reynolds are former Pulitzer Prize winners—a pattern the Pulitzer Board encourages as a likely means of perpetuating its standards.

When convenient, the music jurors attend live performances of compositions submitted for prizes. Only two finalists have been nominated in the 1990 competition, and at least one of the jurors attended a performance of each. They are Mel Powell's "Duplicates: A Concerto for Two Pianos and Orchestra," which premiered on January 26, 1990, performed by the Los Angeles Philharmonic, and Ralph Shapey's "Concerto for Cello, Piano and String Orchestra," which premiered on July 31, 1989, at Tanglewood Music Center.

However, the jury members listen to recordings of the overwhelming majority of entries. Composers must submit a score and a recording, along with a $20 fee. As in the drama category, the music compositions must be performed within a twelve-month period ending in March.

The identities of all arts and letters and music jurors are kept secret each year until the prizes are announced. This policy, according to Christopher, helps eliminate lobbying of jurors by publishers, writers' groups, play producers, and other interests. These juries' formal written reports—summarizing the thinking behind their nominations—are kept sealed for three years to help shield the jurors from controversy.

7:30 A.M.—March 6, 1990

A few early risers begin arriving to get a head start on the second day of judging in the World Room and elsewhere in the journalism building. Most jurors will not show up until nine o'clock or even 9:30, so these first arrivals are the truly dedicated, the orange-juice drinkers, the ones who didn't stay out all night.

Most of the early birds are on the juries that have the most reading to do—for the various reporting prizes. Many of the entries are astonishingly long-winded—multipart series that run several thousand words in length. Joseph Pulitzer, who posted "terseness" exhortations on his newsroom walls, would have been appalled at this verbiage. "Condense, condense!" he used to shout at his reporters. His style, in the words of biographer Swanberg, was "brief, breezy and briggity," and his will directed that the Pulitzer Prize for news reporting go to work meeting the test of "strict accuracy, terseness and the accomplishment of some public good...."

But over the past two decades, Pulitzer judges began straying from the "terseness" requirement and actually fostered the trend to more long-winded journalism by honoring it with prizes. The tribute to verbiage reached a crescendo of sorts in 1984 when the *Los Angeles Times* was given the public service gold medal for a twenty-seven-part, book-length series called "Latinos." Other Pulitzers that year went to a racial discrimination story that filled ten pages of the *Boston Globe* and a series on how a new airplane is developed, which filled sixteen pages of the *Seattle Times*.

Oddly, after announcing those prizes, the Pulitzer Board's spokesman, Christopher, publicly criticized what he called "a disturbing tendency for stories to run on interminably" in the journalism entries. He did not explain why the board, though bothered by the trend, went ahead and continued to encourage it by honoring mostly opus-length journalism that year.

Since then, the board has put some limits on length. Newspapers, however, have continued submitting prize entries of daunting verbiage, and the Pulitzer judges have continued to reward them.

8:05 A.M.

The jurors with the lightest duty, frankly, are those judging photography and editorial cartoons. Those exhibits remain locked securely in separate rooms upstairs, and none of those jury members have shown up at this early hour.

In an interesting twist of logic, the Pulitzer Board hasn't placed any editorial cartoonists on the jury screening the 129 entries for the cartoon prize. Christopher explains it this way:

"We don't put cartoonists on the jury for essentially the same reason we don't put syndicated columnists on the commentary jury. And that is that the universe of practitioners in both fields is a relatively small one, and they all know each other or know of each other. And they all tend to have feelings about each other."

It wouldn't be desirable, he says, to have cartoonists and columnists "passing judgment on the work of their direct competitors."

So this year's cartoon jury includes two news executives, two journalism educators, and one syndicated columnist—the *Miami Herald*'s Dave Barry. By the board's way of thinking, he is better suited to judge cartoonists than columnists.

For somewhat different reasons, the board also avoids placing many photographers on juries screening the two photo prizes. Christopher says editors are more "dispassionate" judges of pictures. And that explains why only one of this year's five photography jurors—Manny Crisostomo of the *Detroit Free Press*—is a photographer. The other four are news executives.

"Our feeling," Christopher says, "is that the people who are the consumers in a sense—the editors who choose photographs and cartoons—are probably as dispassionate as any judges you're going to find."

The Pulitzer Board applies a converse rule to other categories, such as international reporting. No jurors from smaller, local-oriented newspapers are placed on this jury for fear that they do not properly understand foreign correspondence. Hence this year's international reporting jurors are from the *New York Times, Newsday,* and *New York Daily News,* the *Baltimore Sun,* and Boston University.

Meanwhile, Benjamin J. Burns, editor and publisher of the little daily paper in Mt. Clemens, Michigan, finds himself on the jury for feature writing.

9:30 A.M.

By now, all five members of the specialized reporting jury are hard at work in the World Room. Yesterday, they winnowed 164 entries down to about fifty. This day, they will reduce those to the final three.

The previous day's huge task was managed efficiently by the jury's chairman, Leonard Downie Jr., the *Washington Post*'s managing editor. He has served as a Pulitzer juror before and knows a few tricks. Yesterday, he had his jury divide the 164 entries into five roughly equal stacks. Then everybody started reading as swiftly as possible. On a sheet of paper attached to each exhibit, jurors would mark "yes" or "no," indicating whether they considered it worth keeping on the table as a possible finalist. Once any exhibit received three "no" marks, even if the other two jurors hadn't read it yet, it was off the table.

Downie's four colleagues on the jury are Walt Bogdanich, a reporter for the *Wall Street Journal;* David Hall, editor and vice president of the *Record* of Hackensack, New Jersey; Al Johnson, vice president and executive editor of the *Post-Tribune* of Gary, Indiana, and David R. Witke, executive sports editor of the *Des Moines Register.*

It's an experienced jury. Downie, Johnson, and Witke were jurors last year. And Bogdanich enjoys a different kind of experience: He won the 1988 Pulitzer in this same prize category, for his specialized health-care reporting.

The medical-related entries by Claire Spiegel and Tamar Stieber obviously qualify in this category. Jim Dwyer's subway columns also seem to fit, although some judges will question whether his work is really "specialized reporting."

If biases truly come into play in jury screening, as some critics suggest, Jim would seem to be in a better position than Claire or Tamar. All five jurors are male, and four out of the five are from east of the Mississippi. Additionally, Jim used to work at juror Hall's New Jersey paper, the *Record.*

On the other hand, Claire and Tamar might have an ally in juror Bogdanich. His specialty is medical reporting. In fact, he won his 1988 Pulitzer for reports on faulty testing by American medical laboratories. If any juror is likely to appreciate the two women's health-related news coverage, it is Bogdanich.

12:15 P.M.

After grinding away all morning, Downie's jury is down to eight exhibits still on the table.

Overall, the task so far has not been terribly agonizing for the jury. The truly difficult decisions lie ahead after the lunch break. With only a couple of brief disagreements, the chore of moving 156 of the 164 exhibits "off the table" has gone smoothly and fairly quickly over the past day and a half, and especially this morning. A couple of the jurors wanted to keep a *New York Times* entry on the table—U.S. Supreme Court coverage by reporter Linda Greenhouse. But with some reluctance, the majority voted it down. The same thing happened with an exhibit of work by the staff of the *Fort Worth* (Tex.) *Star-Telegram,* which did a technically impressive job of covering the city's Van Cliburn International Piano Competition. That big scrapbook, too, is now on the floor.

The jurors have arrived at this point by identifying several clearly superior entries and then using them as the standard to help eliminate others. In many cases, jurors have needed to read only the first ten or twenty paragraphs of an entry to determine whether it measures up. The entries' cover letters— so carefully composed, so full of hyperbole and catchwords like "compelling" and "riveting"—receive little attention from the jurors. Nor do they seem the least bit impressed by fancy, expensive packaging. Many of the most elaborately prepared exhibits have been piled on the floor since yesterday.

The eight remaining exhibits are the ones that gradually emerged as the standard against which all others were gauged. These eight are now getting an additional, beginning-to-end reading by Downie and his jurors. This afternoon, they will struggle to reduce these eight to only three, and it is not going to be easy.

Two of the eight are *Washington Post* entries, one by sports reporter Bill Brubaker and the other by staff writer Cynthia Gorney. Two are *Wall Street Journal* entries, one by reporter Gary Putka and the other by reporter Johnnie Roberts. One exhibit is an *Albuquerque Tribune* entry, reporting by Eileen Welsoe, Mark Taylor, and Shonda Novak.

That's five. The other three scrapbooks display the work of Jim Dwyer, Claire Spiegel, and Tamar Stieber.

12:30 P.M.

This day's luncheon, once again at the Faculty House, features slightly improved cuisine and a warm greeting from Columbia president Michael Sovern, who is a member of the Pulitzer Board. He tells jurors how valued their role is in screening the prizes and how important the prizes are to the university and its Graduate School of Journalism.

Actually, Sovern understates the importance a bit. The

prizes are hugely important to Columbia. Each April when the Pulitzers are announced, the university is prominently mentioned in every daily newspaper, news magazine, and publishing trade journal as well as on every major radio and television news broadcast in the country. Regardless of Pulitzer controversies, Columbia always looks good—the respected institution where America's most prestigious awards are handed out each year. For the university and its journalism school, the public relations value of these prizes is immeasurable.

Over lunch, several jurors are overheard discussing the journalism school's sagging reputation. Snatches of the conversation are quite negative:

"Deadwood on the faculty ... "

"Instructors who couldn't cut it at the *Times* ... "

"A lot of better schools out there ... "

Then follows a game of naming the "better schools"—North Carolina, Stanford, Maryland, U.C.–Berkeley, Indiana, Oregon, USC, Northwestern, and Missouri.

Says one editor, in a remark certainly not meant for Michael Sovern to hear: "I'd guess that Columbia needs the Pulitzer Prizes a lot more than the prizes need Columbia."

2:30 P.M.

All the jurors are back at work in the journalism building, trying mightily to finish the job this afternoon so they won't have to return for a third day tomorrow. For most of them, two days of this mind-numbing decision-making is all they can handle.

The specialized reporting jury is ready to begin voting on its remaining eight entries.

Each vote is phrased as a question: "Shall we eliminate it?" For each decision the jury engages in a thoughtful discussion, sometimes an outright debate, of the entry's attributes.

Tamar Stieber's *Albuquerque Journal* entry survives with ease. There is no debate. The vote to keep it is unanimous. Chairman Downie pays it the highest tribute, calling it "investigative reporting where a difference is made." The link between L-Tryptophan and eosinophilia "would not have been discovered without that reporter's work," he says. "Here was a reporter from a relatively smaller newspaper without the big support systems. It was more of a lonely path."

Downie hopes at least one of the *Washington Post* entries will survive. But to avoid any conflict of interest, he has to leave the table while the other jurors discuss Bill Brubaker's sparkling sports reporting and Cynthia Gorney's complex coverage of family law issues. They are impressive exhibits that receive many compliments during Downie's absence. But when he returns to the table, both entries are on the floor.

The *Albuquerque Tribune* entry is next up. It is a strong piece of work on economic forces that threaten New Mexico's wildlife, such as the poaching and farming of elk for their antlers. The stories are well-displayed with high-impact color photography, and more than one juror questions whether he might have been initially swayed a little by that. Nobody comes right out and says so, but the jurors also seem a little uncomfortable with the idea of having two of their three finalists be from Albuquerque newspapers, even though the two papers are direct competitors. Downie calls it a compliment to New Mexico journalism that both Albuquerque papers end up with strong contenders for the same Pulitzer Prize. Jurors agree unanimously, though, to eliminate the *Tribune's* entry.

Next, Jim Dwyer's subway columns come up for discussion, and jurors seem overwhelmingly impressed with his exposé on worker fatigue. One jury member, Al Johnson, is particularly enthusiastic, pointing out to the others how much hard work and time went into Jim's investigation. Nobody disagrees.

However, a snag develops. A couple of jurors question whether Jim's columns have been entered in the proper category. Maybe his work really belongs in the competition for the commentary prize. Downie artfully steers the jury away from that idea. He points out that it's getting awfully late in the process to switch such a good entry. Doing so might doom it. And that would be a shame, Downie says, because Jim's lively "cowboy style" of writing and hard-nosed reporting strikes him as "classic tabloid journalism—the good kind that makes a difference." Jurors vote unanimously to keep Jim's entry on the table.

Now the *Wall Street Journal's* two entries are to be discussed, so *Journal* reporter Walt Bogdanich must leave the table. Bogdanich has high hopes for his newspaper's two entries—especially a series by reporter Johnnie Roberts on how Dun & Bradstreet Corp., an unregulated monopoly, abused its credit-rating power. While Bogdanich is out of earshot, fellow jurors express admiration for the work of both Roberts and fellow staffer Gary Putka, whose education coverage is exceptional, particularly a report on how colleges collude on scholarship decisions. However, when Bogdanich returns to the table, he is disappointed to discover that both entries are now on the floor.

Claire Spiegel's entry draws mixed reviews, at first. Two jurors, Johnson and Bogdanich, rave about it, but the others are not so enthusiastic. Briefly, there is talk of bringing one or more entries back up from the floor for reconsideration against Claire's work. Bogdanich certainly recognizes this as a window of opportunity—one more chance for consideration of his own newspaper's entries, but he is above such political maneuvering, and he finds himself championing Claire's exposé on the problems at Martin Luther King Jr.–Drew Medical Center. Pushing hard, he tells the other jurors he knows from personal experience how difficult such reporting can be. He says he has been researching a book on the hospital industry and has never seen a more original, more dogged example of hospital investigative reporting than Claire's. Bogdanich's passion for her entry leads to a unanimous vote by the jury to keep her on the table.

And that leaves the final three: Claire, Jim, and Tamar, all nominated for the Pulitzer Prize.

4:45 P.M.

Downie, in his role as chairman, begins filling out the one-page form that serves as the jury's formal report to the board. As the other jurors offer helpful comments, he writes the following nominations in bold, neat handwriting and in alphabetical order, as required by the rules:

JIM DWYER, special writer, *Newsday,* for his series of stories and columns on safety problems, malfunctions, rider outrages and official unresponsiveness in the New York subways. For several years, Dwyer has made a lively specialized beat out of a subject all New Yorkers complain about but few reporters covered—the dysfunction of the subway system. His style is unorthodox, adopting the point of view of an angry subway rider, but his reporting is thoroughgoing—exposing in this entry, for example, the serious, deadly safety problem caused by the fatigue of overworked Transit Authority workers.

CLAIRE SPIEGEL, health services writer, *Los Angeles Times*, for her coverage of dangerously substandard patient care, mismanagement and questionable ethics in the Los Angeles emergency health care system. She went beyond describing once again that the public emergency care system was overcrowded and underfunded to showing through original research how much of the problem could be traced to official mismanagement of resources and questionable practices by physicians using their positions in the system to increase their incomes. Her series on the Martin Luther King Jr.–Drew Medical Center led to local, state and federal investigations that produced significant improvement in policies and care.

TAMAR STIEBER, staff reporter, *Albuquerque Journal*, for her persistent, enterprising reporting that solved a significant medical mystery by linking a rare blood disorder afflicting a few local women, eosinophilia myalgia syndrome, to a common, over-the-counter dietary supplement often recommended for premenstrual syndrome, L-Tryptophan. Her reporting led to a national FDA recall of L-Tryptophan and national investigation of a serious threat to women that otherwise would have gone undiscovered.

5:30 P.M.

A light snow is falling on the Columbia campus as all five jury members sign their names at the bottom of the report.

Finished, they say their farewells and start bundling up. By morning, when the snow begins sticking, they'll all be back in their newsrooms in Des Moines, Hackensack, Gary, Washington, and downtown Manhattan.

The five men leave Columbia with their integrity intact. They passed over a total of twenty entries from their own newspapers. And two of their three finalists are not only women—they're from the West.

So much for the theory of Eastern-male bias.

11

Columbia, the Prizes, and the Times

O N ONE LEVEL, Jim Dwyer, Claire Spiegel, and Tamar Stieber—now locked in final competition for a Pulitzer Prize—couldn't be less alike.

Married man, married woman, single woman.

Yankees fan, ballet patron, jogger.

Catholic, Protestant, Jew.

The list of differences goes on, but there is one major common denominator linking the three finalists for the prize in specialized reporting: In an odd coincidence, all three attended Columbia University.

In the 1970s, Jim and Claire received master's degrees from the Graduate School of Journalism. Both of them look back warmly on their time at Columbia as a demanding educational experience that was invaluable in getting their careers started.

Tamar, meanwhile, never set foot in the journalism building, majoring instead in linguistics and Romance languages. But she, too, has positive memories of the high stature the Columbia journalism program enjoyed when she was on campus.

There is no question that Columbia has been a sort of grandfather of serious journalism schools. It is one of the oldest—operating since 1912, shortly after the University of Missouri opened the world's first school of journalism. And Columbia for many years was universally regarded as one of the three best journalism schools, along with Missouri and Northwestern.

Columbia has always enjoyed the advantage of being in New York, once considered the acme of American journalism and the center of the communications industry. Many of Columbia's graduates have become distinguished writers, editors, and publishers. The school annually confers several prestigious prizes, including the Pulitzers, the National Magazine Awards, and the Alfred I. duPont–Columbia University Awards in broadcast journalism. And Columbia has long benefited from an extremely close relationship with the *New York Times,* regarded by many as the nation's best newspaper.

These three institutions—Columbia, the Pulitzers, and the *Times*—fused over the decades into a sort of Holy Trinity of journalism, deified and inextricably linked in an oddly synergistic relationship. Year after year, in a constantly repeated process, each somehow amassed increased holiness from being entwined with the others:

Columbia lent prestige to the prizes.

The prizes conferred glory on the *Times.*

The *Times* hired Columbia's graduates.

And Columbia gained more prestige.

But something finally interrupted that synergy, and the journalism program now finds itself being sniped at by Pulitzer Prize jurors at Faculty House luncheons.

What happened? Somehow, during the 1980s, Joseph Pulitzer's journalism school managed to damage its once-lustrous reputation.

An awakening occurred in journalism education in the seventies and eighties. Many educators and media people began to argue that the challenges facing American mass communications required that university journalism programs be more than glorified trade schools that dutifully trained young people to go out into the world and practice journalism. Many began pushing journalism schools away from that time-honored practical role and toward a more academic emphasis requiring research and published debate of issues important to the mass media and society.

Caught in that intellectual conflict, Columbia's Graduate School of Journalism faculty—famous for its practical, how-to approach—dug in. And while many other journalism schools around the nation were changing, Columbia fell farther and farther out of the mainstream.

Columbia's administration tried throughout the 1980s to get the school's faculty to perform more research and to publish articles and books of critical commentary on journalism. The administration also wanted more emphasis on specialization, in such areas as science and foreign affairs, and demanded more courses on such theoretical issues as journalistic ethics. But that pressure brought extreme resistance from the faculty, which vigorously opposed any cutback in the school's tight focus on basic reporting and editing skills.

To traditionalists on the faculty, the administration's big push was the naive, misguided thinking of people who knew too little about the news business and what it takes to train students to become reporters and editors.

To Columbia administrators, it seemed that education and research, not job training, were the university's primary roles, and the faculty curmudgeons who didn't fully accept that were viewed as turf-protecting anti-intellectuals.

Even today, most of the journalism school's twenty-two full-time professors do not hold doctoral degrees. Most secured their jobs many years ago on the basis of their experience as journalists rather than on academic or research credentials. At least four of the school's sixty adjunct professors are former reporters and editors widely known to have been fired at New York newspapers.

The burgeoning tension between Columbia's faculty and administration erupted publicly during the eighties.

In 1981, the accrediting committee of the American Council on Education for Journalism warned of the "gulf" between faculty and administration and concluded that the school was "adrift."

In 1983, the *New York Times* quoted a former Columbia professor who called the journalism school an "intellectually

stifling" program providing the equivalent of on-the-job training with little journalistic introspection. The former professor,
Lawrence Pinkham, also was quoted as saying the newspaper
industry was disappointed in Columbia's journalism school but
was "loathe to criticize it because it administers the most
prominent and coveted awards"—the Pulitzers.

Also in 1983, the school's associate dean, Carolyn Lewis,
resigned after a rancorous tug-of-war with tenured faculty
members, whom she criticized as wanting "total control of the
school." The faculty had demanded her resignation.

In 1986, the school's dean, Osborn Elliott, resigned amid
continuing deep tension between his administration and the
faculty.

In 1987, a respected North Carolina journalism professor,
Philip Meyer, was publicly disclosed as Columbia's first choice
to replace Elliott as dean. A few days later, Meyer declined the
university's offer.

A year later, the dean's position still hadn't been filled, and
the journalism school's reputation was in tatters as it observed
its seventy-fifth anniversary. In a *New York Times* article on the
somber occasion, media writer Alex Jones noted that a journalism degree from Columbia "no longer automatically opens
doors at the nation's better news organizations."

In the 1950s and 1960s, the journalism school practically
served as a training annex for larger papers, especially the *New
York Times,* which routinely hired beginning reporters right out
of Columbia. Back then, the university's formula was highly
attractive to newspapers. Many editors today, in fact, still
revere Columbia's vocational-school approach and its refusal to
broaden the curriculum to include courses in advertising and
public relations, which most other journalism schools have
added.

Columbia offers a one-year master's degree program for
about 180 graduate students, equally divided in their pursuit
of newspaper, broadcasting, and magazine careers. The program is based on the premise that undergraduates should get
firm liberal arts educations and then learn the nuts and bolts
of journalism in an intensive, nine-month experience often
described as a "journalistic boot camp." The school takes
advantage of the city itself as a sort of laboratory, in which

students are sent to the United Nations, Times Square, City Hall, or the South Bronx on daily assignments.

Students are required to take basic courses in reporting, writing, editing, and broadcasting, and they must write a master's thesis, such as Claire Spiegel's story (later published by the *Daily News*) on plans to store liquefied natural gas on Staten Island. Students also are exposed to numerous lectures by prominent broadcast, newspaper, wire service, and magazine people who normally don't accept such invitations at journalism schools outside New York. By the time they graduate, Columbia's better students are able to walk into most newsrooms and start producing entry-level work right away.

But by 1980, as journalism became more popular and news organizations became flooded with applications from educated, experienced applicants, the Columbia journalism degree was no longer a quick ticket to employment. A promising young graduate such as Jim Dwyer, for example, could not carry his diploma up to 43rd Street in 1980 and go to work for the *New York Times*. He had to go across the river, to Hudson County, and start out at the *Dispatch* for $147.50 a week.

Editors at many of the big newspapers began changing their hiring criteria, sometimes looking for people with special training in such fields as science, politics, the arts, international relations, business, and law. Many newspapers began hiring from a larger pool, in some cases searching for bright, inquisitive people with broad liberal arts backgrounds—beginners such as Tamar Stieber—instead of those with formal journalism training. Some editors began saying, "We'll take the smartest, best-educated people available—those with good instincts and the ability to think—and we'll make better journalists out of them than any J-school can."

Then came the eighties and the increasingly public clash between Columbia's administration and journalism faculty. That stripped even more lustre from Joseph Pulitzer's school.

Pulitzer himself would have been heartsick over the conflict. He was both pragmatic and intellectual—qualities he sought for his journalism school. In his will, he directed that it provide "intellectual training." Today he would probably ask: Why not preserve the best of Columbia's practical instruction, add more curricula to challenge the intellect, and increase the emphasis on publishing and research to expand the body of knowledge about mass communication?

That appears to be the mission Columbia embarked on in 1988 when Joan Konner, the university's second choice for journalism dean, accepted the job. Initially, her appointment raised eyebrows among critics who felt the journalism school needed outside blood. Konner was a trustee of the university, a graduate of the journalism school, and a popular choice among its faculty—not necessarily a good sign. On top of that, she had no background in journalism education. And her professional experience was not in print journalism but in broadcasting, which made many newspaper editors cringe. Konner was president of Public Affairs Television, an independent production company associated with broadcast journalist Bill Moyers. She also had been a writer, director, and producer of documentaries at NBC News for twelve years and had won several prestigious broadcasting awards.

Although lacking in academic credentials, Konner had considerable experience in fund-raising, which has become a major part of the journalism dean's job at Columbia. Much of the school's problem is related to money—a lack of resources to continue the traditional training while expanding curriculum and encouraging research and publishing. Konner accepted the dean's job with a promise to go after more money for the school and to spend the first dollars raised on a new paint job for the shabby building.

She kept her promise about the fresh paint and set about making other changes that have brought praise from some and shudders from others. One thing in Konner's favor is the small number of tenured faculty members, many of them nearing retirement. As they are replaced—an attrition that has already begun—she has an opportunity to further shape the school's direction.

New paint, new programs, and new professors won't be enough, however. Konner admits the school still faces steep challenges as it seeks to rebuild, and lack of money remains a major worry.

As an investor, Joseph Pulitzer was a virtuoso. He had a

brilliant mind for money, and if he hadn't been so passionate about journalism, there's little doubt he could have made a far bigger fortune as a financier. The man obviously assumed Columbia would manage his endowment wisely so it would be sufficient for all time. He left plenty of money, by 1912 standards—$1 million to build the school, $500,000 to run it, and $500,000 for the Pulitzer Prizes. In 1990 dollars, that totaled more than $26 million.

But in the early half of the century, Columbia spent too much of the income from Pulitzer's endowment and failed to put adequate earnings back into it to protect against inflation. And as the school grew and added expenses, administrators failed to raise adequate funds to bolster the original endowment to safeguard its future. By the 1970s, both the school and the prize administration were running deficits.

Such shortsightedness in the management of old endowments is by no means unique to Columbia. Other universities are similarly stuck with the poor financial decisions of campus administrators decades ago. But that fact would come as little solace to Joseph Pulitzer, who would have been appalled to see the dean of his school out hustling for cash for a paint job.

The school's dire need for money, along with its diminished reputation, make the Pulitzer Prizes more important than ever to Columbia. And this helps explain why the university seems to be increasingly defensive about the prizes, as reflected in some of the editorial decisions that appear in the *Columbia Journalism Review*, published by the school of journalism.

CJR, as the publication calls itself, has been described by the *New York Times* as "the nation's most widely known journal of press criticism." It vigorously skewers all sorts of flaws and foibles of the American mass media—bad headlines, insensitive pictures, unethical news decisions, sexist language, biased reporting, conflicts of interest, and so forth. The magazine takes on newspapers, chains, networks, wire services, magazines, and even press clubs and professional associations.

However, *CJR* never criticizes the Pulitzer Prizes. And it never publishes a word when *others* criticize the prizes.

Occasionally, in a column called "Darts and Laurels," the magazine will toss a critical comment at a newspaper or an individual for Pulitzer Prize–related acts of pettiness, such as these:

DART: to the *San Diego Union,* for curiously omitting, from a 23-paragraph story announcing the Pulitzer Prizes for 1985, two awards involving other California papers— the *Los Angeles Times,* whose TV columnist Howard Rosenberg was honored for his criticism, and the Orange County *Register,* whose staff was singled out in the category for spot news photography.

DART: to the *Chicago Tribune,* for peevishly withdrawing its Pulitzer Prize nomination of media critic Gary Deeb after the columnist announced plans to switch to the rival *Sun-Times.*

Readers of *CJR,* however, will never see a "dart" aimed at any aspect of the Pulitzer Prize process or administration, even though there are opportunities aplenty. And the magazine never runs an article that might be considered the least bit offensive to any member of the Pulitzer Board.

It is no coincidence that the publisher of the *Columbia Journalism Review* is a member of the Pulitzer Board. She also is top boss of the journalism school—dean Joan Konner. That is why *CJR's* "Darts and Laurels" never offers such items as:

DART: to members of the Pulitzer Board, for upholding a 1988 prize to the board chairman's *Philadelphia Inquirer* for a Pentagon "black budget" report that was essentially a rehash of reporting already published by *National Journal* magazine.

DART: to the entire Pulitzer Prize judging system, for a 1988 award to the *Lawrence* (Mass.) *Eagle-Tribune* for its fear-mongering, irresponsibly lopsided stories on Willie Horton and prison furloughs.

Any readers who want their journalism review to take an honest look at the Pulitzer Prizes will do far better to subscribe to the *Washington Journalism Review,* published at the University of Maryland's journalism school. It has occasionally published criticism of prize decisions by the Pulitzer Board while *CJR* has remained silent.

It's unfair, of course, to expect the Columbia magazine to offer criticism of its own publisher and her fellow board members. But the absence of even straightforward news of Pulitzer Prize controversies smacks of self-serving news suppression. *CJR* ought to at least acknowledge such prize flaps in its news briefs, as the magazine occasionally did under previous administrations. Better yet, the dean should step out of the publisher's role and give it to a tenured professor with no ties to the Pulitzer Prizes, freeing the magazine to do its job.

In a 1990 subscription sales promotion, *CJR* called itself "the nation's most respected press monitor." It is too bad it doesn't monitor the nation's most respected press awards.

Just as cozy is Columbia's relationship with the *New York Times.*

Every year, in full-page "house ads"—advertisements promoting itself—the *Times* repeatedly boasts about its ever-growing collection of Pulitzer Prizes. In 1990 it climbed to a staggering total of sixty-three, three times as many as any other newspaper.

Half of that statistic has to do with the *Times* being what it is: one of the nation's best newspapers. A lot of journalists consider it *the* best. It is often too wordy, as many readers are aware, and its editing is sometimes surprisingly lax, but no other newspaper can match its depth and breadth, its accuracy and sure news judgment, or its intangible qualities such as courage, responsibility, credibility, and intelligence. As a result of all that, press critic David Shaw speculates that some Pulitzer judges may automatically vote for the paper's entries, "swayed by the quality, prestige, and mystique of the *Times,* and confident that no one could quibble with a vote for so august and excellent a newspaper."

But sixty-three Pulitzer Prizes?

The other half of that statistic has to do with the *Times* having a special niche—a favored position—at Columbia and in the Pulitzer Prize bureaucracy.

It is risky but not entirely impossible to document at least a strong whiff of favoritism toward the *Times* in Pulitzer Prize decisions over the decades. Here are a few such figures:

- The *Times* has been represented on the Pulitzer Board, which wields absolute power over the entire prize-judging hierarchy, in all but seven of its seventy-five years. No other newspaper, except for the *St. Louis Post-Dispatch* (run by Joseph Pulitzer's heirs), has enjoyed such a favored role.

- Over a twenty-year period, from 1970 through 1990, no other newspaper matched the *Times's* total of thirty-eight journalism jurors.

- The *Times* has benefited more than any other paper from board votes overturning jury recommendations for prizes, according to research by David Shaw for his book *Press Watch*.

- The *Times* has benefited from some extraordinarily friendly decisions by the Pulitzer Board, such as the 1951 prize to fellow board member Arthur Krock of the *Times* "for his exclusive interview with President Truman."

None of the above proves anything. But when a newspaper wins *three times* more Pulitzer Prizes than any other paper, a pattern of favored treatment certainly puts a cloud over the honors. That is especially true in light of the following:

- Arthur Ochs Sulzberger, publisher of the *New York Times,* is a 1951 graduate of Columbia University.

- Sulzberger also is on Columbia's board of trustees.

- Sulzberger received Columbia's highest honor, the Alexander Hamilton Medal, in 1982. His father, former *Times* publisher Arthur Hays Sulzberger, received the medal in 1953.

- Sulzberger and the *Times* contribute generously to Columbia, most recently announcing a new $25,000 law school fellowship for print journalists.

- Sulzberger's father also contributed generously to Columbia, and the journalism school's library is named after him.

- The *Times* has more Columbia graduates on its staff than any other newspaper.
- The *Times* has more Pulitzer winners on its staff than any other newspaper. Even its media critic, Alex Jones, has received a Pulitzer Prize.

Despite the Columbia journalism school's problems, the triumvirate keeps going: prizes for the newspaper, rewards for the school, prestige for the prizes.

So what's wrong with this coziness? Nothing, perhaps. Or, at the opposite extreme, maybe this preoccupation with prizes isn't such a good thing. Maybe it introduces a little-understood, corrupting influence into American journalism at its highest level, in the fiber of its most-admired newspaper, and spreading outward from there into the souls of all the others.

Published research on the question has been limited, but some of it certainly suggests a need for concern. For example, a 1988 report by David C. Coulson, director of graduate studies in the Reynolds School of Journalism at the University of Nevada–Reno, found that most U.S. newspapers surveyed— particularly larger ones—have policies encouraging prize-seeking.

That raises troubling questions about effects on reporter performance, news decisions, editorial ethics, and allocation of newsroom resources:

Don't journalism prizes subtly influence the reporting process by introducing a personal-gain motive where none should exist? Don't prizes expose reporters to an unwholesome pressure to cut corners on honesty and fairness?

Wasn't Tamar Stieber tiptoeing around the edges of truth when she said prizes, such as her free trip to Key West, may be all right for travel agents and realtors, but not for reporters?

Don't editors, in pursuit of prizes, push for showy projects likely to win recognition at the expense of routine but important news that their communities need? Doesn't a prize-seeking climate foster the kind of sloppy ethics that led to the *Washington Post's* fake story about an eight-year-old heroin addict?

Isn't it true that newspaper chains seek prizes to create a perception that they are doing great public good, while in fact their newspapers are drastically diminishing news content and quality in their pursuit of high profits?

These are concerns that dramatize the challenge still facing the school Joseph Pulitzer endowed.

Instead of being the "journalistic boot camp" renowned for its prestigious prizes, Columbia perhaps should become known as the university breaking new ground with research on the effects of media prize-giving.

12

The All-Powerful Board

7:25 A.M.—April 9, 1990

SUNLIGHT BREAKS OVER the tops of buildings on the east side of the Columbia University campus, bathing the journalism school's eastern entry in pale yellow radiance. Facing east, two Muslims say their dawn prayers near an appropriate symbol of their religious freedom, a statue of Thomas Jefferson, erected near the building's entrance by decree of Joseph Pulitzer.

Indoors, another aspect of the publisher's will is being carried out. Bud Kliment is readying the World Room for the arrival of the eighteen members of the Pulitzer Prize Board, due to show up soon to judge the 1990 finalists.

Kliment, assistant administrator of the prizes, briskly surveys the room. Everything appears to have been arranged as he directed: one long table surrounded by eighteen chairs, exhibits of the finalists neatly presented on side tables, coffee and rolls and juice (both orange and tomato again) available nearby.

Unlike a month ago, when the Pulitzer juries came, the World Room on this day is tidy. The carpeting has been vacuumed, at least, and there is no clutter of cardboard boxes.

Kliment tenses up when he notices an unexpected visitor standing in the doorway, looking around the room.

"I'm afraid you can't be in here," Kliment says, hurrying to the door. "This room's off limits."

No part of the Pulitzer Prize process is more secretive than the final deliberation that is about to begin in the World Room. The judging hierarchy has been aptly described as a "journalistic priesthood" in which members of the board serve as high priests who insist on being tightly cloistered as they wield their power.

It is a fair description. The board's meetings are closed. No observers are allowed. No outsider may address the board. Minutes of board meetings are confidential. There is no written record of individual board members' votes. And members on this day will add one more layer of privacy by voting to limit all public comment on board business to the chairman and secretary.

The hierarchy has one hidden level: the board's three-member subcommittees. There are seven of them—one for each of the prizes in letters, drama, and music. The membership of these subcommittees is kept officially secret even after the prizes are given.

Against the backdrop, Bud Kliment can be forgiven for seeming a little anxious as he whisks the visitor away from the World Room. The high priests will be here soon.

8:30 A.M.

Outside on Broadway at 116th Street, the newsstands are doing well this morning with a punchy front-page tabloid story, courtesy of Donald Trump. He opened the Taj Mahal casino yesterday in Atlantic City, and the debut was a masterpiece of mismanagement. Thousands of slot machines ran out of money and shut down as workers failed to keep them adequately loaded and running. The resulting firings of Trump employees and furor among unhappy gamblers make for lively Monday morning reading. The *New York Daily News* has the best headline: GOOF AT TAJ! HEADS ROLL!

The tabloid's publisher, James Hoge Jr., is one of the first Pulitzer Board members to arrive at the university gates, along with Michael Gartner, president of NBC News; Robert Maynard, editor and publisher of the *Tribune* of Oakland, California; Walter Rugaber, president and publisher of the *Roanoke* (Va.) *Times & World-News*, and David Laventhol, president of the Times Mirror Company.

Five of the arriving board members are Pulitzer Prize winners themselves: Russell Baker, columnist for the *New York Times;* Meg Greenfield, editorial page editor for the *Washington Post;* Peter Kann, publisher of the *Wall Street Journal;* James Risser, Knight Fellowships director at Stanford University; and Claude Sitton, editor of the *News and Observer* of Raleigh, North Carolina.

Three represent Columbia: Michael Sovern, university president; Joan Konner, dean of journalism; and Robert Christopher, prize administrator and secretary to the board.

One board member, Sissela Bok, is a Brandeis University professor. There are two other women, Geneva Overholser, editor of the *Des Moines Register,* and Charlotte Saikowski, former Washington bureau chief for the *Christian Science Monitor.*

Among the last to arrive is the board chairman, Eugene Roberts, executive editor and president of the *Philadelphia Inquirer.*

The eighteenth board member, Burl Osborne, editor and president of the *Dallas Morning News,* will not arrive today. He is still in Texas, testifying in a court case.

Unlike the sixty-five prize jurors who showed up at Columbia one month ago in taxis and even by subway, many of the board members come in limousines. The symbolism is perfect: taxis for the monks, limos for the high priests. There is no higher status in American journalism than appointment to the Pulitzer Prize Board.

Over the seventy-five years of these prizes, fewer than one hundred people have served on the board. It has always been a self-perpetuating body, choosing its own members—white, male, senior journalists replaced by more white, male, senior journalists for the first sixty-five years of prizes. Of all the facts and figures in Pulitzer Prize history, the most astonishing is that the board did not accept its first woman, first nonwhite, and first nonjournalist until 1980.

The board assembling at Columbia on this April morning is still weighted the historic way. And most members, as always, are from the eastern half of the United States. Heavily outnumbered among elected members of the board are its five women, one black (Maynard), one nonjournalist (Bok), and five members from west of the Mississippi.

Besides Bok, Sovern also is a nonjournalist, but he was not elected to the board as Professor Bok was. He serves automatically because he is Columbia's president. He is eligible to vote on board issues, but the other two Columbia representatives, Konner and Christopher, are nonvoting members.

In its early decades, members could stay on the board as long as they pleased. The board decided in 1954 to limit members to three terms of four years each. In 1979 the terms were shortened to three years.

Originally, the body was called the Advisory Board of the Graduate School of Journalism, and part of its mission was to make sure Columbia ran Joseph Pulitzer's school the way he would have wanted it run. In practice, however, the board left academic matters to the university and concentrated instead on the prizes.

To reflect that reality, the board in 1950 changed its name to the Pulitzer Prize Advisory Board. In 1975 the name was shortened to the Pulitzer Prize Board after Columbia's trustees withdrew from the process and delegated their responsibility to the university president, who has always been on the board. In briefest outline, that leaves the journalistic priesthood working like this:

- The contestants at the bottom of the hierarchy submit their work for screening by prize juries.
- The juries turn in slates of nominees for review by the board's secret subcommittees.
- The subcommittees suggest winners to the full board.
- The full board "recommends" final prizes to the university president.
- The president announces them to the public.

- Every year, Columbia's formal announcement declares that the prizes are "awarded on the recommendation" of the Pulitzer Board, but that is misleading. All the power is held by the board. Since 1975, the university's role has been no more than a rubber stamp.

8:50 A.M.

As the board gets settled in the World Room, its chairman, Eugene Roberts, looking a bit haggard, has a quiet conversation in the hallway outside.

"I've been on the witness stand for fourteen straight days. I had to get excused to come here," he tells a visiting journalist.

Testifying in the $34 million libel suit against his paper, the *Philadelphia Inquirer,* doesn't appear to have been much fun for the fifty-eight-year-old Roberts. Nor does he seem to be enjoying his present task in the hallway, explaining why the board won't allow an outsider to sit in on its meeting, or observe even part of its discussion, or even speak to the board for five minutes to ask for help on some book research.

Roberts graciously explains that he has no problem with allowing an observer in the meeting, but the rest of the board members are opposed to it. They feel it would inhibit discussion and set a precedent which would lead to other reporters asking to sit in, too, he says.

As he explains the board's fear of turning the judging "into a circus," Roberts is clearly uncomfortable. Shutting out journalists who are trying to obtain information does not come naturally to this man, widely respected as one of the nation's best editors.

He is held in almost mystical esteem within the newspaper industry, viewed by many as a sort of wizard who discovered how to magically transform a bad newspaper into a very good one.

Roberts began building that reputation in 1972 when he gave up a good job as national editor of the *New York Times* and became editor of the *Philadelphia Inquirer.* At that time it was an undistinguished, financially troubled operation, considered by many to be among the nation's weakest metropolitan papers. One piece of evidence, according to some who measure success by prizes, was that the *Inquirer* had never won a Pulitzer.

Roberts, along with a lot of other people, helped the *Inquirer* move ahead of the market-dominating *Philadelphia Bulletin.* After the *Bulletin* folded in 1982, the *Inquirer* emerged as the city's monopoly daily and became one of the Knight-Ridder newspaper chain's most profitable operations.

One of the gifts Roberts contributed was an uncanny sense of the kind of journalism that would win Pulitzer Prizes—*lots* of them. In the era that began with Roberts, the once-lowly newspaper won so many Pulitzers—seventeen—and other national media awards that critics began to call it a "prize factory."

The wizard chuckles modestly at such talk. He says his paper never did a story to win a prize, only to do good journalism. And if it was good enough, the company would push it hard for recognition. That happened often enough, and with such success, that the *Inquirer* started winning respect within two years of Roberts's arrival. And within five years, it was obvious something special was happening in Philadelphia.

Before 1972, the *Inquirer* was mired in mediocrity. Standards were low. Respect was hard to find. The staff was discouraged and unmotivated. It was not the kind of place where outstanding people would seek work—or stay if they were already there.

Then came Roberts. And prizes. He admits he aggressively applied for them "as a way of building in a tradition, of making people care."

In a profession not known for its high pay, journalists crave recognition, so Roberts's strategy worked wonders at Philadelphia. When *Inquirer* staffers suddenly started receiving national awards, the change had a snowball effect.

Pride took root. Reporters tried harder. Standards were raised. More prizes came. The paper won respect. Talented people began joining the staff. And the prizes kept coming.

Prizes, of course, are only one measure of a newspaper's quality. There are many newspapers that have never won a Pulitzer Prize but in several ways serve their readers better than the *Philadelphia Inquirer* serves its readers. More than one press critic, in fact, has labeled the *Inquirer* as a paper edited for the prize judges, not for the readers.

There is a formula, in a positive sense, to Roberts's success at winning prizes. The secret is not in fancy display of the news or packaging of entries, as envious rivals have sniped. It is

Roberts's excellent vision of what makes a great news story and his ability to communicate that vision to his staff. The secret, according to a wonderful definition written by Roberts's editors, is his dedication "to the story of the untold event that oozes instead of breaks; to the story that reveals, not repeats; to the reporter who zigs instead of zags; to the truth as opposed to the facts; to the forest, not just the trees; to the story they'll be talking about in the coffee shop on Main Street; to the story that answers not just who, what, where, when and why, but also 'so what?'; to efforts at portraying real life itself; to journalism that wakes me up and makes me see; to the revival of the disappearing storyteller."

Roberts himself has never won a Pulitzer Prize. But a look at a few of the Pulitzers his paper has won reveals much about the kind of journalism he seeks:

- A revelation that Philadelphia police dogs had attacked more than 350 people led to an investigation of the city's K-9 force and removal of a dozen officers. The story by William Marimow won the 1985 prize for investigative reporting.
- Disclosure of massive deficiencies in the Internal Revenue Service's processing of tax returns eventually brought about major changes in IRS procedures and prompted the agency's public apology to taxpayers. The story by Arthur Howe won the 1986 prize for national reporting.
- A revelation of hidden tax breaks for the wealthy in the Tax Reform Act of 1986 led to congressional rejection of proposals giving special tax breaks to many politically connected individuals and businesses. The series by Donald Barlett and James Steele won the 1989 prize for national reporting.

As the list goes on, a distinct pattern emerges. Most of the *Philadelphia Inquirer's* seventeen Pulitzer Prizes were won by news stories with three common ingredients:

1. They revealed information that readers would ardently want to know.

2. They revealed information that others would not want disclosed.

3. Publishing the information somehow made a difference.

Roberts has built his entire career around turning reporters loose to gather information that institutions, both public and private, seek to conceal. It is easy to believe he disagrees with the clandestine nature of the Pulitzer Prize administration and feels uncomfortable saying no to requests for access and records.

The board as a group, not Eugene Roberts, is perpetuating a tradition of secrecy that goes back to Joseph Pulitzer himself and his paranoid insistence on secret codes. Every day, these board members' news organizations expect their reporters to pry information out of uncooperative sources, so there is an awkward irony to seeing such important news executives behaving that way themselves.

"The board, I'm afraid, is not willing to make an exception," Roberts tells the fellow journalist in the hallway.

The wizard of the Pulitzer Prizes looks faintly embarrassed as he excuses himself and steps into the World Room, latching the heavy doors behind him.

9:15 A.M.

Safely sequestered, the board begins two days of hard work, picking the final winners of the 1990 Pulitzers.

The board used to do the job in one day. But in 1981, after being criticized for its role in awarding a Pulitzer Prize to Janet Cooke's fraudulent story about a nonexistent, eight-year-old heroin addict, the board expanded its judging to two days. The extra day, board secretary Christopher said at the time, would help the board "to review nominations even more exhaustively than in the past." The announcement was the closest the Pulitzer Board has ever come to admitting a mistake.

On one level, it is hard to fault board members for wanting to make their decisions in private with voting by individual board members shielded from public exposure. Why be subjected to any more second-guessing than absolutely necessary?

"The pay ain't worth it," quips Christopher.

What he means, of course, is that service on the board is

unpaid. Even travel expenses are the responsibility of members or their companies. Prestige and power are a board member's sole rewards, and although they are immense, so is the amount of work that goes with the job.

For board members, judging the Pulitzers requires much more than these two days of deliberation each April on the Columbia campus. Their work actually begins in January, when each of the five book juries submits its slate of three finalists. That is a total of fifteen books that all board members, ideally, should read over the next ninety days, by April.

Before then, however, the drama and music juries submit their lists of finalists on March 1. That means the board members, in addition to the books they need to read, now have three plays to see (or at least read), and three audio recordings to review.

And one week after those juries report, the fourteen journalism juries submit *their* nominees—a total of forty-two finalists. The Pulitzer office sends each board member a hefty set of photocopies of all forty-two exhibits, which are supposed to be read before the final judging in April at Columbia.

Obviously, few high-powered executives have time for that much prize-related homework. And that explains the system of subcommittees. The board divides itself into seven groups of three, with some members serving on more than one committee, to judge the books, plays, and musical compositions.

All three members of the biography subcommittee, for example, are assigned to read all three books nominated for that prize and offer a recommendation to the full board. Members of the music subcommittee will do likewise, after listening to recordings of the three finalists, and members of the drama subcommittee will recommend a play, presumably after viewing all three finalists.

Under informal board rules, members are expected to abstain from passing judgment on any book they haven't read or play they haven't seen. That rule was born in 1964 after the Pulitzer Board came under fire for rejecting a prize for Edward Albee's *Who's Afraid of Virginia Woolf?*—a play that at least one board member later admitted he had not seen but had voted against anyway because he had heard it contained offensive language.

As a result of that rule, according to Roberts, the board usually accepts its subcommittee recommendations. Exceptions occur most often in fiction and drama—categories in which many board members *not* on the subcommittees are often familiar with the finalists and may have differing opinions.

There are no subcommittees for the journalism awards. All board members are expected to read the forty-two exhibits and come prepared to vote on them. The original exhibits are on display during judging in the World Room in case board members need to refresh their memories or otherwise refer to them.

12:30 P.M.

At the lunch break, Roberts reveals that the board spent the morning on the books, drama, and music prizes.

"We got most of 'em out of the way," he says in a gentle North Carolina accent.

If almost anybody else said that, admitting that judgment on much of the nation's culture had been neatly dispatched by lunchtime, it would sound artless or even outrageous. Somehow, though, coming from Roberts, the comment seems reasonable. The man has enough charisma and kindly charm to make you think ten minutes of judging would be adequate, if that's what he wanted you to think.

There is an engaging lilt to his speech, only occasionally giving away his Southern roots when he says something like "foreign news," which comes out "farrin news." He graduated in journalism from the University of North Carolina at Chapel Hill and began his newspaper career nearby as a farm reporter at the *Goldsboro News-Argus* in 1956. He worked at the *Virginian-Pilot* in Norfolk, the *News and Observer* in Raleigh, North Carolina, and the *Detroit Free Press* before joining the *New York Times,* for which he covered both the civil rights struggle in the South and the war in Vietnam.

Roberts views himself, correctly, as a career newspaperman, not as an arts critic. And he seems almost apologetic about the speed with which the board got the arts and letters awards "out of the way." There is in fact something astonishing about what has transpired: A group of news executives, aided by a college president and a professor, just finished identifying the best of American culture for 1990.

Presumptuous? Roberts agrees that it is, indeed, for a group of generalists—nonexperts, all—to pass judgment on the nation's literature, drama, and music. He points out, however, that in doing so the board is merely carrying out Joseph Pulitzer's wishes, as expressed in his will. He also emphasizes that the board relies heavily on recommendations of its expert juries in the nonjournalism awards—especially music.

"We try hard to get a good jury in that area," Roberts says.

That is reassuring. It does not take brilliant investigative reporting to discover that members of the board's music subcommittee—James Hoge, Walter Rugaber, and Charlotte Saikowski—have no formal music education, other than childhood piano lessons and experience in a school orchestra.

Prior to the board meeting, the three subcommittee members listened to recordings of the music finalists, then endorsed the jury's recommendation for a prize to Mel Powell for "Duplicates: A Concerto for Two Pianos and Orchestra." Technically, juries are not asked to make recommendations—just to submit finalists in alphabetical order. But in practice, almost all of the arts and letters and music juries rank their finalists, much to the pleasure of the Pulitzer Board members, none of whom has ever composed a concerto.

The full board accepted its subcommittee's recommendation without listening to any recordings. Why make a pretense? This is one Pulitzer Prize that is decided by the jury.

Different versions of that same scenario were played out throughout the morning on the books and drama prizes. The process was more thoughtful and deliberate, however, perhaps because the board members do read books—even write them, in a few cases—and some do go to plays, all of which makes many of them feel qualified to pass judgment on literature and works of the stage.

Besides the music award, the board tentatively approved several other prizes by lunchtime. Members approved a history prize for *In Our Image: America's Empire in the Philippines* by Stanley Karnow, a biography prize for *Machiavelli in Hell* by Sebastian de Grazia, a poetry prize for *The World Doesn't End* by Charles Simic, and a general nonfiction prize for *And Their Children After Them* by Dale Maharidge and Michael Williamson.

The glamour prizes—fiction and drama—are saved for later.

2:30 P.M.

Columbia University clearly feeds Pulitzer Board members better than it feeds Pulitzer jurors. Board members return from the president's mansion raving about his elegant luncheon of crab and stuffed red snapper. No "broccoli with something white on it" for this group.

Now the board gets down to the business that suits them best, handing out the journalism awards.

Disasters figure prominently among this year's winners. The board votes a general news reporting prize to the staff of the *San Jose Mercury News* for its coverage of the Bay Area earthquake of October 17, 1989. The photo staff of the *Tribune* of Oakland wins the spot news photography prize for its visual coverage of the same quake. And four reporters at the *Seattle Times*—Ross Anderson, Bill Dietrich, Mary Ann Gwinn, and Eric Nalder—receive the national reporting prize for coverage of the *Exxon Valdez* oil spill and its aftermath.

Overseas political upheaval also emerges as a theme. The board gives its international reporting prize to Nicholas Kristof and Sheryl WuDunn of the *New York Times* for reporting from China on the mass movement for democracy and its subsequent suppression. And the feature photography prize goes to David Turnley of the *Detroit Free Press* for his photos of the political uprisings in China and Eastern Europe.

As always, muckraking journalism wins some honors. The board gives its investigative reporting prize to Lou Kilzer and Chris Ison of the *Star Tribune* of Minneapolis–St. Paul for exposing a network of citizens who had links to the St. Paul fire department and profited from fires, including some described by the fire department itself as being of suspicious origin. The explanatory journalism prize goes to David Vise and Steve Coll of the *Washington Post* for stories scrutinizing the Securities and Exchange Commission and the way it has been affected by the policies of its former chairman, John Shad.

The feature-writing prize is awarded to Dave Curtin of the *Colorado Springs Gazette Telegraph* for his story of a family's struggle to recover after its members were burned in an explosion that devastated their home.

Thomas Hylton of the Pottstown, Pennsylvania *Mercury* wins the prize for editorial writing, for his pieces on a local bond issue for the preservation of farmland and other open space in rural Pennsylvania.

Architecture critic Allan Temko of the *San Francisco Chronicle* is given the prize for criticism, and seventy-year-old sports columnist Jim Murray of the *Los Angeles Times* is awarded a long-overdue prize for commentary.

Throughout all these deliberations, board members take turns parading out to the hallway, recusing themselves while their own newspapers are up for prizes. They must leave the World Room under a written policy that says members of the board may "take no part whatever in either the discussion or judgment of any exhibit that may even remotely involve a conflict of interest."

When it is safe for board members to return to the table, Pulitzer Prize office assistant Claudia Stone steps out into the hallway and summons them, much like a bailiff.

Over the next day and a half, Russell Baker has to excuse himself from the room three times, as his paper, the *New York Times,* has finalists in three different prize categories. Meg Greenfield of the *Washington Post* tops him, having to leave the room four times.

But one board member, Roberts, tops them all. He excuses himself seven times, because his Philadelphia paper is part of the Knight-Ridder newspaper chain, which has finalists in seven different categories. Roberts's presence during those discussions would be a clear conflict, so he spends considerable time out in the hallway throughout the journalism judging.

One thing that becomes clear as the day passes is that no board members excuse themselves from certain instances of voting that would seem to be precluded by the strongly worded policy on conflicts.

During the deliberations on book prizes, for example, no board members left the World Room to avoid a conflict. Meanwhile, two of the board members have financial relationships with publishers whose books were up for awards. Random House and its subsidiary, Pantheon, have published four books for board member Sissela Bok, who participated in the discussions that led to a Pulitzer history prize for one Random House title, *In Our Image: America's Empire in the Philippines,* and a general nonfiction prize for one Pantheon title, *And Their Children After Them.* And board secretary Robert Christopher's publisher is Alfred A. Knopf, which had a title among the biography finalists. (It should be noted that the Knopf book did not win, and Christopher is a nonvoting member.)

Russell Baker, who has written a dozen books for a variety of publishers, did not have any apparent conflicts among the 1990 titles. However, in previous years since he joined the board in 1985, some of his publishers have been among the finalists.

When asked about the apparent conflict, Baker says it frankly never occurred to him. Roberts and Christopher echo the sentiment. Nobody has ever brought it up, they say.

But any author who has a contract with a book publisher, or who is seeking such a contract, ought not to be in a position to help that publisher win a Pulitzer Prize for a book. That would be a significant financial favor. That's a violation of the board's own policy banning "judgment of any exhibit that may even remotely involve a conflict of interest."

Some board members who have syndicated columns also take part in judgment of exhibits involving their own syndicates. Robert Maynard, for example, did not recuse himself from action on a Pulitzer for cartoonist Tom Toles, whose work is syndicated by Universal Press, which syndicates Maynard's twice-weekly column. Is that doing a favor for one's syndicate? The Pulitzer certainly didn't hurt Universal Press. (Maynard later refuses to discuss his voting and directs all inquiries to Christopher.)

Board members also participate in judgment of the work of their direct competitors—sometimes voting for it, but just as often against it. This practice would appear to be a conflict.

"There has been discussion about that from time to time," Roberts says. "But I've never seen an instance of anyone even remotely doing anything unseemly. There is a tendency, if anything, to be muted [in discussions about competitors], and the only times I have heard a lot of conversation from people in competitive situations is when they support their competitors."

But why don't board members recuse themselves in those situations, just as they do when their own newspapers are up for discussion? Roberts replies:

"One of the problems in just saying that you have to leave the room when your competition is involved is how do you define competition? For example, you can make a case to some degree that a paper like the *Philadelphia Inquirer* competes against half of the papers in the state of Pennsylvania. Or that the *Los Angeles Times* competes against literally dozens of papers in the state of California. And no one has really known where you draw the line."

4:15 P.M.

Perhaps the line could be drawn at head-to-head competition for survival on the streets of New York. In deliberation on the prize for specialized reporting, Times Mirror president David Laventhol leaves the room, because two of the finalists are from his papers, Jim Dwyer of *New York Newsday,* and Claire Spiegel of the *Los Angeles Times.* No others recuse themselves, however. That includes *New York Daily News* publisher James Hoge. Even though his tabloid is a bitter rival of Laventhol's, Hoge sits through the discussion—quietly, but still creating a presence that could subtly influence the outcome.

This prize category is decided with surprising speed, in less than ten minutes. Hoge is mute during the discussion, and his preference does not determine the outcome. However, he casts his vote in favor of giving the specialized reporting Pulitzer to someone other than Jim Dwyer, the rival columnist who once turned down Hoge's offer to leave *Newsday* and join the *Daily News.*

Later, Hoge repeatedly rejects opportunities to explain this apparent conflict of interest or any of his other voting on Pulitzer Prizes. He dodges requests for an interview on the subject during the judging at Columbia and in communication by telephone and by mail. A final attempt to discuss the matter with him brings the following terse telephoned response from his secretary, Betty Boudekian: "Mr. Hoge suggests that you direct your questions to Mr. Christopher at Columbia University."

9:30 A.M.—April 10, 1990

Day Two is reserved for finishing up prize categories that were not judged yesterday and then ratifying all the decisions for the twenty-one prize categories.

The board also takes care of ancillary business, such as a few financial matters and discussion of appointments to the board. In an unexpected move, the board also adopts a new policy that all inquiries about this year's judging be funneled through Roberts and Christopher. No other board members are to attempt to handle reporters' questions. The policy decision arises after a number of board members become uncomfortable with a visiting journalist's questions out in the corridor and about the personal letters he distributes to each board member, asking for cooperation on his book research.

Later, Christopher says the policy springs from "one of the more news-oriented board members, somebody I wouldn't have expected to be that concerned." He declines to name the board member.

Roberts says the policy is not the idea of one board member but "several of them—it was everybody's idea, actually."

Board members later will faithfully comply with their new policy and direct all inquiries to Roberts and Christopher.

According to Christopher, he is also directed to keep his written minutes of the meeting strictly confidential. These records do not reveal how individuals vote, but the minutes do reflect financial business and personality discussions that the board "does not want splashed all over the place," he says.

"The thing is, one of the reasons they have closed meetings is because there are things they want to discuss freely—more freely than they could if they were in the public eye. For example, there is discussion of who to elect to vacancies and some other future actions, sometimes policy actions, sometimes even budgetary questions, which, you know, they just don't want to have as a matter of public record, because it would inhibit their debate," Christopher says.

Without being permitted to attend the board's meeting, or

review its minutes or even interview members in the corridors, a reporter finds it difficult to reconstruct the board's second day of deliberation. However, according to Christopher and Roberts, it is a smooth day of decision-making with comparatively little disagreement—one of the most harmonious days of Pulitzer Prize judging in recent years.

The fiction prize is awarded to *The Mambo Kings Play Songs of Love* by Oscar Hijuelos. This year's jurors—Joel Conarroe, president of the John Simon Guggenheim Memorial Foundation; Diane Johnson, a San Francisco writer and critic; and Philip O'Connor, a professor at Bowling Green State University in Ohio—offered only one other finalist: *Billy Bathgate* by E. L. Doctorow. Some board members prefer the Doctorow novel. Other board members say they don't care for either book. A majority, however, supports Hijuelos.

The drama prize is given to *The Piano Lesson* by August Wilson, even though few board members have seen it because the play has not opened in New York yet. And few board members have seen the jury's other leading contender, *And What of the Night?* by Maria Irene Fornes, because it also was an out-of-town play that closed before the board received the drama jury's report. Board members, however, are quite taken with the jury's passionate report, written by *Time*'s Pulitzer-winning critic, William Henry III. He hails *The Piano Lesson* as "probably the best American play of my adult lifetime" and says August Wilson is without doubt the most important American playwright of the past decade, if not longer. So Wilson, who received the 1987 Pulitzer for his play *Fences,* becomes a two-time winner.

With arts and letters judging now completed, the board finishes up the journalism awards.

As always, there are a couple of snags in the judging.

Board members are not satisfied with the three finalists nominated by the jury for editorial cartooning. (But what did the board expect? There are no cartoonists on the jury.) Editorial cartoons by finalists Chan Lowe of the Fort Lauderdale, Florida *Sun-Sentinel* and Jim Morin of the *Miami Herald* fail to win sufficient votes. Some board members admire the entry by the third finalist, "Doonesbury" cartoonist Garry Trudeau, but the majority either don't care for his work or don't want to give him a second Pulitzer Prize. He won in 1975.

By this point, it is obvious that the board is not going to approve an editorial cartooning prize this year unless the jury can suggest an alternate. So Christopher hurries to his office and calls the jury chairman, Richard Leonard, a journalism professor at Marquette University. After discussing the stalemate, Christopher returns, and the board approves a Pulitzer for an alternate choice, Tom Toles of the *Buffalo News*. He is honored for the body of his work, as exemplified by a cartoon titled "First Amendment," ridiculing efforts to abridge freedom of speech by banning desecration of the American flag.

The board also does some juggling with the photo prizes. Members want very much to give the spot news photography award to fellow board member Robert Maynard's *Tribune* for its Bay Area quake coverage. The *Tribune* has not won a Pulitzer in forty years, and there may not be another chance to give a boost to the financially troubled paper for many more years— if indeed Maynard manages to keep it alive. But the best spot news photo exhibit—clearly superior to any other photography submitted this year—is David Turnley's emotional, visually smashing work in China and Europe.

No problem, however. The board has the power to move finalists to different prize categories. Thus Turnley's spot news photography is conveniently declared "feature photography" and is moved to the feature-photo category, where it wins. To the board, it makes no difference that Turnley's pictures are really "spot" or "breaking" news.

Later, Christopher vigorously denies that there is any hint of cronyism involved in this photo-prize juggling act that benefited a board member's newspaper. But it is exactly the kind of behind-closed-doors maneuvering that casts suspicion on the Pulitzer Board.

The judging of the entries for meritorious public service— generally considered the most prestigious Pulitzer Prize—also results in an unusual decision. For only the fifth time in seventy-five years, two newspapers end up sharing the honor.

Board members find themselves split over whether to give the gold medal to their chairman's *Philadelphia Inquirer* or to a little paper in North Carolina, the *Washington Daily News*.

Some on the board favor the *Inquirer*'s entry of reporting by Gilbert Gaul, disclosing how the American blood industry operates with little governmental regulation or supervision.

Gaul, whose reporting won a Pulitzer in 1979, filed forty separate Freedom of Information requests in documenting his series, which helped lead to a congressional investigation of the blood industry.

Others on the board favor giving the gold medal to the small, family-owned North Carolina paper. It showed considerable courage in revealing that the town's water supply was contaminated with carcinogens, a problem that the local government had neither disclosed nor corrected over a period of eight years. The *Daily New*'s month-long reports led to new Environmental Protection Agency regulations for smaller city water systems, requiring more stringent testing nationwide.

Faced with equally persuasive arguments on behalf of each newspaper, the board votes to let them share the prize.

And Christopher, the board secretary, flinches a little. He knows that sharing the prize doesn't mean the two papers share the gold-plated silver medal. They *each* get one, and the medals nick Christopher's tight operating budget by about $1,700 apiece, depending on the current prices of gold and silver. Benjamin Franklin's profile is on one face of each medal, and a printer operating a flatbed press is depicted on the other. Metallic Arts of Danbury, Connecticut, strikes the medals for the prizes each year, customizing them with the date and the name of the winning newspaper.

For Christopher, the man who minds the budget, the extra medal is a setback but no fiscal calamity. The prize administration is in fine shape financially, he says.

Such was not the case a decade ago. In the 1970s, the income from Joseph Pulitzer's original $500,000 endowment—bolstered by $100,000 from a beer company—was all there was for continuing the prizes.

"Before I came aboard, they were running a little bit short each year of meeting their operating expenses out of income," Christopher says. "Things reached a point where they were having to dip into capital. The endowment was beginning to shrink. If that continued very much longer, they would be broke."

In 1911, the year he died, Pulitzer's original endowment for the prizes was plenty of money for the program—a little over

$6.1 million in 1990 dollars. But a number of things occurred that Pulitzer had not anticipated:

- The university would not have the foresight to protect the endowment adequately against inflation by reinvesting enough of the income each year.
- During the first six decades of prizes, neither the Pulitzer Board nor the university mounted any significant fund drives to increase the original endowment so it could keep up with inflation.
- To free them of the details of managing the prizes, the board and university developed an administrative office that now has annual operating expenses of about $200,000 on top of the cash prizes.
- Over the decades, the board increased Joseph Pulitzer's original nine prizes to twenty-one, drawing criticism from some quarters that the proliferation has somewhat diluted the prestige of the prize. By contrast, the original five Nobel Prizes were increased by only one— an economics prize—while the Pulitzer Prizes were ballooning. All of the additional prizes have been in journalism except for two, the music and poetry prizes, which Joseph Pulitzer never asked for.

In his will, Pulitzer set the original prizes at $1,000 each, except for the history prize, which he put at $2,000 for reasons never explained.

If the board and university had managed Pulitzer's money the way he had hoped, and had adhered to the financial wishes expressed in his will, a Pulitzer Prize today—adjusted for inflation—would be worth $13,290, except for the history prize, which would bring $26,580.

However, the prizes were not increased until 1988, and then only to $3,000. There are many other, far less prestigious journalism prizes that pay considerably more than that.

For sixty-five years, the only significant increase in Joseph Pulitzer's endowment was a $100,000 contribution from Schlitz beer in 1950 when it sponsored a short-lived ABC television program, "Pulitzer Prize Playhouse."

In 1970 the Pulitzer Board launched its first significant fund-raising drive, "but just about then the economy went all to hell, so they suspended it," Christopher says. "In 1983, after I got here, the economy picked up again and we revived the capital fund drive and raised enough dough so that we now are able to meet expenses out of the income."

The campaign raised about $3 million, he says. (It would have had to raise twice that to restore the cash value of the prizes to the level intended by Joseph Pulitzer.) All the money was from newspaper enterprises—independent papers and chains.

"We put a cap of $150,000 on individual contributions," Christopher says. "That was the maximum we would accept from any single source in the endowment drive, primarily to avoid any appearance of anybody buying influence. There were a number of newspapers and chains that contributed up to the maximum."

The identity of contributors is confidential, he says.

So is the 1990 amount of the endowment. "The best that I can do," Christopher says, "is tell you that it's several million dollars."

An educated guess is about $4 million.

In 1987, the school of journalism received $1 million from a donor who wanted part of the money used to increase the Pulitzer Prizes, and they were boosted to $3,000 the following year. Neither Christopher nor Roberts will reveal the identity of the donor, who insisted on anonymity. Christopher reveals only that the source is not a newspaper enterprise.

"There was nothing sinister about it," Roberts says. "Some people are very modest and believe philosophically that philanthropy should be from the heart and not for publicity."

That is quite true, of course. But isn't there something unseemly about bankrolling cash prizes for America's most distinguished investigative reporting with money contributed from sources that cannot be disclosed?

"I don't think any questionable donors have come up within the Pulitzer program," Roberts says. "Also, in a manner of speaking, the university effectively launders the money in dispensing it, and I literally don't know where it all came from," so there is no possibility of a contributor buying influence that way.

Given time, a good reporter could find out where the Pulitzer contributions have come from. But the more important question is not "who gave how much," but "why keep it secret?" Doing so sends the following statement to winners: "For your distinguished work, please accept this Pulitzer Prize and a check for $3,000. Unfortunately, the money is not really from Joseph Pulitzer's endowment but from revenue earned on funds from other, more recent contributors whom we must not reveal. But trust us. Most of the donors are newspaper companies. We cannot disclose which ones, but you can probably guess who they are. As for the nonnewspaper contributors, we assure you we would never accept money that would compromise your ethics in any way."

There is no record of any journalists ever questioning the source of their Pulitzer Prize checks before pocketing them. But they are in effect being asked to make a leap of faith. With a little imagination, the board could erase that problem. For instance, the board could let the prize bureaucracy operate off income from the anonymous donations and pay out prize money from a combination of Joseph Pulitzer's original endowment and entry fees.

And while the board is at it, it could raise the fees for the big metro papers. Why should North Carolina's tiny *Washington Daily News* have to pay the same fee as the *Philadelphia Inquirer,* which is rich enough to flood the competition with thirty-four entries it presumably deems to be worthy of Pulitzer Prizes?

In the 1990 competition the $20 fees for each of the 1,770 journalism entries, 590 book entries, and 129 music entries add up to nearly $50,000, which is short of the $63,400 paid out in prize money and gold medals. If the entry fee for papers with more than 250,000 circulation were raised to $50, rough calculations show that the entry fees overall would then generate nearly $90,000—enough to clear up the ethical glitch and even increase the prizes themselves.

Of course, there is always the chance that the $50 fee would make the big papers quit flooding the contest. That seems highly unlikely. But if it happened, the sixty-five screening jury members—monks who do most of the priests work—would probably stand and applaud.

4:45 P.M.

The board's work is done.

Now it is up to the Pulitzer office and Columbia University to keep a lid on all these prize decisions for another two days—until Thursday, April 12, at 3 P.M., Pulitzer Prize Day, when the 1990 winners will be announced.

To get full public relations impact, the board must keep its choices secret for the next forty-eight hours. In reality, however, some members won't be able to resist confiding in someone, who will tell someone else.

"If loose lips could sink ships, we'd all be dead around here," Christopher mutters.

Board members say their goodbyes and head out for their respective corners of the country, where they can brace themselves for whatever may occur when the prizes are revealed.

For their effort, board members can usually count on being criticized for one or more of their choices. That's the nature of prize-giving, and the bigger the prizes, the bigger the complaints, most often involving accusations of racism, sexism, elitism, regionalism, and cronyism.

A case might be made for the last of those "isms," but the other charges do not hold up, not this year at least. The record for 1990 prizes looks respectable:

Racism? A black playwright wins the drama prize and a Hispanic novelist receives the fiction award.

Sexism? Women win Pulitzers in four out of the five journalism categories in which women were finalists.

Elitism? The most prestigious prize—the gold medal for public service—is shared by a tiny paper, the *Washington Daily News*, with only 10,000 circulation in Beaufort County, North Carolina.

Regionalism? Half of the journalism prizes, for the first time in Pulitzer history, go to papers west of the Mississippi.

Cronyism? The board looks vulnerable on that score. Eight of the fourteen journalism awards go to newspapers represented by members of the board. The winning work by those eight papers appears to be superb, of course, but their overwhelming link to the powerful board inevitably raises protests that it is a self-congratulatory club of big newspapers, presenting most of the awards to each other and giving what's left to a few outsiders.

Board members also seem exposed on other issues: There is hypocrisy in honoring investigative journalism with prizes administered in secret. There is arrogance in the notion of news executives being qualified to pass final judgment on American literature, drama, and music. And there is recklessness in board members' casual handling of their abundant conflicts of interest.

In fairness, it should be emphasized that none of the 1990 board members created the aura of secrecy surrounding the prizes. Nor did they invent the judging procedures which established them as arbiters of culture and which threaten to trip them up, sooner or later, in embarrassing ethical conflicts that could seriously tarnish the prizes.

Board members inherited all this.

They do, however, have the same mighty weapon that a previous board used when it added women and minorities to its ranks in 1980: the power to change traditions that are wrong.

13

Pulitzer Prize Day Revisited

3:05 P.M. EST—April 12, 1990

ASSOCIATED PRESS BULLETINS begin appearing on the screen of Jim Dwyer's home computer, linked by modem to *New York Newsday* in downtown Manhattan. As usual, the moment the Pulitzer Prizes are announced each year, AP starts off transmitting the news of the winners in one-paragraph takes:

> NEW YORK (AP)—Reporters and photographers covering the San Francisco Bay Area earthquake, the *Exxon Valdez* tanker spill and the suppression of democracy in China dominated the Pulitzer Prizes for journalism today....

Jim sees a separate bulletin on the drama prize. The second Pulitzer for playwright August Wilson is treated as big news. And there is a separate bulletin on the book awards, leading off with the fiction prize to Cuban-American Oscar Hijuelos, apparently the first Hispanic to win this Pulitzer category.

Each of the fourteen prizes in journalism moves as a separate wire item, called an "add," which is just a paragraph or two:

> The *San Jose Mercury News* won the prize for general news reporting for its coverage of the Oct. 17 earthquake, while the *Tribune* of Oakland won for its spot news photography for pictures of devastation caused by the temblor.
>
> An elated, cheering staff at the *Tribune* spritzed newspaper executives and editors with champagne....

As he scrolls the wires, Jim considers whether he might be some sort of journalistic masochist. He knows he didn't win. In the same way he had been tipped off in March that he was a finalist, he was tipped off again yesterday that he had lost. His editor, Donald Forst, phoned and left the message with Cathy, Jim's wife.

Jim does not know, however, that the Pulitzer board decided on the specialized reporting prize with little discussion— mainly a lament by some that perhaps Jim's columns should have been submitted instead in the commentary category, according to both Eugene Roberts and Robert Christopher. Any talk of transferring his work to that category was squelched by the fact that the board had already decided to give the commentary prize this year to Jim Murray of the *Los Angeles Times*. Both Roberts and Christopher say the vote was unanimous, by show of hands, with no abstentions.

And Jim at this moment still does not know who *did* win. That helps explain the butterflies as he watches the AP bulletins. He is hoping the winner, whoever it is, got the prize for something terrific. Something *fabulous*, actually. That would be about the only news that could relieve some of the crushing dejection he has felt for the past twenty-four hours.

12:05 P.M. PST

To Claire Spiegel's great disappointment, as she stares at the TV set in her Manhattan Beach home, Cable News Network isn't offering a word on the Pulitzer Prizes. But that makes sense, she knows. These are print-media, not broadcast, awards. CNN will report the arts and letters Pulitzers later this day, but the journalism prizes will get short shrift.

Claire goes channel surfing, trying to find the Pulitzer announcements on another news program, but without luck.

Frustrated, she finally gives up. But Claire already knows what happened to her Pulitzer entry. In much the same manner she had been told in March that she was a finalist, she was tipped off yesterday by *Los Angeles Times* editor Shelby Coffey that she had not won.

Like Jim Dwyer, Claire was searching the news to find out who *had* won.

There may be no worse cliché than "leaks like a sieve," nor any better way to describe the porosity of the Pulitzer Prize system. Of twenty-eight journalism finalists who responded to a survey by the author, twenty-one indicated they had been tipped off before the formal announcements on Pulitzer Prize Day. Those twenty-one even include the Pulitzer Board chairman's reporter, Gilbert Gaul of the *Philadelphia Inquirer*, who admits that his editors tipped him off early when he became a finalist and then again when his work was chosen for the public service prize.

Another of those twenty-one, Claire Spiegel, will have to take her baby, Leslie, to a doctor for treatment of a stomach ailment later on this day. While driving there, listening to the car radio, Claire will hear a news item on the Pulitzer winners and finally discover who received the prize that she had spent the past month hoping for. And Claire will later tell people that upon hearing the news, she instantly felt better.

1:05 P.M. MST

Picking at a traditional Passover meal of gefilte fish and matzo in her Santa Fe apartment, Tamar Stieber has the chills. She tries to concentrate on work, focusing her thoughts on the county dog-license hearing she is supposed to cover tonight. But she can't stop thinking about what happened to her—or *almost* happened to her—four days ago on Interstate 25. As hard as she tries to push it out of her mind, the terrifying memory keeps leaping back. And every time, it gives her shivers.

Last Sunday, on the black, blustery night before Passover, Tamar drove hurriedly down that freeway to Albuquerque to pick up a friend at the airport. She recalls that she was speeding a little, thinking about her falling-out with her sister Sharon and worrying about the lump-removal surgery facing her other sister, Carrie, in a few days.

Tamar was lost in thought when out of nowhere a large, ghostlike tumbleweed bounced into her headlight beams. Most Southwesterners are used to tumbleweeds. You just drive right on through them. But Tamar, a New York native, had no time to remember such advice. Badly startled, she swerved instinctively. The car lurched out of control and rolled three times with a sickening screech of bending metal and shattering glass.

Demolished, the car came to a rest in the freeway median. No other cars were hit. Tamar, who had been wearing a seat belt, walked away from the wreck. She was literally unscratched.

On this day, however, she is concerned about the chills that sweep over her every time her thoughts go back to Sunday night. In an almost desperate search for serenity, she has decided to observe Passover, even though she considers her beliefs to be "somewhere between agnosticism and atheism." But over the past few days she has been finding comfort in the religious tradition, and she has vowed to eat no leavened bread all this week.

When not dwelling on the accident, Tamar can't quit worrying about her two sisters. Sharon still isn't speaking to her. Carrie is scheduled to have her breast lump removed this afternoon. Tamar's chills come back, and she finds herself saying a silent prayer.

The telephone rings. She jumps, nerves shot.

"Congratulations," the caller says. Tamar recognizes the voice of Ed Mareno, Santa Fe correspondent for the Associated Press.

"Thanks a lot," she replies, slightly annoyed. Tamar assumes Ed has called to tease her about the car wreck.

"Now I suppose you'll get your own parking space at the *Journal*," he quips.

"Very funny, Ed," she says, not really thinking he is all that humorous.

"You haven't heard yet?" he asks. "You've just won the Pulitzer Prize."

He says he needs a few comments from her for the story he is writing on the first Pulitzer ever won by a New Mexico newspaper. Tamar is convinced Ed is joking. She is becoming irritated. She needs to get to work. But he insists it is true and begins reading Associated Press bulletins to her. She still thinks he is playing some sort of cruel prank on her when the telephone's call-waiting program beeps.

It is CBS News. A reporter wants a comment on how she broke the L-Tryptophan story that won the Pulitzer Prize.

Now Tamar knows. But she is stunned. She tells the reporter her mind just went blank, and she switches back to Ed.

"Ed, I can't give you a comment now. I want to find out if I should give it to my paper first," she says, then hangs up.

Later, she will realize that was a silly reaction, and she will apologize to Ed Mareno. But at this moment, her mind is not processing information in its usual fashion.

Dazed, Tamar rushes out the door, heading for work. On the way, she stops off at the Post Office to mail a payment that is overdue. While there, she discovers she has a spot on her skirt. "My God," she says to herself. "What if they want to take my picture?"

She heads back home and changes into something neater—a longer black skirt with a kick pleat and a white silk shirt with a belt. As she heads out the door again, the phone starts going crazy.

First is Tamar's city editor, Howard Houghton. He is jubilant. That strikes Tamar as funny. Howard is not known as an editor who ever publicly expresses so much enthusiasm.

That call is interrupted by another, from the bureau managing editor, Tim Coder, who played such a vital role in the L-Tryptophan story.

"Nice going," he says, not mentioning the word "Pulitzer."

"My God," Tamar says, "can you believe this?"

"Sure," replies Coder. He is an exceptionally calm editor who almost became a Jesuit priest.

More calls interrupt: a close friend, then a fellow reporter, then one of the *Journal* photographers, Neil Jacobs.

"Goddam it, get down here," Jacobs says. "They're all waiting for you!"

Now it really begins to sink in. Tamar decides she should call her parents in New York so that they don't hear the news from somewhere else. Her mother, reached at home in Peekskill in Putnam County, simply screams. Tamar's father, reached at his office in Manhattan, becomes emotional. Lovingly, he tells her, "This makes up for all the *tsuris* [Yiddish for "worries"] you've given us."

Tamar spends a moment composing herself. Then she goes out to the rental car she has been using this week and heads for the office. The mile-and-a-half drive provides her a few more precious moments for deep breathing.

2:15 P.M.

As a remarkably composed Tamar Stieber walks through the door of the *Albuquerque Journal's* bureau office in downtown Santa Fe, the entire news staff begins clapping. Almost everyone has come in, even the city editor, Houghton, who usually does not arrive until four.

Somebody has brought some bottles of champagne and plastic cups. As Tamar is hugged and congratulated, corks start popping and bubbly begins flowing. Like most modern newspapers, the *Journal* has strict rules against alcohol during working hours. The days of Hildy Johnson and *The Front Page* are long gone. An employee can be fired for having a beer at lunch. But Pulitzer Prize Day is the one day of the year when reporters and editors can drink openly in the center of the newsroom without fear of losing their jobs.

At this exact moment in thirteen other newsrooms around the nation, similar Pulitzer Prize parties are happening. Perhaps the wildest jubilation is occurring at papers in Oakland and San Jose, where entire staffs share in prizes for their earthquake coverage. But as those Bay Area journalists pour champagne over themselves in photos that are transmitted around the world, others can only wonder about the appropriateness of such ecstatic celebration of awards made possible through a terrible calamity that killed over two hundred people.

The *Albuquerque Journal's* festivities, though, do not seem callous. The L-Tryptophan stories saved lives. That is indeed something to celebrate.

Tamar, however, abstains from the champagne. She is taking

medication that her doctor said should not be mixed with alcohol.

Among the little bureau staff of twelve, the celebration is heartfelt and real. They're all happy for Tamar, of course. But they're also elated for the bureau, for "Journal North," as they call themselves.

"Four people had to cover my beat for me at different times during the L-Tryptophan story," Tamar says later. "That's the way it is in the bureau. You work long hours, you write a lot of stories, you crank it out, and if you have to cover somebody else's beat, that goes with the territory. So winning the prize really created a feeling of 'we did it' among the entire staff."

Bureau employees feel they are regarded in Albuquerque as sort of second-class citizens, staffing an outpost. For reasons hard to articulate, they say, the bureau has lower status than the main newsroom in the city. So harvesting the Pulitzer Prize is especially sweet for all who work in "Journal North."

But the joyful celebration in Santa Fe is interrupted by a call from Albuquerque. Executives in top management would like their Pulitzer Prize winner to make an appearance in the main newsroom, pronto.

3:20 P.M.

Neil Jacobs, the photographer, drives Tamar the sixty miles from Santa Fe to Albuquerque. On the way, they receive a call on his car phone. It is from New Mexico's governor, Garrey Carruthers. He congratulates Tamar for being the first Pulitzer Prize winner from New Mexico, and he jokes with her.

"You're going to ask them to give you a handsome raise now, aren't you?"

"Well, Governor," she shoots back, "I think it would have a lot more impact if *you* asked them to give me a handsome raise."

He laughs. "You tell them that Garrey Carruthers said they should double your salary."

That will not happen. However, the company will match Tamar's $3,000 cash prize, doubling it to $6,000. That has become a widespread newspaper tradition—a response to the feeling that the Pulitzer's cash value has not adequately kept up with inflation over the years.

3:45 P.M.

Tamar begins tensing up as soon as she and Jacobs get out of his car in the *Albuquerque Journal*'s parking lot. A couple of staff photographers are waiting there, taking her picture as she walks from the car to the building. One of them follows her every move with a video camera. She laughs. It strikes her as funny.

The attention terrifies Tamar, however. She loves going to parties and talking with people, but she abhors being the center of a crowd. And she is petrified at the thought of speaking in public. That is her worst nightmare.

As Tamar enters the newsroom, the staff gives her a standing ovation. This is a much bigger group than the little Santa Fe crew. There are well over a hundred staffers here in Albuquerque. Tamar knows hardly any of them.

Several staffers approach Tamar and take turns giving her hugs. There's Gerald Crawford, the editor. And Kent Walz, the assistant editor, and Rod Deckert, one of the managing editors. And several others. Then comes an awkward silence.

"You're not waiting for a speech, are you?" Tamar asks.

Yes, of course, they are. Her worst fear has come true.

She takes a deep breath. Then, in a thin voice, she mentions that at least half of the prize really belongs to Tim Coder, the editor who handed her the L-Tryptophan story in the first place and who did so much to help her report it.

"This was a two-person story," she tells the staff. "I'm going to split my award with Tim. If he doesn't accept it, I'll donate it to his favorite charity or something like that."

Coder enters the newsroom as she is talking. As she sees him, her voice get shaky, and she has to stop.

She and Tim hug. No words have to be spoken.

Somebody wheels out a sheet cake and some sparkling grape juice, and now an awkward little party begins. Many of the staffers walk over, congratulate Tamar, and take some cake back to their desks.

Tamar's nervousness increases as she realizes this isn't a real celebration. Few of these staff members have ever spoken to her. They don't know her. They are not really happy for her. They might even be envious. Whatever they are feeling, it isn't the jubilation that Tamar sensed among her fellow staffers back at Santa Fe.

The *Journal's* choice of beverage provides a good symbol of the difference between the Albuquerque and Santa Fe operations. The corporate celebration has grape juice. The real celebration has champagne. Albuquerque keeps emotions in check and company policy firmly in place. Santa Fe gets a little crazy, bends a few of the rules, wins a Pulitzer Prize.

Tamar apologizes to the Albuquerque editors about abstaining from the cake. Leavened bread, she explains. Overhearing that, the paper's arts writer, David Steinberg, comes over to Tamar.

"Look," he says, "I read in the Talmud where it says you can't eat leavened bread during Passover *unless* you've won the Pulitzer Prize. Then you are *supposed* to eat it."

Crews from all three Albuquerque television stations have arrived. Each wants to tape an interview with Tamar.

She seems numb as she submits to the interviews. All three TV reporters ask her what she plans to do, now that she has won the coveted prize.

"Well," she tells them, "tonight I'm covering the county hearing on dog licensing. But someday I think I might like to be a foreign correspondent for the *New York Times.*"

Later, Tamar kicks herself for saying the part about the *New York Times.* What would her bosses think of that? But it was the truth, and she always tries to tell the truth.

Now the *Journal* assigns a reporter to interview Tamar for the paper's own coverage of the prize. The story will run the following morning in a four-column box on the top of the front page. The interview will be accompanied by a color photograph of Tamar and Tim Coder, posing as if they are helping each other open a bottle of sparkling grape juice. In the foreground are the sheet cake and several other bottles of juice—all with the "Welch's" labels carefully turned toward the camera. The accompanying headline is straight to the point: JOURNAL REPORTER WINS PULITZER.

The city's competing newspaper, the *Albuquerque Tribune*, will come out this evening with a much more subdued story, displayed much more modestly. And that account will illustrate one of the universal truths of media prizes: Those that win them treat it as major news; those that lose them play it down.

This is the one day of the year when normally ethical news executives suspend their objective judgment for twenty-four hours.

Tamar endures a couple more interviews, one of them by Ed Mareno, the AP's reporter, to whom she apologizes for her earlier brush-off. Then she is asked to read over the *Journal* reporter's copy that will appear on tomorrow's front page. This time, Tamar notes with satisfaction, "Stieber" is spelled correctly.

6:15 P.M.

None of the brass in Albuquerque has suggested any celebratory dining this evening, much to Tamar's relief. She urgently wants to get back to Santa Fe and relax before going to her assignment, the county hearing.

Neil Jacobs is waiting, equally anxious to return. He, too, senses that the Pulitzer Prize celebration, at least in Albuquerque, has formally ended.

7:15 P.M.

When Tamar walks back into the bureau office in Santa Fe, she is surprised to find a mountain of flowers—many from friends all around the country, and many from businesses and professional firms. Among all the flowers are two dozen long-stem roses from the *Journal*'s publisher, Thompson Lang.

Dozens of telephone messages also await her, along with several gifts. The Albuquerque staff, for example, has sent something called a "Trauma Bear," which Tamar is supposed to squeeze at appropriate times. And David Steinberg, the arts critic, has sent some matzo and a book on the Holocaust.

Tamar has some time before her meeting, so she tries to do some work that piled up during her chaotic day. Howard Houghton, the bureau city editor, sees her and walks over.

"What are you doing?"

"Trying to get at least one story done before I go to my meeting tonight," she replies.

"No you're not," he says.

Houghton tells her to forget the dog-license hearing. "There will be lots more of those," he says, "but who knows when we'll win another Pulitzer?" He orders her to put on her coat. They're going out for what he calls "beverage therapy."

"I can't drink," she says.

"I can," he replies.

A few reporters and friends join them at a downtown bar called The Pink Adobe.

9:15 P.M. EST

In Manhattan, meanwhile, Jim and Cathy Dwyer have a quiet dinner with a friend at a favorite Italian restaurant on Spring Street in SoHo.

Jim is feeling a little less depressed about his close brush with Pulitzer acclaim. Good Italian food always lifts his spirits, especially at this great little place.

Unintentionally, his mother has also helped cheer him up tonight. When Jim called her and told her who had beaten him out for the prize, Mary Dwyer, a nurse, exclaimed: "Oh, L-Tryptophan. That *was* a big story!"

6:15 P.M. PST

But in the California coastal town of Manhattan Beach, Claire Spiegel is not having as much success as Jim Dwyer at getting over her disappointment tonight.

While Tamar goes out for "beverage therapy" and Jim salves his wounds with SoHo cannelloni, Claire is at home on the telephone, alternately calling her husband, Brad, and a real estate broker. Claire and Brad are bidding on a house they hope to buy in Pasadena.

Claire desperately wants the place. It is a big, old, English manor on an acre of land, just fifteen minutes from downtown Los Angeles—less than one-third of her present commute. This would be an enormous advantage to her when she resumes her juggling act, career versus parenthood.

The bidding on the house, however, does not seem to be going in her favor, Claire senses.

"Gee," she tells herself, "today I lost out on a Pulitzer Prize, and tonight I'm going to lose out on the house we really want."

Claire cannot remember the last time she felt so depressed.

3:30 A.M. MST—April 13, 1990

It is Friday the thirteenth, the Day After Pulitzer Prize Day, and Tamar Stieber is finally getting to bed. She and her *Journal* colleagues closed down The Pink Adobe, then continued the party at a private home. There will be some memorable hangovers later on in the Santa Fe bureau office, although not for Tamar Stieber. She drank only mineral water.

Tamar will become exhausted over the next week or so, however. She finds she cannot sleep.

Lying there in the darkness, staring up at the ceiling, she feels her body literally buzzing after the most incredible day of her life. Her mind races over the past twenty-four hours, sorting through the events and images and emotions.

Ed Mareno's phone call. Her mother screaming. Her father choking up. The call from sister Carrie. The strained party in Albuquerque. The warm emotions in Santa Fe. The tumbleweed. The car rolling. Passover. Not hearing from Sharon, her estranged sister.

Tamar's chills return, and she fights depression. "What's wrong with me?" she asks. Tamar does not know it yet, but she is experiencing an early bout of the post-Pulitzer blues. Like others who have suffered it, she can't feel happy, she can't cry, she can't get in touch with her emotions.

Her thoughts keep returning to Sharon. That is what's wrong, Tamar thinks. She needs to talk to Sharon, but she doesn't know how to reach her. Or what she would say if she did.

Tamar imagines the phone jangling in the darkness. The voice on the other end of the line sounds familiar: "Way to go, Tamar. I always knew you were special. And I love you."

The imagined voice is Sharon's. And then, finally, in her fantasy, Tamar Stieber lets go.

Epilogue

AS 1990 CAME TO A CLOSE, Eugene Roberts, chairman of the Pulitzer Prize Board, quit the newspaper business.

His resignation as editor and president of the *Philadelphia Inquirer* was accompanied by suggestions in the trade press that his paper's prize-winning news formula was at odds with the financial expectations of Knight-Ridder, the *Inquirer's* notoriously profit-oriented publisher. Roberts, however, repeatedly denied that any conflicts with the newspaper chain led to his decision. He said only that he wanted to do something different, and he picked teaching.

Roberts accepted a position as tenured professor at the University of Maryland's College of Journalism—widely viewed as one of the nation's best programs. It has no connection with the Pulitzer Prizes, and neither does Roberts, effective in April 1991. His final term on the Pulitzer Board expired, and he was replaced as chairman by James Hoge, whose *New York Daily News* entered the new year gripped in a vicious strike that threatened the tabloid's continued existence.

During the five-month walkout, the *Daily News* plunged into even more precarious financial health, losing half its 1.1 million circulation and much of its advertising revenue. British publisher Robert Maxwell took over the paper from the Tribune Company and kept it in business after its nine striking unions agreed to sacrifice a third of their jobs. The paper's future remains very much in jeopardy.

If New York loses the *Daily News*, the city loses one more irreplaceable link to the journalism of Joseph Pulitzer.

* * *

Jim Dwyer spent little time brooding about his lost Pulitzer. He instantly recognized Tamar Stieber's L-Tryptophan story for what it was: one of those amazing journalistic lightning bolts that strike only rarely. If the story comes to a reporter who has the necessary talent and readiness, as Tamar Stieber did, nothing is going to stop it on its path to the Pulitzer Prize.

"It was one hell of a story, and she did an incredible job with it," Jim says.

He ended his leave of absence shortly after Pulitzer Prize Day and went back to work at *New York Newsday* as a general columnist. His book on the subways was scheduled for fall 1991 publication.

One of the advantages of his new general-interest column, Jim discovered, was the vastly increased opportunity for new experiences. For example, after New York rabbi Meir Kahane was assassinated by a young Arab on November 5, 1990, *Newsday* sent Jim to Israel to cover the funeral.

Although he was no longer the subway columnist, Jim found himself writing about the subject again after a twenty-two-year-old Utah tourist was slain on September 2 when he and his family were attacked by a gang of knife-wielding youths on a Manhattan subway platform. *Time* subsequently published a cover story called "The Rotting of the Big Apple," and Jim answered with a stirring column listing many positive things that happened in New York on September 2 but were ignored by the magazine. Wrote Jim:

"They [*Time* executives] do not know, at last, sitting in the tower at Rockefeller Center, or in their air-conditioned cars with the smoked windows, that the city rides on the quiver of immigrant hopes, never straight, not always clean and true, but still soaring."

Jim and Cathy Dwyer still fervently hope to have a larger family, and they purchased a larger apartment to get ready for the day that dream comes true.

* * *

Claire Spiegel was a runner-up for the Pulitzer Prize but not for the house in Pasadena. She and Brad won the bidding war. They moved in with Allison and Leslie and the girls' nanny, Amy Caffee, at the end of the summer of 1990.

To Claire's considerable relief, the *Los Angeles Times* granted her request for a three-day workweek. She returned to her former health-care beat in early 1991 under a special job-sharing arrangement with the reporter who had covered the subject during Claire's maternity leave.

She resumed her career with great expectations. The shorter commute from Pasadena was a huge improvement over the drive from Manhattan Beach. Allison and Leslie seemed to be adjusting well to having their mother gone part of the week. And for Claire, it felt wonderful to be back reporting news.

This time, Claire told her friends, everything is going to work out.

* * *

Within days of winning her prize, Tamar Stieber heard the apocalyptic story of a young newspaper photographer who won a Pulitzer in the 1970s and found himself showered with adulation, promotions, and offers of lucrative new jobs. The world's expectations of him changed overnight, creating extraordinary stress for the man, still in his twenties. Amplified by other emotional problems, the pressure grew until a climactic day when he called a news conference to announce that he was Jesus Christ.

The story of his breakdown, unfortunately quite true, serves as an extreme illustration of the fact that winning the Pulitzer does not always change lives for the better.

Tamar herself became intimate quickly with the psychological penalties that come with the prize. Once her euphoria passed, all sorts of questions began rolling out of nowhere like tumbleweeds in the night:

What should she do next? Go back to covering sewage meetings and dog-license hearings?

Should she demand a raise? Ask for a better beat?

What if her next work doesn't live up to the new standard that has been set for her?

Should she cash in on her prize and seek a higher-paying job at a bigger newspaper? What if she stays in Santa Fe? Will people think she's a failure?

Tamar was not able to sleep soundly for eight days after winning the prize. By then she had heard from previous winners about the so-called post-Pulitzer blues. Some recipients have reported steep emotional letdowns and sudden confusion about what they should do with the rest of their lives.

Those blues intensified for Tamar during the blur of events following Pulitzer Prize Day. She went to celebratory lunches with the publisher and the editor and other top managers. A colleague put on a dinner in her honor. The staff threw a party. There were endless congratulatory phone calls and interviews with media from around the country. The *Journal* had her pose beside the printing presses for promotional photos. Much of it was fun, but the cumulative effect on Tamar was overpowering.

"I didn't know what all this really meant, but I knew it was bringing a major change in my life, all of a sudden, on top of all my other crises," Tamar says. "All my friends were saying to me, 'Doors are going to open up for you. You can do whatever you want now. You can write your own ticket.' I felt like the Dustin Hoffman character in *The Graduate*. Everyone was telling me, 'plastics, plastics, plastics.' Emotionally, I was starting to crash, like a plane coming down."

Maturity was on Tamar's side. After years of waiting tables and going back to school and working in dead-end clerical jobs, she was no stranger to life's ups and downs. After winning the Pulitzer, she allowed herself eight disoriented days and sleepless nights, then took what she calls a "mental health day." She resumed her jogging—a four-mile morning run that she had been neglecting—and spent the rest of the day alone in her apartment. She reflected on things, watched a little TV, caught up on some reading, and answered no phone calls.

The next day, she made a decision: "I wasn't going to dump on my newspaper just because I had won a damn Pulitzer Prize."

By her way of thinking, the *Albuquerque Journal* had taken a chance on a somewhat desperate, thirty-four-year-old beginning reporter and had given her an opportunity to reach for the highest honor in journalism. She was not going to ask for a raise, a promotion, a different beat, or even an extra day off.

Without her asking, however, the paper did offer her an attractive new assignment as a roving special-projects reporter, looking for important and interesting stories throughout northern New Mexico. She gladly accepted.

A month later, in May, Tamar attended a Pulitzer Prize luncheon for all the 1990 winners at Columbia University. Editors Gerald Crawford, Kent Walz, and Tim Coder accompanied her. Tamar's parents also were there, beaming proudly as she received her prize certificate from Columbia president Michael Sovern.

While she was in New York, Fred and Florence Stieber put on a party in Tamar's honor at a clubhouse on Lake Peekskill. Her sister Carrie, whose tumor had turned out to be benign, was also there that night—a joyous occasion in all respects but one. The other sister, Sharon, who had been expected to come, called at the last minute and said she could not make it.

Tamar was disappointed but philosophical:

"About eighty others came—people I had not seen in years, mostly from New York, so it was wonderful. My mother gave a speech, then my father gave a speech. He was funny and very good. I had no idea. And they presented a plaque to me. It says something like, 'You used to be known as Fred and Florence Stieber's daughter, and now we are known as Tamar Stieber's parents.'

"They also gave me a pen holder made out of petrified wood, and they had my name put on it—Tamar P. Stieber. I don't have a middle name so they gave me the initial. They knew I always did wish I had one, so they had the engraver insert the P. It stands for 'Pulitzer.'"

Throughout the rest of 1990, prospective employers did not line up at Tamar's door, trying to lure her away from Santa Fe. However, she received several "get acquainted" invitations from editors at other papers, all of which she declined.

In the fall, she received a letter from Robert Christopher, secretary to the Pulitzer Board, inviting her to serve on one of the juries screening the 1991 prizes. She turned him down.

"I'm absolutely not doing it. I'd feel ridiculous. I haven't been in this business long enough to judge anybody else."

As the first anniversary of her prize passes, Tamar says she is still happy at the *Albuquerque Journal*, still living in her tiny adobe apartment, and still deeply in debt, although she has a savings account for the first time in her life, thanks to her prize money.

She continues to dream of someday working for one of the nation's great papers, perhaps as a foreign correspondent. That is a notion she has had since the *New York Times* published her first piece of journalism, a letter to the editor when she was fifteen years old. She never forgot the thrill, although it took her another fifteen years to become a reporter.

She says she probably will try for such a job after gaining a little more experience. Her tenure as a reporter has been limited, she realizes, but she has had a good formal education and has traveled much of the world. She also speaks Spanish, French, Italian, and Japanese, with varying degrees of fluency. And she has good employer references, which she figures will help.

Her Pulitzer Prize probably won't hurt, either.

A Complete Record of Pulitzer Prize Winners 1917–1991

ARTS AND LETTERS AND MUSIC

Novels

1917   No award
1918   *His Family*, by Ernest Poole
1919   *The Magnificent Ambersons*, by Booth Tarkington
1920   No award
1921   *The Age of Innocence*, by Edith Wharton
1922   *Alice Adams*, by Booth Tarkington
1923   *One of Ours*, by Willa Cather
1924   *The Able McLaughlins*, by Margaret Wilson
1925   *So Big*, by Edna Ferber
1926   *Arrowsmith*, by Sinclair Lewis
1927   *Early Autumn*, by Louis Bromfield
1928   *The Bridge of San Luis Rey*, by Thornton Wilder
1929   *Scarlett Sister Mary*, by Julia Peterkin
1930   *Laughing Boy*, by Oliver LaFarge
1931   *Years of Grace*, by Margaret Ayer Barnes
1932   *The Good Earth*, by Pearl S. Buck
1933   *The Store*, by T. S. Stribling
1934   *Lamb in His Bosom*, by Caroline Miller
1935   *Now in November*, by Josephine Winslow Johnson
1936   *Honey in the Horn*, by Harold L. Davis
1937   *Gone with the Wind*, by Margaret Mitchell
1938   *The Late George Apley*, by John Phillips Marquand
1939   *The Yearling*, by Marjorie Kinnan Rawlings

1940   *The Grapes of Wrath*, by John Steinbeck
1941   No award
1942   *In This Our Life*, by Ellen Glasgow
1943   *Dragon's Teeth*, by Upton Sinclair
1944   *Journey in the Dark*, by Martin Flavin
1945   *A Bell for Adano*, by John Hersey
1946   No award
1947   *All the King's Men*, by Robert Penn Warren

(Note: The following year, the name of this category was changed to "Fiction.")

Fiction

1948   *Tales of the South Pacific*, by James A. Michener
1949   *Guard of Honor*, by James Gould Cozzens
1950   *The Way West*, by A. B. Guthrie Jr.
1951   *The Town*, by Conrad Richter
1952   *The Caine Mutiny*, by Herman Wouk
1953   *The Old Man and the Sea*, by Ernest Hemingway
1954   No award
1955   *A Fable*, by William Faulkner
1956   *Andersonville*, by MacKinlay Kantor
1957   No award
1958   *A Death in the Family*, by James Agee
1959   *The Travels of Jaimie McPheeters*, by Robert Lewis Taylor
1960   *Advise and Consent*, by Allen Drury
1961   *To Kill a Mockingbird*, by Harper Lee
1962   *The Edge of Sadness*, by Edwin O'Connor
1963   *The Reivers*, by William Faulkner
1964   No award
1965   *The Keepers of the House*, by Shirley Ann Grau
1966   *Collected Stories*, by Katherine Anne Porter
1967   *The Fixer*, by Bernard Malamud
1968   *The Confessions of Nat Turner*, by William Styron
1969   *House Made of Dawn*, by N. Scott Momaday
1970   *Collected Stories*, by Jean Stafford
1971   No award
1972   *Angle of Repose*, by Wallace Stegner
1973   *The Optimist's Daughter*, by Eudora Welty
1974   No award
1975   *The Killer Angels*, by Michael Shaara
1976   *Humboldt's Gift*, by Saul Bellow
1977   No award

1978 *Elbow Room*, by James Alan McPherson
1979 *The Stories of John Cheever*, by John Cheever
1980 *The Executioner's Song*, by Norman Mailer
1981 *A Confederacy of Dunces*, by John Kennedy Toole
1982 *Rabbit Is Rich*, by John Updike
1983 *The Color Purple*, by Alice Walker
1984 *Ironweed*, by William Kennedy
1985 *Foreign Affairs*, by Alison Lurie
1986 *Lonesome Dove*, by Larry McMurtry
1987 *A Summons to Memphis*, by Peter Taylor
1988 *Beloved*, by Toni Morrison
1989 *Breathing Lessons*, by Anne Tyler
1990 *The Mambo Kings Play Songs of Love*, by Oscar Hijuelos
1991 *Rabbit at Rest*, by John Updike

Drama

1917 No award
1918 *Why Marry?* by Jesse Lynch Williams
1919 No award
1920 *Beyond the Horizon*, by Eugene O'Neill
1921 *Miss Lulu Bett*, by Zona Gale
1922 *Anna Christie*, by Eugene O'Neill
1923 *Icebound*, by Owen Davis
1924 *Hell-Bent for Heaven*, by Hatcher Hughes
1925 *They Knew What They Wanted*, by Sidney Howard
1926 *Craig's Wife*, by George Kelly
1927 *In Abraham's Bosom*, by Paul Green
1928 *Strange Interlude*, by Eugene O'Neill
1929 *Street Scene*, by Elmer L. Rice
1930 *The Green Pastures*, by Marc Connelly
1931 *Alison's House*, by Susan Glaspell
1932 *Of Thee I Sing*, by George S. Kaufman, Morrie Ryskind, and Ira Gershwin
1933 *Both Your Houses*, by Maxwell Anderson
1934 *Men in White*, by Sidney Kingsley
1935 *The Old Maid*, by Zoë Akins
1936 *Idiot's Delight*, by Robert E. Sherwood
1937 *You Can't Take It with You*, by Moss Hart and George S. Kaufman
1938 *Our Town*, by Thornton Wilder
1939 *Abe Lincoln in Illinois*, by Robert E. Sherwood
1940 *The Time of Your Life*, by William Saroyan
1941 *There Shall Be No Night*, by Robert E. Sherwood

1942 No award
1943 *The Skin of Our Teeth,* by Thornton Wilder
1944 No award
1945 *Harvey,* by Mary Chase
1946 *State of the Union,* by Russel Crouse and Howard Lindsay
1947 No award
1948 *A Streetcar Named Desire,* by Tennessee Williams
1949 *Death of a Salesman,* by Arthur Miller
1950 *South Pacific,* by Richard Rodgers, Oscar Hammerstein II, and Joshua Logan
1951 No award
1952 *The Shrike,* by Joseph Kramm
1953 *Picnic,* by William Inge
1954 *The Teahouse of the August Moon,* by John Patrick
1955 *Cat on a Hot Tin Roof,* by Tennessee Williams
1956 *Diary of Anne Frank,* by Albert Hackett and Frances Goodrich
1957 *Long Day's Journey into Night,* by Eugene O'Neill
1958 *Look Homeward, Angel,* by Ketti Frings
1959 *J.B.,* by Archibald MacLeish
1960 *Fiorello!* Book by Jerome Weidman and George Abbott, music by Jerry Bock, and lyrics by Sheldon Harnick
1961 *All the Way Home,* by Tad Mosel
1962 *How to Succeed in Business Without Really Trying,* by Frank Loesser and Abe Burrows
1963 No award
1964 No award
1965 *The Subject Was Roses,* by Frank D. Gilroy
1966 No award
1967 *A Delicate Balance,* by Edward Albee
1968 No award
1969 *The Great White Hope,* by Howard Sackler
1970 *No Place to Be Somebody,* by Charles Gordone
1971 *The Effect of Gamma Rays on Man-in-the-Moon Marigolds,* by Paul Zindel
1972 No award
1973 *The Championship Season,* by Jason Miller
1974 No award
1975 *Seascape,* by Edward Albee
1976 *A Chorus Line,* by Michael Bennett, James Kirkwood, Nicholas Dante, Marvin Hamlisch, and Edward Kleban
1977 *The Shadow Box,* by Michael Cristofer
1978 *The Gin Game,* by Donal L. Coburn
1979 *Buried Child,* by Sam Shepard

1980   *Talley's Folley*, by Lanford Wilson
1981   *Crimes of the Heart*, by Beth Henley
1982   *A Soldier's Play*, by Charles Fuller
1983   *'Night, Mother*, by Marsha Norman
1984   *Glengarry Glen Ross*, by David Mamet
1985   *Sunday in the Park with George*, music and lyrics by Stephen Sondheim, book by James Lapine
1986   No award
1987   *Fences*, by August Wilson
1988   *Driving Miss Daisy*, by Alfred Uhry
1989   *The Heidi Chronicles*, by Wendy Wasserstein
1990   *The Piano Lesson*, by August Wilson
1991   *Lost in Yonkers*, by Neil Simon

History

1917   *With Americans of Past and Present Days*, by J. J. Jusserand
1918   *A History of the Civil War, 1861–1865*, by James Ford Rhodes
1919   No award
1920   *The War with Mexico*, 2 vols., by Justin H. Smith
1921   *The Victory at Sea*, by William Sowden Sims in collaboration with Burton J. Hendrick
1922   *The Founding of New England*, by James Truslow Adams
1923   *The Supreme Court in United States History*, by Charles Warren
1924   *The American Revolution—A Constitutional Interpretation*, by Charles Howard McIlwain
1925   *A History of the American Frontier*, by Frederic Paxson
1926   *The History of the United States*, by Edward Channing
1927   *Pinckney's Treaty*, by Samuel Flagg Bemis
1928   *Main Currents in American Thought*, 2 vols., by Vernon Louis Parrington
1929   *The Organization and Administration of the Union Army, 1861–1865*, by Fred Albert Shannon
1930   *The War of Independence*, by Claude H. Van Tyne
1931   *The Coming of the War: 1914*, by Bernadotte Schmitt
1932   *My Experiences in the World War*, by John J. Pershing
1933   *The Significance of Sections in American History*, by Frederick J. Turner
1934   *The People's Choice*, by Herbert Agar
1935   *The Colonial Period of American History*, by Charles McLean Andrews
1936   *The Constitutional History of the United States*, by Andrew C. McLaughlin
1937   *The Flowering of New England*, by Van Wyck Brooks

1938   *The Road to Reunion, 1865–1900,* by Paul Herman Buck
1939   *A History of American Magazines,* by Frank Luther Mott
1940   *Abraham Lincoln: The War Years,* by Carl Sandburg
1941   *The Atlantic Migration, 1607–1860,* by Marcus Lee Hansen
1942   *Reveille in Washington,* by Margaret Leech
1943   *Paul Revere and the World He Lived In,* by Esther Forbes
1944   *The Growth of American Thought,* by Merle Curti
1945   *Unfinished Business,* by Stephen Bonsal
1946   *The Age of Jackson,* by Arthur Meier Schlesinger Jr.
1947   *Scientists Against Time,* by James Phinney Baxter III
1948   *Across the Wide Missouri,* by Bernard DeVoto
1949   *The Disruption of American Democracy,* by Roy Franklin Nichols
1950   *Art and Life in America,* by Oliver W. Larkin
1951   *The Old Northwest, Pioneer Period 1815–1840,* by R. Carlyle Buley
1952   *The Uprooted,* by Oscar Handlin
1953   *The Era of Good Feelings,* by George Dangerfield
1954   *A Stillness at Appomattox,* by Bruce Catton
1955   *Great River: The Rio Grande in North American History,* by Paul Horgan
1956   *Age of Reform,* by Richard Hofstadter
1957   *Russia Leaves the War: Soviet-American Relations, 1917–1920,* by George F. Kennan
1958   *Banks and Politics in America,* by Bray Hammond
1959   *The Republican Era: 1869–1901,* by Leonard D. White and Jean Schneider
1960   *The Days of McKinley,* by Margaret Leech
1961   *Between War and Peace: The Potsdam Conference,* by Herbert Feis
1962   *The Triumphant Empire, Thunder-Clouds in the West,* by Lawrence H. Gipson
1963   *Washington, Village and Capital, 1800–1878,* by Constance McLaughlin Green
1964   *Puritan Village: The Formation of a New England Town,* by Sumner Chilton Powell
1965   *The Greenback Era,* by Irwin Unger
1966   *Life of the Mind in America,* by Perry Miller
1967   *Exploration and Empire: The Explorer and the Scientist in the Winning of the American West,* by William Goetzmann
1968   *The Ideological Origins of the American Revolution,* by Bernard Bailyn
1969   *Origins of the Fifth Amendment,* by Leonard W. Levy
1970   *Present at the Creation: My Years in the State Department,* by Dean Acheson

1971   *Roosevelt, the Soldier of Freedom,* by James MacGregor Burns

1972   *Neither Black nor White,* by Carl N. Degler

1973   *People of Paradox: An Inquiry Concerning the Origins of American Civilization,* by Michael Kammen

1974   *The Americans: The Democratic Experience,* by Daniel J. Boorstin

1975   *Jefferson and His Times: Vols. I–V,* by Dumas Malone

1976   *Lamy of Santa Fe,* by Paul Horgan

1977   *The Impending Crisis,* by David M. Potter (published posthumously, the manuscript was completed by Don E. Fehrenbacher)

1978   *The Visible Hand: The Managerial Revolution in American Business,* by Alfred D. Chandler Jr.

1979   *The Dred Scott Case,* by Don E. Fehrenbacher

1980   *Been in the Storm So Long: The Aftermath of Slavery,* by Leon F. Litwack

1981   *American Education: The National Experience, 1783–1876,* by Lawrence A. Cremin

1982   *Mary Chesnut's Civil War,* edited by C. Vann Woodward

1983   *The Transformation of Virginia, 1740–1790,* by Rhys Isaac

1984   No award

1985   *Prophets of Regulation,* by Thomas K. McCraw

1986   *...the Heavens and the Earth: A Political History of the Space Age,* by Walter A. McDougall

1987   *Voyagers to the West: A Passage in the Peopling of America on the Eve of the Revolution,* by Bernard Bailyn

1988   *The Launching of Modern American Science 1846–1876,* by Robert V. Bruce

1989   *Parting the Waters: America in the King Years 1954–63,* by Taylor Branch, and *Battle Cry of Freedom: The Civil War Era,* by James M. McPherson

1990   *In Our Image: America's Empire in the Philippines,* by Stanley Karnow

1991   *A Midwife's Tale: The Life of Martha Ballard, Based on Her Diary 1785-1812,* by Laurel Thatcher Ulrich

Biography

1917   *Julia Ward Howe,* by Laura E. Richards, Maude Howe Elliott, and Florence Howe Hall

1918   *Benjamin Franklin, Self-Revealed,* by William Cabell Bruce

1919   *The Education of Henry Adams,* by Henry Adams

1920   *The Life of John Marshall,* 4 vols., by Albert J. Beveridge

1921   *The Americanization of Edward Bok,* by Edward Bok

1922   *A Daughter of the Middle Border,* by Hamlin Garland

1923 *The Life and Letters of Walter H. Page,* by Burton J. Hendrick
1924 *From Immigrant to Inventor,* by Michael Idvorsky Pupin
1925 *Barrett Wendell and His Letters,* by M. A. DeWolfe Howe
1926 *The Life of Sir William Osler,* 2 vols., by Harvey Cushing
1927 *Whitman,* by Emory Holloway
1928 *The American Orchestra and Theodore Thomas,* by Charles Edward Russell
1929 *The Training of an American: The Earlier Life and Letters of Walter H. Page,* by Burton J. Hendrick
1930 *The Raven,* by Marquis James
1931 *Charles W. Eliot,* by Henry James
1932 *Theodore Roosevelt,* by Henry F. Pringle
1933 *Grover Cleveland,* by Allan Nevins
1934 *John Hay,* by Tyler Dennett
1935 *R. E. Lee,* by Douglas S. Freeman
1936 *The Thought and Character of William James,* by Ralph Barton Perry
1937 *Hamilton Fish,* by Allan Nevins
1938 *Pedlar's Progress,* by Odell Shepard, and *Andrew Jackson,* 2 vols., by Marquis James
1939 *Benjamin Franklin,* by Carl Van Doren
1940 *Woodrow Wilson, Life and Letters, Vols. VII and VIII,* by Ray Stannard Baker
1941 *Jonathan Edwards,* by Ola Elizabeth Winslow
1942 *Crusader in Crinoline,* by Forrest Wilson
1943 *Admiral of the Ocean Sea,* by Samuel Eliot Morison
1944 *The American Leonardo: The Life of Samuel F. B. Morse,* by Carleton Mabee
1945 *George Bancroft: Brahmin Rebel,* by Russel B. Nye
1946 *Son of the Wilderness,* by Linnie Marsh Wolfe
1947 *The Autobiography of William Allen White*
1948 *Forgotten First Citizen: John Bigelow,* by Margaret Clapp
1949 *Roosevelt and Hopkins,* by Robert E. Sherwood
1950 *John Quincy Adams and the Foundations of American Foreign Policy,* by Samuel Flagg Bemis
1951 *John C. Calhoun: American Portrait,* by Margaret Louise Coit
1952 *Charles Evans Hughes,* by Merlo J. Pusey
1953 *Edmund Pendleton 1721–1803,* by David J. Mays
1954 *The Spirit of St. Louis,* by Charles A. Lindbergh
1955 *The Taft Story,* by William S. White
1956 *Benjamin Henry Latrobe,* by Talbot Faulkner Hamlin
1957 *Profiles in Courage,* by John F. Kennedy

1958 *George Washington, Volumes I–VI*, by Douglas Southall Freeman, and *Volume VII*, by John Alexander Carroll and Mary Wells Ashworth

1959 *Woodrow Wilson, American Prophet*, by Arthur Walworth

1960 *John Paul Jones*, by Samuel Eliot Morison

1961 *Charles Sumner and the Coming of the Civil War*, by David Donald

1962 No award

1963 *Henry James*, by Leon Edel

1964 *John Keats*, by Walter Jackson Bate

1965 *Henry Adams*, 3 vols., by Ernest Samuels

1966 *A Thousand Days*, by Arthur M. Schlesinger Jr.

1967 *Mr. Clemens and Mark Twain*, by Justin Kaplan

1968 *Memoirs*, by George F. Kennan

1969 *The Man from New York: John Quinn and His Friends*, by Benjamin Lawrence Reid

1970 *Huey Long*, by T. Harry Williams

1971 *Robert Frost: The Years of Triumph, 1915–1938*, by Lawrance Thompson

1972 *Eleanor and Franklin*, by Joseph P. Lash

1973 *Luce and His Empire*, by W. A. Swanberg

1974 *O'Neill, Son and Artist*, by Louis Sheaffer

1975 *The Power Broker: Robert Moses and the Fall of New York*, by Robert Caro

1976 *Edith Wharton: A Biography*, by R. W. B. Lewis

1977 *A Prince of Our Disorder: The Life of T. E. Lawrence*, by John E. Mack

1978 *Samuel Johnson*, by Walter Jackson Bate

1979 *Days of Sorrow and Pain: Leo Baeck and the Berlin Jews*, by Leonard Baker

1980 *The Rise of Theodore Roosevelt*, by Edmund Morris

1981 *Peter the Great: His Life and World*, by Robert K. Massie

1982 *Grant*, by William S. McFeely

1983 *Growing Up*, by Russell Baker

1984 *Booker T. Washington: The Wizard of Tuskegee, 1901–1915*, by Louis R. Harlan

1985 *The Life and Times of Cotton Mather*, by Kenneth Silverman

1986 *Louise Bogan: A Portrait*, by Elizabeth Frank

1987 *Bearing the Cross: Martin Luther King Jr. and the Southern Christian Leadership Conference*, by David J. Garrow

1988 *Look Homeward: A Life of Thomas Wolfe*, by David Herbert Donald

1989 *Oscar Wilde*, by Richard Ellmann

1990 *Machiavelli in Hell*, by Sebastian de Grazia
1991 *Jackson Pollock: An American Saga*, by Steven Naifeh and Gregory White Smith

General Nonfiction

1962 *The Making of the President 1960*, by Theodore H. White
1963 *The Guns of August*, by Barbara W. Tuchman
1964 *Anti-Intellectualism in American Life*, by Richard Hofstadter
1965 *O Strange New World*, by Howard Mumford Jones
1966 *Wandering Through Winter*, by Edwin Way Teale
1967 *The Problem of Slavery in Western Culture*, by David Brion Davis
1968 *Rousseau and Revolution*, by Will and Ariel Durant
1969 *So Human an Animal*, by René Jules Dubos, and *Armies of the Night*, by Norman Mailer
1970 *Gandhi's Truth*, by Erik H. Erikson
1971 *The Rising Sun*, by John Toland
1972 *Stilwell and the American Experience in China, 1911–1945*, by Barbara W. Tuchman
1973 *Children of Crisis, Vols. II and III*, by Robert Coles, and *Fire in the Lake: The Vietnamese and the Americans in Vietnam*, by Frances FitzGerald
1974 *The Denial of Death*, by Ernest Becker
1975 *Pilgrim at Tinker Creek*, by Annie Dillard
1976 *Why Survive? Being Old in America*, by Robert N. Butler
1977 *Beautiful Swimmers*, by William W. Warner
1978 *The Dragons of Eden*, by Carl Sagan
1979 *On Human Nature*, by Edward O. Wilson
1980 *Gödel, Escher, Bach: An Eternal Golden Braid*, by Douglas R. Hofstadter
1981 *Fin-de-Siècle Vienna: Politics and Culture*, by Carl E. Schorske
1982 *The Soul of a New Machine*, by Tracy Kidder
1983 *Is There No Place on Earth for Me?* by Susan Sheehan
1984 *The Social Transformation of American Medicine*, by Paul Starr
1985 *The Good War: An Oral History of World War Two*, by Studs Terkel
1986 *Move Your Shadow: South Africa, Black and White*, by Joseph Lelyveld, and *Common Ground: A Turbulent Decade in the Lives of Three American Families*, by J. Anthony Lukas
1987 *Arab and Jew: Wounded Spirits in a Promised Land*, by David K. Shipler
1988 *The Making of the Atomic Bomb*, by Richard Rhodes
1989 *A Bright Shining Lie: John Paul Vann and America in Vietnam*, by Neil Sheehan

1990 *And Their Children After Them,* by Dale Maharidge and Michael Williamson

1991 *The Ants,* by Bert Holldobler and Edward O. Wilson

Poetry

1922 *Collected Poems,* by Edwin Arlington Robinson

1923 *The Ballad of the Harp-Weaver; A Few Figs from Thistles;* Eight Sonnets in *American Poetry, 1922, A Miscellany,* by Edna St. Vincent Millay

1924 *New Hampshire: A Poem with Notes and Grace Notes,* by Robert Frost

1925 *The Man Who Died Twice,* by Edwin Arlington Robinson

1926 *What's O'Clock,* by Amy Lowell

1927 *Fiddler's Farewell,* by Leonora Speyer

1928 *Tristram,* by Edwin Arlington Robinson

1929 *John Brown's Body,* by Stephen Vincent Benét

1930 *Selected Poems,* by Conrad Aiken

1931 *Collected Poems,* by Robert Frost

1932 *The Flowering Stone,* by George Dillon

1933 *Conquistador,* by Archibald MacLeish

1934 *Collected Verse,* by Robert Hillyer

1935 *Bright Ambush,* by Audrey Wurdemann

1936 *Strange Holiness,* by Robert P. Tristram Coffin

1937 *A Further Range,* by Robert Frost

1938 *Cold Morning Sky,* by Marya Zaturenska

1939 *Selected Poems,* by John Gould Fletcher

1940 *Collected Poems,* by Mark Van Doren

1941 *Sunderland Capture,* by Leonard Bacon

1942 *The Dust Which Is God,* by William Rose Benét

1943 *A Witness Tree,* by Robert Frost

1944 *Western Star,* by Stephen Vincent Benét

1945 *V-Letter and Other Poems,* by Karl Shapiro

1946 No award

1947 *Lord Weary's Castle,* by Robert Lowell

1948 *The Age of Anxiety,* by W. H. Auden

1949 *Terror and Decorum,* by Peter Viereck

1950 *Annie Allen,* by Gwendolyn Brooks

1951 *Complete Poems,* by Carl Sandburg

1952 *Collected Poems,* by Marianne Moore

1953 *Collected Poems 1917–1952,* by Archibald MacLeish

1954 *The Waking,* by Theodore Roethke

1955 *Collected Poems,* by Wallace Stevens

1956 *Poems—North & South*, by Elizabeth Bishop
1957 *Things of This World*, by Richard Wilbur
1958 *Promises: Poems 1954–1956*, by Robert Penn Warren
1959 *Selected Poems 1928–1958*, by Stanley Kunitz
1960 *Heart's Needle*, by W. D. Snodgrass
1961 *Times Three: Selected Verse from Three Decades*, by Phyllis McGinley
1962 *Poems*, by Alan Dugan
1963 *Pictures from Breughel*, by William Carlos Williams
1964 *At the End of the Open Road*, by Louis Simpson
1965 *77 Dream Songs*, by John Berryman
1966 *Selected Poems*, by Richard Eberhart
1967 *Live or Die*, by Anne Sexton
1968 *The Hard Hours*, by Anthony Hecht
1969 *Of Being Numerous*, by George Oppen
1970 *Untitled Subjects*, by Richard Howard
1971 *The Carrier of Ladders*, by William S. Merwin
1972 *Collected Poems*, by James Wright
1973 *Up Country*, by Maxine Kumin
1974 *The Dolphin*, by Robert Lowell
1975 *Turtle Island*, by Gary Snyder
1976 *Self-Portrait in a Convex Mirror*, by John Ashbery
1977 *Divine Comedies*, by James Merrill
1978 *Collected Poems*, by Howard Nemerov
1979 *Now and Then*, by Robert Penn Warren
1980 *Selected Poems*, by Donald Rodney Justice
1981 *The Morning of the Poem*, by James Schuyler
1982 *The Collected Poems*, by Sylvia Plath
1983 *Selected Poems*, by Galway Kinnell
1984 *American Primitive*, by Mary Oliver
1985 *Yin*, by Carolyn Kizer
1986 *The Flying Change*, by Henry Taylor
1987 *Thomas and Beulah*, by Rita Dove
1988 *Partial Accounts: New and Selected Poems*, by William Meredith
1989 *New and Collected Poems*, by Richard Wilbur
1990 *The World Doesn't End*, by Charles Simic
1991 *Near Changes*, by Mona Van Duyn

Music

1943 "Secular Cantata No. 2," by William Schuman
1944 "Symphony No. 4, Opus 34," by Howard Hanson
1945 "Appalachian Spring," by Aaron Copland
1946 "The Canticle of the Sun," by Leo Sowerby

1947 "Symphony No. 3," by Charles Ives
1948 "Symphony No. 3," by Walter Piston
1949 "Louisiana Story," by Virgil Thomson
1950 "The Consul," by Gian Carlo Menotti
1951 "Giants in the Earth," by Douglas S. Moore
1952 "Symphony Concertante," by Gail Kubik
1953 No award
1954 "Concerto for Two Pianos and Orchestra," by Quincy Porter
1955 "The Saint of Bleecker Street," by Gian Carlo Menotti
1956 "Symphony No. 3," by Ernst Toch
1957 "Meditations on Ecclesiastes," by Norman Dello Joio
1958 "Vanessa," by Samuel Barber and Gian Carlo Menotti
1959 "Concerto for Piano and Orchestra," by John LaMontaine
1960 "Second String Quartet," by Elliott Carter
1961 "Symphony No. 7," by Walter Piston
1962 "The Crucible," by Robert Ward and Bernard Stambler
1963 "Piano Concerto No. 1," by Samuel Barber
1964 No award
1965 No award
1966 "Variations for Orchestra," by Leslie Bassett
1967 "Quartet No. 3," by Leon Kirchner
1968 "Echoes of Time and the River," by George Crumb
1969 "String Quartet," by Karel Husa
1970 "Time's Encomium" by Charles Wuorinen
1971 "Synchronisms No. 6 for Piano and Electronic Sound," by Mario Davidovsky
1972 "Windows," by Jacob Druckman
1973 "String Quartet No. 3," by Elliott Carter
1974 "Notturno," by Donald Martino
1975 "From the Diary of Virginia Woolf," by Dominick Argento
1976 "Air Music," by Ned Rorem
1977 "Visions of Terror and Wonder," by Richard Wernick
1978 "Déjà Vu for Percussion Quartet and Orchestra," by Michael Colgrass
1979 "Aftertones of Infinity," by Joseph Schwantner
1980 "In Memory of a Summer Day," by David Del Tredici
1981 No award
1982 "Concerto for Orchestra," by Roger Sessions
1983 "Symphony No. 1 (Three Movements for Orchestra)," by Ellen Taaffee Zwilich
1984 "Canti del Sole" for Tenor and Orchestra, by Bernard Rands
1985 "Symphony, RiverRun," by Stephen Albert
1986 "Wind Quintet IV," by George Perle

1987 "The Flight into Egypt," by John Harbison
1988 "12 New Etudes for Piano," by William Bolcom
1989 "Whispers out of Time," by Roger Reynolds
1990 "Duplicates: A Concerto for Two Pianos and Orchestra," by Mel Powell
1991 "Symphony," by Shulamit Ran

Special Citations

1944 *Oklahoma!* by Richard Rodgers and Oscar Hammerstein II
1957 Kenneth Robert, historian
1960 *The Armada*, by Garrett Mattingly
1961 *The American Heritage Picture History of the Civil War*
1973 *George Washington, Vols. I–IV*, by James Thomas Flexner
1974 Roger Sessions, composer
1976 Scott Joplin, composer
1977 Alex Haley, author
1978 E. B. White, essayist and author
1982 Milton Babbitt, composer
1984 Theodor Seuss Geisel (Dr. Seuss), author
1985 William Schuman, composer

JOURNALISM

Meritorious Public Service

1917 No award
1918 *New York Times*, for publishing many official reports, documents, and speeches by European statesmen on the progress and conduct of World War I.
1919 *Milwaukee Journal*, for its campaign for Americanism.
1920 No award
1921 *Boston Post*, for exposing the operations of Charles Ponzi in a series of articles that led to his arrest.
1922 *New York World*, for exposing the operations of the Ku Klux Klan.
1923 *Commercial Appeal*, Memphis, Tenn., for news and editorial cartoons involving the Ku Klux Klan.
1924 *New York World*, for exposing Florida peonage abuse.
1925 No award
1926 *Columbus* (Ga.) *Enquirer Sun*, for its crusades against the Ku Klux Klan, lynching, corrupt public officials, and a law barring the teaching of evolution.

1927 *Canton* (Ohio) *Daily News*, for its fight against collusion between city officials and criminal elements, which led to assassination of the paper's editor, Don R. Mellett.

1928 *Indianapolis Times*, for exposing political corruption in Indiana.

1929 *New York Evening World*, for its various campaigns to correct abuses in the administration of justice.

1930 No award

1931 *Atlanta Constitution*, for exposing municipal graft.

1932 *Indianapolis News*, for its campaign to eliminate waste from city management and reduce the tax levy.

1933 *New York World-Telegram*, for articles on veterans' relief, real estate bond abuses, lottery schemes, and the municipal write-in campaign for Joseph V. McKee.

1934 *Medford* (Ore.) *Mail-Tribune*, for its campaign against unscrupulous politicians in Oregon's Jackson County.

1935 *Sacramento Bee*, for its campaign against political influence in the naming of federal judges in Nevada.

1936 *Cedar Rapids* (Iowa) *Gazette*, for its crusade against corruption and poor government in Iowa.

1937 *St. Louis Post-Dispatch*, for exposing fraudulent voter registration in St. Louis.

1938 *Bismarck* (N.D.) *Tribune*, for news reports and editorials titled "Self Help in the Dust Bowl."

1939 *Miami Daily News*, for its campaign for the recall of the Miami City Commission.

1940 *Waterbury* (Conn.) *Republican-American*, for its campaign exposing municipal graft.

1941 *St. Louis Post-Dispatch*, for its campaign against smoke polluting the city's air.

1942 *Los Angeles Times*, for its campaign for press freedom.

1943 *Omaha World-Herald*, for its statewide campaign to collect scrap metal for the war effort.

1944 *New York Times*, for its survey of the teaching of American history.

1945 *Detroit Free Press*, for its investigation of legislative graft and corruption at Lansing, Mich.

1946 *Scranton* (Pa.) *Times*, for its investigation of judicial practices in a U.S. District Court, resulting in removal of a district judge and indictment of others.

1947 *Baltimore Sun*, for articles by Howard M. Norton on unemployment compensation in Maryland, resulting in criminal convictions of ninety-three persons.

1948   *St. Louis Post-Dispatch*, for its coverage of the mine disaster in Centralia, Ill., and its follow-up resulting in reforms in mine safety laws and regulations.

1949   *Nebraska State Journal*, for its campaign to establish the Nebraska presidential primary.

1950   *Chicago Daily News* and *St. Louis Post-Dispatch*, for the work of George Thiem and Roy J. Harris, respectively, in exposing thirty-seven Illinois newspapermen on the state payroll.

1951   *Miami Herald* and *Brooklyn Eagle*, for crime reporting.

1952   *St. Louis Post-Dispatch*, for exposing corruption in the Internal Revenue Bureau and other governmental agencies.

1953   *Whiteville News Reporter* and *Tabor City Tribune*, two North Carolina weeklies, for their campaigns against the Ku Klux Klan, resulting in more than one hundred arrests.

1954   *Newsday*, for exposing race track scandals and labor racketeering, which led to imprisonment of New York labor racketeer William C. DeKoning Sr.

1955   *Columbus* (Ga.) *Ledger* and *Sunday Ledger-Enquirer*, for campaigning against widespread corruption in neighboring Phenix City, Ala.

1956   *Watsonville* (Calif.) *Register-Pajaronian*, for exposing corruption in public office.

1957   *Chicago Daily News*, for exposing a $2.5 million fraud resulting in the conviction of the Illinois state auditor and reorganization of state procedures.

1958   *Arkansas Gazette*, for its objective news coverage and calming editorial leadership during the Little Rock school integration crisis.

1959   *Observer-Dispatch*, Utica, N.Y., and *Utica Daily Press*, for their campaign against corruption, gambling, and vice in Utica, leading to sweeping civic reforms.

1960   *Los Angeles Times*, for its editorial campaign and reporting by Gene Sherman on the flow of illegal drugs from Mexico into border states.

1961   *Amarillo* (Tex.) *Globe Times*, for exposing lax local law enforcement, leading to election of reform candidates.

1962   *News-Herald*, Panama City, Fla., for its campaign against corruption in local government.

1963   *Chicago Daily News*, for calling attention to the issue of birth-control services in public health programs.

1964   *St. Petersburg* (Fla.) *Times*, for disclosing widespread illegal acts involving the Florida Turnpike Authority, leading to reorganization of the state's highway program.

1965   *Hutchinson* (Kan.) *News*, for its campaign for more equitable reapportionment of the Kansas legislature.

1966   *Boston Globe*, for its campaign to prevent the confirmation of Francis X. Morrissey as a federal judge.

1967   *Courier-Journal*, Louisville, Ky., for its campaign to control the strip mine industry, and *Milwaukee Journal*, for its fight for stronger water-pollution laws.

1968   *Press-Enterprise*, Riverside, Calif., for exposing court corruption in the handling of the property and estates of an Indian tribe in California.

1969   *Los Angeles Times*, for exposing wrongdoing by city officials, leading to ousters and widespread reforms.

1970   *Newsday*, for exposing secret land deals in eastern Long Island, leading to a series of convictions, firings, and resignations of elected and appointed public officials.

1971   *Winston-Salem* (N.C.) *Journal and Sentinel*, for coverage of environmental concerns, as exemplified by a campaign to block a North Carolina strip mining operation.

1972   *New York Times*, for publishing the Pentagon Papers.

1973   *Washington Post*, for its Watergate investigation.

1974   *Newsday*, for a report on illicit narcotics traffic.

1975   *Boston Globe*, for news coverage of the city's school desegregation crisis.

1976   *Anchorage Daily News*, for disclosing the influence of the Teamsters Union on Alaska's economy and politics.

1977   *Lufkin* (Tex.) *Daily News*, for an obituary of a local man who died in Marine boot camp, leading to an investigation and reform in Marine Corps training.

1978   *Philadelphia Inquirer*, for disclosing abuses of power by Philadelphia police.

1979   *Point Reyes* (Calif.) *Light*, for its probe of Synanon, the controversial drug-rehabilitation center.

1980   Gannett News Service, for exposing financial mismanagement of contributions by the Pauline Fathers.

1981   *Charlotte* (N.C.) *Observer*, for its series on "brown lung" disease caused by cotton processing plants.

1982   *Detroit News*, for exposing the U.S. Navy's cover-up of circumstances surrounding deaths of seamen aboard ship.

1983   *Clarion-Ledger*, Jackson, Miss., for its campaign against inadequacies in Mississippi's public schools.

1984   *Los Angeles Times*, for a series on the Latino community.

1985   *Fort Worth* (Tex.) *Star-Telegram*, for reporting by Mark J. Thompson on a design flaw in Bell helicopters, blamed for the deaths of 250 U.S. servicemen.

1986 *Denver Post*, for disclosing inflated estimates of organizations raising money to find missing children.

1987 *Pittsburgh Press*, for exposing threats to airline passenger safety caused by inadequate medical screening of pilots by the Federal Aviation Administration.

1988 *Charlotte* (N.C.) *Observer*, for reporting by Charles Shepard on the PTL ministry of Jim Bakker.

1989 *Anchorage Daily News*, for reporting on the high rates of alcoholism and suicide among Native American Alaskans.

1990 *Philadelphia Inquirer*, for reporting by Gilbert M. Gaul on the American blood industry, and the *Washington* (N.C.) *Daily News*, for disclosing contamination of the local water supply.

1991 *Des Moines Register*, for reporting by Jane Schorer on rape and its aftermath.

Reporting

1917 Herbert Bayard Swope, *New York World*, for articles titled "Inside the German Empire."

1918 Harold A. Littledale, *New York Evening Post*, for exposing abuses in the New Jersey State Prison.

1919 No award

1920 John J. Leary Jr., *New York World*, for reporting on the national coal strike.

1921 Louis Seibold, *New York World*, for an interview with President Wilson.

1922 Kirke L. Simpson, Associated Press, for reporting on the burial of "the Unknown Soldier."

1923 Alva Johnston, *New York Times*, for reports on a scientific convention held in Cambridge, Mass.

1924 Magner White, *San Diego Sun*, for reporting on a solar eclipse.

1925 James Mulroy and Alvin Goldstein, *Chicago Daily News*, for reports that helped solve the murder of Robert Franks Jr. and leading to the conviction of Nathan F. Leopold and Richard Loeb.

1926 William B. Miller, *Courier-Journal*, Louisville, Ky., for reports on the trapping of a man in Sand Cave, Ky.

1927 John T. Rogers, *St. Louis Post-Disptach*, for reports leading to impeachment of a U.S. District Court judge.

1928 No award

1929 Paul Y. Anderson, *St. Louis Post-Dispatch*, for revealing disposition of Liberty Bonds purchased by Continental Trading Co. in connection with naval oil leases.

1930   Russell D. Owen, *New York Times*, for reports on the Byrd Antarctic expedition.

1931   A. B. MacDonald, *Kansas City Star*, for coverage of a murder in Amarillo, Texas.

1932   W. C. Richards, D. D. Martin, J. S. Pooler, F. D. Webb and J. N. W. Sloan, *Detroit Free Press*, for their account of an American Legion parade.

1933   Francis A. Jamieson, Associated Press, for reporting on the kidnapping of the infant son of Charles Lindbergh.

1934   Royce Brier, *San Francisco Chronicle*, for coverage of the lynching of two kidnappers of a merchant's son.

1935   William H. Taylor, *New York Herald Tribune*, for reports on international yacht races.

1936   Lauren D. Lyman, *New York Times*, for disclosing that the Charles Lindbergh family was moving to England.

1937   John J. O'Neill, *New York Herald Tribune;* William L. Laurence, *New York Times;* Howard W. Blakeslee, Associated Press; Gobind Behari Lal, Universal Service; and David Dietz, Scripps-Howard Newspapers, for coverage of science at the tercentenary of Harvard University.

1938   Raymond Sprigle, *Pittsburgh Post-Gazette*, for exposing one-time membership of Justice Hugo L. Black in the Ku Klux Klan.

1939   Thomas L. Stokes, Scripps-Howard Newspapers, for reports on alleged intimidation of workers for the Works Progress Administration in Pennsylvania and Kentucky.

1940   S. Burton Heath, *New York World-Telegram*, for exposing frauds perpetrated by a federal judge.

1941   Westbrook Pegler, *New York World-Telegram*, for reporting on scandals in organized labor.

1942   Stanton Delaplane, *San Francisco Chronicle*, for coverage of a movement by several California and Oregon counties to secede and form a new state.

1943   George Weller, *Chicago Daily News*, for reporting on an appendectomy performed on a submarine under enemy waters.

1944   Paul Schoenstein, *New York Journal-American*, for reports that helped save the life of a girl needing penicillin.

1945   Jack S. McDowell, *San Francisco Call-Bulletin*, for a campaign encouraging blood donations.

1946   William L. Laurence, *New York Times*, for his eyewitness account of the atomic-bombing of Nagasaki.

1947   Frederick Woltman, *New York World-Telegram*, for reports on the infiltration of Communism in the United States.

1948   George E. Goodwin, *Atlanta Journal,* for reporting on county voting fraud.

1949   Malcolm Johnson, *New York Sun,* for a series called "Crime on the Waterfront."

1950   Meyer Berger, *New York Times,* for reports on a mass murder in Camden, N.J.

1951   Edward S. Montgomery, *San Francisco Examiner,* for reports on tax frauds.

1952   George de Carvalho, *San Francisco Chronicle,* for reports on extortion of money from Chinese-Americans.

(NOTE: The following year, this category was split into two new categories—Local General Reporting and Local Specialized Reporting.)

Local General Reporting

1953   Staff, *Journal-Bulletin,* Providence, R.I., for coverage of a bank robbery.

1954   Staff, *Vicksburg* (Miss.) *Sunday Post-Herald,* for coverage of a tornado.

1955   Caro Brown, *Alice* (Tex.) *Daily Echo,* for coverage of a successful attack on one-man political rule in a neighboring county.

1956   Lee Hills, *Detroit Free Press,* for reporting on United Auto Workers' negotiations with Ford and General Motors.

1957   Staff, *Salt Lake Tribune,* for coverage of the collision of two airliners over the Grand Canyon.

1958   Staff, *Fargo* (N.D.) *Forum,* for coverage of a tornado.

1959   Mary Lou Werner, *Washington Evening Star,* for coverage of the racial integration crisis in Virginia.

1960   Jack Nelson, *Atlanta Constitution,* for article on Georgia mental institutions.

1961   Sanche de Gramont, *New York Herald Tribune,* for an article on the death of Leonard Warren on the stage of the Metropolitan Opera.

1962   Robert D. Mullins, *The Deseret News,* Salt Lake City, for reports on a murder-kidnapping at Dead Horse Point, Utah.

1963   Sylvan Fox, Anthony Shannon, and William Longgood, *New York World-Telegram and Sun,* for their reporting on an airplane crash in Jamaica Bay.

1964   Norman C. Miller Jr., *Wall Street Journal,* for his account of a vegetable oil swindle in New Jersey.

1965   Melvin H. Ruder, *Hungry Horse News,* Columbia Falls, Mont., for coverage of a flood disaster.

1966   Staff, *Los Angeles Times*, for Watts riots coverage.

1967   Robert V. Cox, *Public Opinion*, Chambersburg, Pa., for reports on the manhunt for a deranged sniper.

1968   Staff, *Detroit Free Press*, for Detroit riot coverage.

1969   John Fetterman, *Louisville Times* and *Courier-Journal*, for a story on the burial of a soldier killed in Vietnam.

1970   Thomas Fitzpatrick, *Chicago Sun-Times*, for a report on the violence of youthful radicals in Chicago.

1971   Staff, *Beacon Journal*, Akron, Ohio, for coverage of the shootings at Kent State University.

1972   Richard Cooper and John Machacek, *Times-Union*, Rochester, N.Y., for coverage of the Attica prison riot.

1973   Staff, *Chicago Tribune*, for uncovering violations of voting procedures in a primary election.

1974   Arthur M. Petacque and Hugh F. Hough, *Chicago Sun-Times*, for revealing evidence leading to renewed efforts to solve the 1966 murder of Valerie Percy.

1975   Staff, *Xenia* (Ohio) *Daily Gazette*, for coverage of a tornado.

1976   Gene Miller, *Miami Herald*, for reporting that cleared two men wrongfully convicted of murdering two gas station employees.

1977   Margo Huston, *Milwaukee Journal*, for reports on the elderly and the process of aging.

1978   Richard Whitt, *Courier-Journal*, Louisville, Ky., for coverage of the Beverly Hills Supper Club fire.

1979   Staff, *San Diego Tribune*, for reporting on the collision of a jetliner and a small plane over the city.

1980   Staff, *Philadelphia Inquirer*, for coverage of the Three Mile Island nuclear accident.

1981   Staff, *Daily News*, Longview, Wash., for coverage of the eruption of Mount St. Helens.

1982   Staff, *Kansas City Star* and *Kansas City Times*, for reports on the Hyatt Regency Hotel skywalk collapse.

1983   Staff, *News-Sentinel*, Fort Wayne, Ind., for coverage of a flood that ravaged the city.

1984   Staff, *Newsday*, for coverage of the Baby Jane Doe case and its social and political implications.

1985   Thomas Turcol, *Virginian-Pilot* and *Ledger-Star*, Norfolk, Va., for exposing the corruption of a local economic development official.

1986   Edna Buchanan, *Miami Herald*, for police reporting.

1987   Staff, *Beacon Journal*, Akron, Ohio, for coverage of the attempted takeover of Goodyear Tire and Rubber Co. by a European financier.

1988   Staff, *Alabama Journal*, Montgomery, Ala., for reports on Alabama's unusually high infant-mortality rate, and staff, *Lawrence* (Mass.) *Eagle-Tribune*, for reports on the Massachusetts prison furlough system.

1989   Staff, *Courier Journal*, Louisville, Ky., for coverage of a bus crash that claimed twenty-seven lives.

1990   Staff, *San Jose* (Calif.) *Mercury News*, for coverage of the October 17, 1989, Bay Area earthquake and its aftermath.

1991   Staff, *Miami Herald*, for coverage of the rise and fall of local cult leader Yahweh Ben Yahweh.

(Note: The title of this category, Local General Reporting, was changed this year to Spot News Reporting.)

Local Specialized Reporting

1953   Edward J. Mowery, *New York World-Telegram*, for reports that vindicated an unjustly convicted man.

1954   Alvin Scott McCoy, *Kansas City Star*, for reports that led to the Republican national chairman's resignation.

1955   Roland Kenneth Towery, *Cuero* (Tex.) *Record*, for exposing a scandal in the Veterans' Land Program in Texas.

1956   Arthur Daley, *New York Times*, for sports reporting.

1957   Wallace Turner and William Lambert, *Oregonian*, for exposing vice and corruption involving Portland city officials and organized labor.

1958   George Beveridge, *Washington Evening Star*, for a series titled "Metro, City of Tomorrow."

1959   John Harold Brislin, *Scranton* (Pa.) *Tribune* and the *Scrantonian*, for his campaign to halt labor violence.

1960   Miriam Ottenberg, *Washington Evening Star*, for exposing a used-car racket.

1961   Edgar May, *Buffalo* (N.Y.) *Evening News*, for reporting on New York State's public welfare services.

1962   George Bliss, *Chicago Tribune*, for uncovering scandals in Chicago's Metropolitan Sanitary District.

1963   Oscar Griffin Jr., *Pecos* (Tex.) *Independent and Enterprise*, for exposing the Billie Sol Estes scandal.

1964   James Magee, Albert Gaudiosi, and Frederick Meyer, *Philadelphia Bulletin*, for exposing a numbers racket.

1965   Gene Goltz, *Houston Post*, for exposing government corruption in Pasadena, Texas.

1966   John Anthony Frasca, *Tampa* (Fla.) *Tribune*, for reports that freed an innocent man accused of two robberies.

1967   Gene Miller, *Miami Herald*, for reporting that helped free a man in Florida and a woman in Louisiana, who both were wrongfully convicted of murder (in separate trials).

1968   J. Anthony Lukas, *New York Times*, for reporting on the Linda Fitzpatrick murder case.

1969   Albert Delugach and Denny Walsh, *St. Louis Globe-Democrat*, for their campaign against fraud and abuse of power within the St. Louis Steamfitters Union.

1970   Harold Eugene Martin, *Montgomery Advertiser* and *Alabama Journal*, for exposing a commercial scheme using state prisoners for drug experimentation.

1971   William Jones, *Chicago Tribune*, for exposing collusion between police and private ambulance companies.

1972   Timothy Leland, Gerard O'Neill, Stephen Kurkjian, and Ann DeSantis, *Boston Globe*, for exposing widespread corruption in Somerville, Mass.

1973   Staff, *Sun* newspapers, Omaha, Neb., for revealing the large financial resources of Boys Town, Neb.

1974   William Sherman, *New York Daily News*, for exposing abuse of the New York Medicaid program.

1975   Staff, *Indianapolis Star*, for disclosing local police corruption and lax law enforcement.

1976   Staff, *Chicago Tribune*, for uncovering abuses in federal housing programs in Chicago and exposing bad conditions at two private Chicago hospitals.

1977   Acel Moore and Wendell Rawls Jr., *Philadelphia Inquirer*, for reports on conditions at a mental hospital.

1978   Anthony R. Dolan, *Advocate*, Stamford, Conn., for a series on municipal corruption.

1979   Gilbert M. Gaul and Elliot G. Jaspin, *Pottsville* (Pa.) *Republican*, for reports on the destruction of the Blue Coal Co. by men with ties to organized crime.

1980   Stephen Kurkjian, Alexander Hawes Jr., Nils Bruzelius, and Joan Vennochi, *Boston Globe*, for exposing mismanagement in Boston's transit system.

1981   Clark Hallas and Robert B. Lowe, *Arizona Daily Star*, Tucson, Ariz., for their investigation of the University of Arizona athletic department.

1982   Paul Henderson, *Seattle Times*, for reports helping to clear a man who had been wrongly convicted of rape.

1983   Loretta Tofani, *Washington Post*, for stories exposing inhumane conditions in a Maryland detention center.

1984   Staff, *Boston Globe*, for a series on race relations in Boston.

1985 Randall Savage and Jackie Crosby, *Macon* (Ga.) *Telegraph and News*, for reporting on academics and athletics at the University of Georgia and Georgia Tech.
1986 Andrew Schneider and Mary Pat Flaherty, *Pittsburgh Press*, for reports on violations and failures in the nation's organ transplant system.
1987 Alex S. Jones, *New York Times*, for reports on the Bingham newspaper family feud and how it led to the sale of a media empire.
1988 Walt Bogdanich, *Wall Street Journal*, for reports on faulty testing by American medical laboratories.
1989 Edward Humes, *Orange County Register*, Santa Ana, Calif., for reporting on the military establishment in Southern California.
1990 Tamar Stieber, *Albuquerque Journal*, for reporting that linked a rare blood disorder to the drug L-Tryptophan.
1991 Natalie Angier, *New York Times*, for reports on a variety of scientific topics; notably, a complicated story on the (human) cell cycle.

(Note: The title of this category was changed this year to Beat Reporting.)

Correspondence

1929 Paul Scott Mowrer, *Chicago Daily News*, for coverage of the Franco-British Naval Pact and Germany's campaign for revision of the Dawes Plan.
1930 Leland Stowe, *New York Herald Tribune*, for reports on conferences on reparations and establishment of the international bank.
1931 H. R. Knickerbocker, *Philadelphia Public Ledger* and *New York Evening Post*, for reports on the Soviet Union's Five-Year Plan.
1932 Walter Duranty, *New York Times*, for Soviet Union reporting, and Charles G. Ross, *St. Louis Post-Dispatch*, for reporting on the U.S. economy.
1933 Edgar Ansel Mowrer, *Chicago Daily News*, for coverage of German political crises.
1934 Frederick T. Birchall, *New York Times*, for his correspondence from Europe.
1935 Arthur Krock, *New York Times*, for his Washington dispatches.
1936 Wilfred C. Barber, *Chicago Tribune*, for reports on the war in Ethiopia.
1937 Anne O'Hare McCormick, *New York Times*, for reports from Europe.

1938   Arthur Krock, *New York Times*, for an interview with President Roosevelt.

1939   Louis P. Lochner, Associated Press, for his dispatches from Berlin.

1940   Otto D. Tolischus, *New York Times*, for his dispatches from Berlin.

1941   American war correspondents, group award, for their reporting from the war zones of Europe, Asia, and Africa.

1942   Carlos P. Romulo, *Philippines Herald*, for reports on developments in the Far East.

1943   Hanson W. Baldwin, *New York Times*, for his report of his wartime tour of the South Pacific.

1944   Ernest Taylor Pyle, Scripps-Howard Newspapers, for his war correspondence.

1945   Harold V. Boyle, Associated Press, for his war correspondence.

1946   Arnaldo Cortesi, *New York Times*, for correspondence as exemplified by his reports from Argentina.

1947   Brooks Atkinson, *New York Times*, for correspondence as exemplified by his series on the Soviet Union.

Telegraphic Reporting (National)

1942   Louis Stark, *New York Times*, for labor reporting.

1943   No award

1944   Dewey L. Fleming, *Baltimore Sun*, for his 1943 work.

1945   James Reston, *New York Times*, for reports on the Dumbarton Oaks security conference.

1946   Edward A. Harris, *St. Louis Post-Dispatch*, for reporting on the Tidewater Oil story.

1947   Edward T. Folliard, *Washington Post*, for reporting on the Columbians, Inc.

National Reporting

1948   Bert Andrews, *New York Herald Tribune*, for articles titled "A State Department Security Case," and Nat S. Finney, *Minneapolis Tribune*, for reports on federal plans to impose secrecy on civilian agencies.

1949   C. P. Trussell, *New York Times*, for his 1948 work.

1950   Edwin O. Guthman, *Seattle Times*, for a series that cleared a professor of charges of being a Communist.

1951   No award

1952   Anthony Leviero, *New York Times*, for disclosing the record of conversations between President Truman and Gen. Douglas MacArthur at Wake Island in 1950.

1953 Don Whitehead, Associated Press, for a report on security to protect President-elect Eisenhower while en route from New York to Korea.

1954 Richard Wilson, Cowles Newspapers, for publication of the FBI report in the Harry Dexter White case.

1955 Anthony Lewis, *Washington Daily News*, for articles that cleared a Navy employee dismissed as a security risk.

1956 Charles L. Bartlett, *Chattanooga Times*, for disclosures leading to resignation of the secretary of the air force.

1957 James Reston, *New York Times*, for his 1956 work, as exemplified by his analysis of the impact of President Eisenhower's illness on the functioning of government.

1958 Relman Morin, Associated Press, for his account of violence in the Little Rock school integration crisis, and Clark Mollenhoff, *Des Moines Register & Tribune*, for investigatory reports on labor racketeering.

1959 Howard Van Smith, *Miami News*, for reporting on poor conditions in a Florida migrant labor camp.

1960 Vance Trimble, Scripps-Howard Newspaper Alliance, for exposing the extent of nepotism in the U.S. Congress.

1961 Edward R. Cony, *Wall Street Journal*, for analysis of a timber transaction that raised ethical questions.

1962 Nathan Caldwell and Gene Graham, *Tennessean*, Nashville, Tenn., for disclosing undercover cooperation between coal industry management and union leaders.

1963 Anthony Lewis, *New York Times*, for coverage of the U.S. Supreme Court during 1962.

1964 Merriman Smith, United Press International, for reporting on the assassination of President John F. Kennedy.

1965 Louis M. Kohlmeier, *Wall Street Journal*, for reports on the growth of the fortune of President Lyndon Johnson.

1966 Haynes Johnson, *Washington Evening Star*, for coverage of the civil rights conflict in Selma, Ala.

1967 Stanley Penn and Monroe Karmin, *Wall Street Journal*, for reporting on the connection between American crime and gambling in the Bahamas.

1968 Howard James, *Christian Science Monitor*, for a series called "Crisis in the Courts," and Nathan Kotz, *Des Moines Register* and *Minneapolis Tribune*, for reporting on unsanitary conditions in meat-packing plants.

1969 Robert Cahn, *Christian Science Monitor*, for reporting on the future of national parks.

1970   William J. Eaton, *Chicago Daily News*, for disclosures on the background of Judge Clement F. Haynesworth in connection with his U.S. Supreme Court nomination.

1971   Lucinda Franks and Thomas Powers, United Press International, for their reporting on the life and death of revolutionary Diana Oughton.

1972   Jack Anderson, syndicated columnist, for reporting on U.S. policy decision-making during the Indo-Pakistan War.

1973   Robert Boyd and Clark Hoyt, Knight Newspapers, for their disclosure of vice presidential nominee Thomas Eagleton's history of psychiatric therapy.

1974   James R. Polk, *Washington Star-News*, for disclosures in the financing of President Nixon's re-election bid, and Jack White, *Providence Journal* and *Evening Bulletin*, for disclosing Nixon's federal income tax payments.

1975   Donald L. Barlett and James B. Steele, *Philadelphia Inquirer*, for exposing the unequal application of federal tax laws.

1976   James Risser, *Des Moines Register*, for disclosing corruption in the American grain exporting trade.

1977   Walter Mears, Associated Press, for coverage of the 1976 presidential campaign.

1978   Gaylord D. Shaw, *Los Angeles Times*, for reports on unsafe structural conditions at the nation's major dams.

1979   James Risser, *Des Moines Register*, for a series on farming damage to the environment.

1980   Bette Swenson Orsini and Charles Stafford, *St. Petersburg (Fla.) Times*, for reporting on the Church of Scientology.

1981   John M. Crewdson, *New York Times*, for reports on illegal aliens and America's immigration problems.

1982   Rick Atkinson, *Kansas City Times*, for reporting on a variety of subjects.

1983   Staff, *Boston Globe*, for reporting on the nuclear arms race.

1984   John Noble Wilford, *New York Times*, for reporting on a variety of scientific topics of national import.

1985   Thomas J. Knudson, *Des Moines Register*, for reports on the dangers of farming as an occupation.

1986   Craig Flournoy and George Rodrigue, *Dallas Morning News*, for disclosing racial bias and segregation in public housing, and Arthur Howe, *Philadelphia Inquirer*, for revealing deficiencies in IRS processing of tax returns.

1987   Staff, *Miami Herald*, for reporting on the nation's Iran-Contra connection, and staff, *New York Times*, for reports on the space shuttle *Challenger* explosion.

1988 Tim Weiner, *Philadelphia Inquirer*, for reporting on a secret Pentagon budget used by the government to sponsor defense research and an arms buildup.

1989 Donald L. Barlett and James B. Steele, *Philadelphia Inquirer*, for revelations about the 1986 Tax Reform Act.

1990 Ross Anderson, Bill Dietrich, Mary Ann Gwinn, and Eric Nalder, *Seattle Times*, for coverage of the *Exxon Valdez* oil spill and its aftermath.

1991 Marjie Lundstrom and Rochelle Sharpe, Gannett News Service, for reporting on deaths caused by child abuse.

Telegraphic Reporting (International)

1942 Laurence Edmund Allen, Associated Press, for reports on the British Mediterranean Fleet.

1943 Ira Wolfert, North American Newspaper Alliance, for his reporting on the fifth battle of the Solomon Islands.

1944 Daniel de Luce, Associated Press, for his 1943 work.

1945 Mark S. Watson, *Baltimore Sun*, for his reports from Washington, London, and the fronts in Italy and France.

1946 Homer William Bigart, *New York Herald Tribune*, for war correspondence from the Pacific.

1947 Eddy Gilmore, Associated Press, for Moscow reporting.

International Reporting

1948 Paul W. Ward, *Baltimore Sun*, for a series called "Life in the Soviet Union."

1949 Price Day, *Baltimore Sun*, for articles on India's first year of independence.

1950 Edmund Stevens, *Christian Science Monitor*, for reports on life in the Soviet Union.

1951 Keyes Beech and Fred Sparks, *Chicago Daily News*; Marguerite Higgins and Homer William Bigart, *New York Herald Tribune;* and Relman Morin and Don Whitehead, Associated Press, for reporting on the Korean War.

1952 John M. Hightower, Associated Press, for the body of his work during 1951.

1953 Austin Wehrwein, *Milwaukee Journal*, for reporting on Canada.

1954 Jim G. Lucas, Scripps-Howard Newspapers, for reporting on the Korean War.

1955 Harrison E. Salisbury, *New York Times*, for reporting on the Soviet Union.

1956 William Randolph Hearst Jr., Kingsbury Smith, and Frank Conniff, International News Service, for their exclusive interviews with Soviet leaders.

1957 Russell Jones, United Press, for reporting on the revolt in Hungary.

1958 Staff, *New York Times*, for its work during 1957.

1959 Joseph Martin and Philip Santora, *New York Daily News*, for disclosing the brutality of Cuba's Batista regime.

1960 A. M. Rosenthal, *New York Times*, for Poland reporting.

1961 Lynn Heinzerling, Associated Press, for reporting on the Congo crisis.

1962 Walter Lippmann, *New York Herald Tribune*, for the body of his work, as exemplified by an interview with Soviet Premier Nikita Khrushchev.

1963 Hal Hedrix, *Miami News*, for revealing Soviet installation of missile launching pads in Cuba.

1964 Malcolm W. Browne, Associated Press, and David Halberstam, *New York Times*, for their reporting on the Vietnam War.

1965 J. A. Livingston, *Philadelphia Bulletin*, for reporting on the economics of Soviet satellite nations in Eastern Europe.

1966 Peter Arnett, Associated Press, for coverage of the Vietnam War.

1967 R. John Hughes, *Christian Science Monitor*, for reports on the attempted Communist coup in Indonesia.

1968 Alfred Friendly, *Washington Post*, for coverage of the Middle East War of 1967.

1969 William Tuohy, *Los Angeles Times*, for his reporting on the Vietnam War.

1970 Seymour M. Hersh, Dispatch News Service, for disclosing the My Lai massacre.

1971 Jimmie Lee Hoagland, *Washington Post*, for coverage of the struggle against apartheid in South Africa.

1972 Peter R. Kann, *Wall Street Journal*, for coverage of the Indo-Pakistan War.

1973 Max Frankel, *New York Times*, for reports on President Nixon's visit to China.

1974 Hedrick Smith, *New York Times*, for coverage of the Soviet Union and its Eastern European allies.

1975 William Mullen and Ovie Carter, *Chicago Tribune*, for coverage of famine in Africa and India.

1976 Sydney H. Schanberg, *New York Times*, for reporting on the Communist takeover in Cambodia.

1977 No award

1978　Henry Kamm, *New York Times*, for reports on the refugee "boat people" from Indochina.

1979　Richard Ben Cramer, *Philadelphia Inquirer*, for reports from the Middle East.

1980　Joel Brinkley and Jay Mather, *Courier-Journal*, Louisville, Ky., for reporting on a Cambodian refugee camp.

1981　Shirley Christian, *Miami Herald*, for coverage of the turbulence in Central America.

1982　John Darnton, *New York Times*, for Poland reporting.

1983　Thomas L. Friedman, *New York Times*, and Loren Jenkins, *Washington Post*, each for his reporting of the Israeli invasion of Beirut and its aftermath.

1984　Karen Elliott House, *Wall Street Journal*, for interviews with Jordan's King Hussein.

1985　Josh Friedman, Dennis Bell, and Ozier Muhammad, *Newsday*, for their series on victims of famine in Africa.

1986　Lewis M. Simons, Pete Carey, and Katherine Ellison, *San Jose* (Calif.) *Mercury News*, for a series documenting transfers of wealth abroad by President Marcos of the Philippines and his associates.

1987　Michael Parks, *Los Angeles Times*, for reporting on South Africa.

1988　Thomas L. Friedman, *New York Times*, for coverage of Israel.

1989　Glenn Frankel, *Washington Post*, for reporting from Israel and the Middle East, and Bill Keller, *New York Times*, for coverage of the Soviet Union.

1990　Nicholas Kristof and Sheryl WuDunn, *New York Times*, for reports from China on the movement for democracy and its subsequent suppression.

1991　Caryle Murphy, *Washington Post*, for coverage of the Iraqi invasion of Kuwait; and Serge Schmemann, *New York Times*, for reporting on the breakdown of East Germany and its merger into the Federal Republic.

Investigative Reporting

1985　William K. Marimow, *Philadelphia Inquirer*, for revealing overzealous use of city police dogs, and Lucy Morgan and Jack Reed, *St. Petersburg* (Fla.) *Times*, for exposing corruption in a county sheriff's office.

1986　Jeffrey A. Marx and Michael M. York, *Lexington* (Ky.) *Herald-Leader*, for a series exposing cash payoffs to University of Kentucky basketball players.

1987   Daniel R. Biddle, H. G. Bissinger, and Fredric N. Tulsky, *Philadelphia Inquirer*, for a series revealing transgressions of justice in the Philadelphia courts, and (in a separate award) John Woestendiek, *Philadelphia Inquirer*, for prison beat reporting.

1988   Dean Baquet, William Gaines, and Ann Marie Lipinski, *Chicago Tribune*, for reporting on self-interest and waste plaguing Chicago's city council.

1989   Bill Dedman, *Atlanta Journal and Constitution*, for his investigation of racial discrimination practiced by lending institutions.

1990   Lou Kilzer and Chris Ison, *Star Tribune*, Minneapolis and St. Paul, Minn., for exposing a network of local citizens with links to members of the St. Paul fire department and who profited from fires, some of suspicious origin.

1991   Joseph T. Hallinan and Susan M. Headden, *Indianapolis Star*, for reporting on medical malpractice in Indiana.

Explanatory Journalism

1985   Jon Franklin, *Baltimore Evening Sun*, for a series on molecular psychiatry.

1986   Staff, *New York Times*, for reports on a space-based missile defense system known as "Star Wars."

1987   Jeffrey R. Lyon and Peter Gorner, *Chicago Tribune*, for a series on the promises of gene therapy.

1988   Daniel Hertzberg and James B. Stewart, *Wall Street Journal*, for stories about an investment banker charged with insider trading.

1989   David Hanners, William Snyder, and Karen Blessen, *Dallas Morning News*, for reporting on a plane crash.

1990   David A. Vise and Steve Coll, *Washington Post*, for reports examining the Securities and Exchange Commission.

1991   Susan C. Faludi, *Wall Street Journal*, for an article on the 1986 leveraged buyout of Safeway Stores, Inc., and its devastating aftermath for Safeway employees.

Editorials

1917   *New York Tribune*, for an editorial on the first anniversary of the sinking of the *Lusitania*.

1918   Henry Watterson, *Courier-Journal*, Louisville, Ky., for editorials titled "Vae Victis!" and "War Has Its Companions."

1919   No award

1920   Havey E. Newbranch, *Omaha Evening World-Herald*, for an editorial called "Law and the Jungle."

1921   No award

1922   Frank M. O'Brien, *New York Herald*, for an article called "The Unknown Soldier."

1923   William Allen White, *Emporia* (Kan.) *Gazette*, for an editorial titled "To An Anxious Friend."

1924   *Boston Herald*, for an editorial called "Who Made Coolidge?" and Frank I. Cobb, *New York World*, for the body of his work.

1925   *The News and Courier*, Charleston, S.C., for an editorial titled "The Plight of the South."

1926   Edward M. Kingsbury, *New York Times*, for an editorial titled "The House of a Hundred Sorrows."

1927   F. Lauriston Bullard, *Boston Herald*, for an editorial called "We Submit."

1928   Grover C. Hall, *Montgomery* (Ala.) *Advertiser*, for editorials against gangsterism, floggings, and racial and religious intolerance.

1929   Louis Isaac Jaffe, *Virginian-Pilot*, Norfolk, Va., for an editorial condemning lynchings.

1930   No award

1931   Charles S. Ryckman, *Fremont* (Neb.) *Tribune*, for an editorial titled "The Gentlemen from Nebraska."

1932   No award

1933   *Kansas City Star*, for a variety of editorials.

1934   E. P. Chase, *Atlantic* (Iowa) *News-Telegraph*, for an editorial called "Where Is Our Money?"

1935   No award

1936   Felix Morley, *Washington Post*, and George B. Parker, Scripps-Howard Newspapers, for their editorials in 1935.

1937   John W. Owens, *Baltimore Sun*, for his work in 1936.

1938   William Wesley Waymack, *Des Moines Register & Tribune*, for his work in 1937.

1939   Ronald G. Callvert, *Oregonian*, Portland, for his work in 1938.

1940   Bart Howard, *St. Louis Post-Dispatch*, for his work in 1939.

1941   Reuben Maury, *New York Daily News*, for his work in 1940.

1942   Geoffrey Parsons, *New York Herald Tribune*, for his work in 1941.

1943   Forrest W. Seymour, *Des Moines Register & Tribune*, for his work in 1942.

1944   Henry J. Haskell, *Kansas City Star*, for his work in 1943.

1945   George W. Potter, *Journal-Bulletin*, Providence, R.I., for his 1944 editorials, especially on press freedom.

1946 Hodding Carter, *Delta Democrat-Times*, Greenville, Miss., for editorials on racial, religious, and economic intolerance.

1947 William H. Grimes, *Wall Street Journal*, for his work in 1946.

1948 Virginius Dabney, *Richmond Times-Dispatch*, for editorials during 1947.

1949 John H. Crider, *Boston Herald*, and Herbert Elliston, *Washington Post*, for their work during 1948.

1950 Carl M. Saunders, *Jackson* (Mich.) *Citizen Patriot*, for his work during 1949.

1951 William H. Fitzpatrick, *New Orleans States*, for a series of editorials on a constitutional issue.

1952 Louis LaCoss, *St. Louis Globe-Democrat*, for an editorial titled "The Low Estate of Public Morals."

1953 Vermont Connecticut Royster, *Wall Street Journal*, for his editorials during 1952.

1954 Don Murray, *Boston Herald*, for editorials on changes in American military policy.

1955 Royce Howes, *Detroit Free Press*, for an editorial on an auto workers' strike against Chrysler Corporation.

1956 Lauren K. Soth, *Des Moines Register & Tribune*, for an editorial inviting Soviet farmers to visit Iowa.

1957 Buford Boone, *Tuscaloosa* (Ala.) *News*, for editorials on the community's segregation issue.

1958 Harry S. Ashmore, *Arkansas Gazette*, Little Rock, Ark., for editorials on the school integration conflict.

1959 Ralph McGill, *Atlanta Constitution*, for the body of his work in 1958, as exemplified by the editorial "One Church, One School."

1960 Lenoir Chambers, *Virginian-Pilot*, Norfolk, Va., for editorials on school segregation in Virginia.

1961 William J. Dorvillier, *San Jose* (P.R.) *Star*, for editorials on clerical interference in the 1960 gubernatorial election in Puerto Rico.

1962 Thomas M. Storke, *Santa Barbara* (Calif.) *News-Press*, for editorials condemning the John Birch Society.

1963 Ira B. Harkey Jr., *Pascagoula* (Miss.) *Chronicle*, for editorials on the integration crisis in Mississippi.

1964 Hazel Brannon Smith, *Lexington* (Miss.) *Advertiser*, for editorials on race relations.

1965 John R. Harrison, *Gainesville* (Fla.) *Sun*, for his campaign for better housing in the community.

1966 Robert Lasch, *St. Louis Post-Dispatch*, for his editorials during 1965.

1967   Eugene Patterson, *Atlanta Constitution,* for his editorials during 1966.

1968   John S. Knight, Knight Newspapers, for his editorials during 1967.

1969   Paul Greenberg, *Pine Bluff* (Ark.) *Commercial,* for his editorials during 1968.

1970   Philip L. Geyelin, *Washington Post,* for his editorials during 1969.

1971   Horance G. Davis Jr., *Gainesville* (Fla.) *Sun,* for editorials supporting peaceful desegregation of schools.

1972   John Strohmeyer, *Bethlehem* (Pa.) *Globe-Times,* for his campaign to reduce racial tensions in his community.

1973   Roger B. Linscott, *Berkshire Eagle,* Pittsfield, Mass., for his editorials during 1972.

1974   F. Gilman Spencer, *Trentonian,* Trenton, N.J., for his campaign to focus attention on scandals in New Jersey's state government.

1975   John Daniell Maurice, *Charleston* (W. Va.) *Daily Mail,* for editorials on a county textbook controversy.

1976   Philip P. Kerby, *Los Angeles Times,* for editorials against government secrecy and judicial censorship.

1977   Warren L. Lerude, Foster Church, and Norman F. Cardoza, *Reno* (Nev.) *Evening Gazette* and *Nevada State Journal,* for editorials challenging a local brothel keeper.

1978   Meg Greenfield, *Washington Post,* for editorials during 1977.

1979   Edwin M. Yoder Jr., *Washington Star,* for editorials during 1978.

1980   Robert L. Bartley, *Wall Street Journal,* for the body of his work in 1979.

1981   No award

1982   Jack Rosenthal, *New York Times,* for writings on a wide range of concerns.

1983   Editorial Board, *Miami Herald,* for its campaign against the Reagan administration's policy of detaining illegal Haitian immigrants.

1984   Albert Scardino, *Georgia Gazette,* Savannah, Ga., for a series on various local and state matters.

1985   Richard Aregood, *Philadelphia Daily News,* for the body of his work in 1984.

1986   Jack Fuller, *Chicago Tribune,* for editorials on constitutional issues.

1987   Jonathan Freedman, *San Diego Tribune,* for editorials urging passage of the first major immigration reform act in thirty-four years.

1988 Jane Healy, *Orlando* (Fla.) *Sentinel*, for editorials protesting overdevelopment of Florida's Orange County.

1989 Lois Wille, *Chicago Tribune*, for editorials on a variety of local issues.

1990 Thomas J. Hylton, *Mercury*, Pottstown, Pa., for his editorials about a local bond issue for the preservation of farmland and other open space in rural Pennsylvania.

1991 Ron Casey, Harold Jackson, and Joey Kennedy, *Birmingham* (Ala.) *News*, for a series of editorials on inequities in Alabama's state tax structure.

(Note: This year, the title of this category was changed to Editorial Writing.)

Editorial Cartoons

1922 Rollin Kirby, *New York World*, for the cartoon "On the Road to Moscow."

1923 No award

1924 Jay N. Darling, *New York Tribune*, for the cartoon, "In Good Old U.S.A."

1925 Rollin Kirby, *New York World*, for the cartoon "News from the Outside World."

1926 D. R. Fitzpatrick, *St. Louis Post-Dispatch*, for the cartoon "The Laws of Moses and the Laws of Today."

1927 Nelson Harding, *Brooklyn Eagle*, for the cartoon "Toppling the Idol."

1928 Nelson Harding, *Brooklyn Eagle*, for the cartoon "May His Shadow Never Grow Less."

1929 Rollin Kirby, *New York World*, for the cartoon "Tammany."

1930 Charles R. Macauley, *Brooklyn Eagle*, for the cartoon "Paying for a Dead Horse."

1931 Edmund Duffy, *Baltimore Sun*, for the cartoon "An Old Struggle Still Going On."

1932 John T. McCutcheon, *Chicago Tribune*, for the cartoon "A Wise Economist Asks a Question."

1933 H. M. Talburt, *Washington Daily News*, for the cartoon "The Light of Asia."

1934 Edmund Duffy, *Baltimore Sun*, for the cartoon "California Points with Pride!"

1935 Ross A. Lewis, *Milwaukee Journal*, for the cartoon "Sure, I'll Work for Both Sides."

1936 No award

1937 C. D. Batchelor, *New York Daily News*, for the cartoon "Come on in, I'll Treat You Right."

1938 Vaughn Shoemaker, *Chicago Daily News*, for work during 1937, as exemplified by the cartoon "The Road Back."

1939 Charles G. Werner, *Daily Oklahoman*, Oklahoma City, for work during 1938, as exemplified by the cartoon "Nomination for 1938."

1940 Edmund Duffy, *Baltimore Sun*, for work during 1939, as exemplified by the cartoon "The Outstretched Hand."

1941 Jacob Burck, *Chicago Times*, for work during 1940, as exemplified by the cartoon "If I Should Die Before I Wake."

1942 Herbert L. Block, NEA Service, for work during 1941, as exemplified by the cartoon "British Plane."

1943 Jay N. Darling, *New York Herald Tribune*, for work during 1942, as exemplified by the cartoon "What a Place for a Waste Paper Salvage Campaign."

1944 Clifford K. Berryman, *Washington Evening Star*, for work during 1943, as exemplified by the cartoon "But Where Is the Boat Going?"

1945 Bill Mauldin, United Feature Syndicate, for 1944 work, as exemplified by the series "Up Front with Mauldin."

1946 Bruce A. Russell, *Los Angeles Times*, for work during 1945, as exemplified by the cartoon "Time to Bridge That Gulch."

1947 Vaughn Shoemaker, *Chicago Daily News*, for the cartoon "Still Racing His Shadow."

1948 Reuben L. Goldberg, *New York Sun*, for the cartoon "Peace Today."

1949 Lute Pease, *Newark Evening News*, for the cartoon "Who, Me?"

1950 James T. Berryman, *Washington Evening Star*, for the cartoon "All Set for a Super-Secret Session in Washington."

1951 Reginald W. Manning, *Arizona Republic*, Phoenix, for the cartoon "Hats."

1952 Fred L. Packer, *New York Mirror*, for the cartoon "Your Editors Ought to Have More Sense Than to Print What I Say!"

1953 Edward D. Kuekes, *Cleveland Plain Dealer*, for the cartoon "Aftermath."

1954 Herbert L. Block, *Washington Post*, for a cartoon condemning Joseph Stalin.

1955 D. R. Fitzpatrick, *St. Louis Post-Dispatch*, for a cartoon opposing U.S. military involvement in Indochina.

1956 Robert York, *Louisville Times*, for a cartoon criticizing low farm prices.

1957 Tom Little, *Tennessean*, Nashville, for a cartoon encouraging polio vaccinations.

1958 Bruce M. Shanks, *Buffalo* (N.Y.) *Evening News*, for a cartoon condemning labor racketeering.

1959   Bill Mauldin, *St. Louis Post-Dispatch*, for the cartoon "I Won the Nobel Prize for Literature. What Was Your Crime?"

1960   No award

1961   Carey Orr, *Chicago Tribune*, for the body of his work, as exemplified by the cartoon "The Kindly Tiger."

1962   Edmund S. Valtman, *Hartford Times*, for his cartoons during 1961, as exemplified by "What You Need, Man, Is a Revolution Like Mine."

1963   Frank Miller, *Des Moines Register*, for his cartoons during 1962, as exemplified by "I Said—We Sure Settled That Dispute, Didn't We!"

1964   Paul Conrad, *Denver Post*, for his cartoons during 1963.

1965   No award

1966   Don Wright, *Miami News*, for his cartoons during 1965, as exemplified by "You Mean You Were Bluffing?"

1967   Patrick B. Oliphant, *Denver Post*, for his cartoons during 1966, as exemplified by "They Won't Get *Us* to the Conference Table, Will They?"

1968   Eugene Gray Payne, *Charlotte* (N.C.) *Observer*, for his cartoons during 1967.

1969   John Fischetti, *Chicago Daily News*, for his cartoons during 1968.

1970   Thomas F. Darcy, *Newsday*, for his cartoons during 1969.

1971   Paul Conrad, *Los Angeles Times*, for his cartoons during 1970.

1972   Jeffrey K. MacNelly, *Richmond* (Va.) *News Leader*, for his cartoons during 1971.

1973   No award

1974   Paul Szep, *Boston Globe*, for his cartoons during 1973.

1975   Garry Trudeau, Universal Press Syndicate, for his comic strip "Doonesbury."

1976   Tony Auth, *Philadelphia Inquirer*, for his cartoons during 1975, as exemplified by "O Beautiful for Spacious Skies, for Amber Waves of Grain."

1977   Paul Szep, *Boston Globe*, for his cartoons during 1976.

1978   Jeffrey K. MacNelly, *Richmond* (Va.) *News Leader*, for his cartoons during 1977.

1979   Herbert L. Block, *Washington Post*, for the body of his work in 1978 and throughout his career.

1980   Don Wright, *Miami News*, for the body of his work in 1979.

1981   Mike Peters, *Dayton* (Ohio) *Daily News*, for a cartoon condemning violence caused by hand guns.

1982   Ben Sargent, *Austin* (Tex.) *American-Statesman*, for the body of his work in 1981.

1983   Richard Locher, *Chicago Tribune*, for his work in 1982.

1984 Paul Conrad, *Los Angeles Times*, for the body of his work during 1983.
1985 Jeffrey MacNelly, *Chicago Tribune*, for the body of his work in 1984.
1986 Jules Feiffer, *Village Voice*, for the body of his work in 1985.
1987 Berke Breathed, *Washington Post* Writers Group, for his comic strip, "Bloom County."
1988 Doug Marlette, *Atlanta Constitution*, for the body of his work in 1987.
1989 Jack Higgins, *Chicago Sun-Times*, for the body of his work in 1988.
1990 Tom Toles, *Buffalo* (N.Y.) *News*, for his work during 1989, as exemplified by the cartoon "First Amendment."
1991 Jim Borgman, *Cincinnati Enquirer*, for the body of his work in 1990.

Photography

1942 Milton Brooks, *Detroit News*, for the photo "Ford Strikers Riot."
1943 Frank Noel, Associated Press, for the photo "Water!"
1944 Frank Filan, Associated Press, for the photo "Tarawa Island," and Earle L. Bunker, *Omaha World-Herald*, for the photo "Homecoming."
1945 Joe Rosenthal, Associated Press, for the photo of the Marines planting the U.S. flag on Mount Suribachi on Iwo Jima.
1946 No award
1947 Arnold Hardy, amateur, Atlanta, Ga., for a hotel fire photo distributed by the Associated Press.
1948 Frank Cushing, *Boston Traveler*, for the photo "Boy Gunman and Hostage."
1949 Nathaniel Fein, *New York Herald Tribune*, for the photo "Babe Ruth Bows Out."
1950 Bill Crouch, *Tribune*, Oakland, Calif., for the photo "Near Collision at Air Show."
1951 Max Desfor, Associated Press, for coverage of the Korean War.
1952 John Robinson and Don Ultang, *Des Moines Register & Tribune*, for a sequence of photos of poor sportsmanship during a college football game.
1953 William M. Gallagher, *Flint* (Mich.) *Journal*, for a photo of presidential candidate Adlai Stevenson with a hole in his shoe.
1954 Virginia Schau, amateur, San Anselmo, Calif., for a rescue photo distributed by the Associated Press.
1955 John L. Gaunt Jr., *Los Angeles Times*, for a photo from a seashore drowning scene.

1956   *New York Daily News,* for its photo coverage in 1955, as exemplified by the picture "Bomber Crashes in Street."

1957   Harry A. Trask, *Boston Traveler,* for photos of the sinking of the liner *Andrea Doria.*

1958   William C. Beall, *Washington Daily News,* for a photo of a policeman talking with a little boy.

1959   William Seaman, *Minneapolis Star,* for a photo of the death of a child in the street.

1960   Andrew Lopez, United Press International, for photos of the execution of a Batista officer by a Castro firing squad in Cuba.

1961   Yasushi Nagao, *Mainichi,* Tokyo, for a photo of a stabbing in Tokyo, distributed by United Press International.

1962   Paul Vathis, Associated Press, for a photo titled "Serious Steps."

1963   Hector Rondon, *La República,* Caracas, Venezuela, for a photo of a priest holding a wounded soldier during an insurrection, distributed by the Associated Press.

1964   Robert H. Jackson, *Dallas Times Herald,* for a photo of the murder of Lee Oswald by Jack Ruby.

1965   Horst Faas, Associated Press, for combat photography from the Vietnam War.

1966   Kyoichi Sawada, United Press International, for combat photography from the Vietnam War.

1967   Jack R. Thornell, Associated Press, for a photo of the shooting of James Meredith in Mississippi.

(NOTE: The following year, this category was split into two new categories, Spot News Photography and Feature Photography.)

Spot News Photography

1968   Rocco Morabito, *Jacksonville* (Fla.) *Journal,* for a photo titled "The Kiss of Life."

1969   Edward T. Adams, Associated Press, for a photograph called "Saigon Execution."

1970   Steve Starr, Associated Press, for a photo titled "Campus Guns."

1971   John Paul Filo, *Valley Daily News* and *Daily Dispatch,* Tarentum and New Kensington, Pa., for photos of the shootings at Kent State University.

1972   Horst Faas and Michel Laurent, Associated Press, for the picture series, "Death in Dacca."

1973   Huynh Cong Ut, Associated Press, for his photo of Vietnamese children in flight from a napalm bomb attack.

1974 Anthony K. Roberts, free-lance, Beverly Hills, Calif., for his photos of the killing of an alleged kidnapper.
1975 Gerald H. Gay, *Seattle Times*, for his photo of four exhausted firemen.
1976 Stanley Forman, *Boston Herald American*, for a sequence of photos of a fire in Boston.
1977 Neal Ulevich, Associated Press, for photos of disorder and brutality in the streets of Bangkok, and Stanley Forman, *Boston Herald American*, for a photo of a youth using the flag as a lance in a street disorder.
1978 John H. Blair, United Press International, for a photo of an Indianapolis broker being held hostage at gunpoint.
1979 Thomas J. Kelly III, *Mercury*, Pottstown, Pa., for a series of photos called "Tragedy on Sanatoga Road."
1980 Anonymous, United Press International, for a photo of an Iranian firing squad executing Kurdish rebels.
1981 Larry C. Price, *Fort Worth* (Tex.) *Star-Telegram*, for photos of a military coup in Liberia.
1982 Ron Edmonds, Associated Press, for photographs of the attempted assassination of President Ronald Reagan.
1983 Bill Foley, Associated Press, for photographs at the Sabra Camp massacre in West Beirut.
1984 Stan Grossfeld, *Boston Globe*, for photographs from Lebanon showing people trapped in the violence of war.
1985 Staff, *Orange County Register*, Santa Ana, Calif., for photographs from the Olympic Games in Los Angeles.
1986 Carol Guzy and Michel duCille, *Miami Herald*, for coverage of the eruption of the Nevado del Ruiz volcano in Colombia.
1987 Kim Komenich, *San Francisco Examiner*, for coverage of the fall of Ferdinand Marcos of the Philippines.
1988 Scott Shaw, *Odessa* (Tex.) *American*, for his photo of the child Jessica McClure being rescued from a well.
1989 Ron Olshwanger, amateur, St. Louis, Mo., for a picture of a firefighter trying to revive a child, published in the *St. Louis Post-Dispatch*.
1990 Staff, *Tribune*, Oakland, Calif., for coverage of the Bay Area earthquake of Oct. 17, 1989.
1991 Greg Marinovich, Associated Press, for a series of photographs taken in the black township of Soweto, in South Africa.

Feature Photography

1968 Toshio Sakai, United Press International, for a Vietnam War photo called "Dreams of Better Times."

1969 Moneta Sleet Jr., *Ebony* magazine, for a photo at the funeral of Dr. Martin Luther King Jr.

1970 Dallas Kinney, *West Palm Beach* (Fla.) *Post*, for a portfolio of photos of Florida migrant workers.

1971 Jack Dykinga, *Chicago Sun-Times*, for photos at schools for the retarded in Illinois.

1972 Dave Kennerly, United Press International, for Vietnam War photography.

1973 Brian Lanker, *Topeka* (Kan.) *Capital-Journal*, for a sequence of photographs at the birth of a child.

1974 Slava Veder, Associated Press, for a photo of the return of an American prisoner of war from captivity in North Vietnam.

1975 Matthew Lewis, *Washington Post*, for a portfolio of photos made during 1974.

1976 Staff, *Courier-Journal* and *Louisville Times*, for photo coverage of busing in Louisville schools.

1977 Robin Hood, *Chattanooga News–Free Press*, for a photo of a disabled veteran and his child at an Armed Forces Day parade.

1978 J. Ross Baughman, Associated Press, for photos from guerrilla areas in Rhodesia.

1979 Staff, *Boston Herald American*, for photo coverage of a blizzard.

1980 Erwin H. Hagler, *Dallas Times Herald*, for a photo series depicting modern Texas cowboys.

1981 Taro M. Yamasaki, *Detroit Free Press*, for photographs made at the State Prison of Southern Michigan.

1982 John H. White, *Chicago Sun-Times*, for photographs covering a range of subjects.

1983 James B. Dickman, *Dallas Times Herald*, for photographs of life and death in El Salvador.

1984 Anthony Suau, *Denver Post*, for photos of starvation in Ethiopia.

1985 Stan Grossfeld, *Boston Globe*, for pictures of famine victims in Ethiopia and illegal aliens on the Mexican border, and Larry Price, *Philadelphia Inquirer*, for war photography from Angola and El Salvador.

1986 Tom Gralish, *Philadelphia Inquirer*, for photographs of Philadelphia's homeless people.

1987 David Peterson, *Des Moines Register*, for photographs depicting the shattered dreams of American farmers.

1988 Michel duCille, *Miami Herald*, for photos of the decay and rehabilitation of a housing project overrun by drugs.

1989 Manny Crisostomo, *Detroit Free Press*, for photos showing student life at Southwestern High School in Detroit.

1990 David C. Turnley, *Detroit Free Press*, for his photos of political uprisings in China and Eastern Europe.

1991 William Snyder, *Dallas Morning News*, for pictures of sick and orphaned children living in Romania.

Commentary

1970 Marquis W. Childs, *St. Louis Post-Dispatch*, for commentary during 1969.

1971 William A. Caldwell, *Record*, Hackensack, N.J., for his daily column in 1970.

1972 Mike Royko, *Chicago Daily News*, for his columns during 1971.

1973 David S. Broder, *Washington Post*, for his columns during 1972.

1974 Edwin A. Roberts Jr., *National Observer*, for commentary on public affairs during 1973.

1975 Mary McGrory, *Washington Star*, for commentary on public affairs during 1974.

1976 Walter Wellesley (Red) Smith, *New York Times*, for his sports commentary during 1975 and throughout his career.

1977 George F. Will, *Washington Post* Writers Group, for commentary during 1976 on a variety of topics.

1978 William Safire, *New York Times*, for commentary on the Bert Lance affair.

1979 Russell Baker, *New York Times*, for the body of his work during 1978.

1980 Ellen H. Goodman, *Boston Globe*, for the body of her work in 1979.

1981 Dave Anderson, *New York Times*, for the body of his work in 1980.

1982 Art Buchwald, *Los Angeles Times* Syndicate, for the body of his work in 1981.

1983 Claude Sitton, *News & Observer*, Raleigh, N.C., for the body of his work in 1982.

1984 Vermont Royster, *Wall Street Journal*, for his weekly column, "Thinking Things Over."

1985 Murray Kempton, *Newsday*, for the body of his work in 1984.

1986 Jimmy Breslin, *New York Daily News*, for the body of his work in 1985.

1987 Charles Krauthammer, *Washington Post* Writers Group, for columns on national issues during 1986.

1988 Dave Barry, *Miami Herald*, for his humor columns in 1987.

1989 Clarence Page, *Chicago Tribune*, for columns on local and national affairs.

1990 Jim Murray, *Los Angeles Times*, for his sports columns.

1991 Jim Hoagland, *Washington Post*, for columns on international issues.

Criticism

1970 Ada Louise Huxtable, *New York Times*, for a variety of criticism during 1969.
1971 Harold C. Schonberg, *New York Times*, for music criticism during 1970.
1972 Frank Peters Jr., *St. Louis Post-Dispatch*, for music criticism during 1971.
1973 Ronald Powers, *Chicago Sun-Times*, for critical writing about television during 1972.
1974 Emily Genauer, *Newsday*, for critical writing about art and artists during 1973.
1975 Roger Ebert, *Chicago Sun-Times*, for his film criticism during 1974.
1976 Alan M. Kriegsman, *Washington Post*, for critical writing about dance during 1975.
1977 William McPherson, *Washington Post*, for his contribution to "Book World."
1978 Walter Kerr, *New York Times*, for drama criticism in 1977 and throughout his career.
1979 Paul Gapp, *Chicago Tribune*, for his critical writing about architecture.
1980 William A. Henry III, *Boston Globe*, for critical writing about television.
1981 Jonathan Yardley, *Washington Star*, for his book reviews.
1982 Martin Bernheimer, *Los Angeles Times*, for his music reviews.
1983 Manuela Hoelterhoff, *Wall Street Journal*, for her reviews on a wide range of subjects.
1984 Paul Goldberger, *New York Times*, for his writing on architecture.
1985 Howard Rosenberg, *Los Angeles Times*, for his television writing.
1986 Donal J. Henahan, *New York Times*, for his music criticism.
1987 Richard Eder, *Los Angeles Times*, for his book reviews.
1988 Tom Shales, *Washington Post*, for his television criticism.
1989 Michael Skube, *News and Observer*, Raleigh, N.C., for his writing about books and other literary topics.
1990 Allan Temko, *San Francisco Chronicle*, for his architecture criticism.
1991 David Shaw, *Los Angeles Times*, for critical writing about the media.

Feature Writing

1979 Jon Franklin, *Baltimore Evening Sun*, for his account of a brain operation.

1980 Madeleine Blais, *Miami Herald*, for a variety of her work in 1979.

1981 Teresa Carpenter, *Village Voice*, New York, for her account of a murder committed by a mental patient.

1982 Saul Pett, Associated Press, for a profile of the American government.

1983 Nan Robertson, *New York Times*, for her personal account of being struck down by toxic shock syndrome.

1984 Peter Mark Rinearson, *Seattle Times*, for a series on development of the Boeing 757.

1985 Alice Steinbach, *Baltimore Sun*, for her account of a blind boy's world.

1986 John Camp, *St. Paul* (Minn.) *Pioneer Press & Dispatch*, for a series on a Minnesota farm family.

1987 Steve Twomey, *Philadelphia Inquirer*, for his profile of life aboard an aircraft carrier.

1988 Jacqui Banaszynski, *St. Paul* (Minn.) *Pioneer Press & Dispatch*, for her series on the life and death of an AIDS victim in a rural farm community.

1989 David Zucchino, *Philadelphia Inquirer*, for his series called "Being Black in South Africa."

1990 Dave Curtin, *Colorado Springs Gazette Telegraph*, for his account of a family's struggle after its members were severely burned in an explosion that wrecked their home.

1991 Sheryl James, *St. Petersburg* (Fla.) *Times*, for a series on a mother who stood trial for abandoning her baby.

Special Awards and Citations

1938 *Edmonton* (Alta.) *Journal*, for its defense of freedom of the press in Canada.

1941 *New York Times*, for the quality of its foreign news reporting.

1944 Byron Price, director of Office of Censorship, for creation and administration of the newspaper and radio codes, and William Allen White, for his services on the Pulitzer Board.

1945 American press cartographers, for their maps of the war fronts.

1947 Columbia University and its Graduate School of Journalism, for efforts to advance the Pulitzer Prizes, and the *St. Louis Post-Dispatch*, for adhering to the ideals of Joseph Pulitzer.

1948   Frank Diehl Fackenthal, for his service as Columbia University president and member of the Pulitzer Board.

1951   C. L. Sulzberger, *New York Times*, for his exclusive interview with Archbishop Stepinac, and Arthur Krock, *New York Times*, for his exclusive interview with President Truman.

1952   Max Kase, *New York Journal-American*, for reports exposing corruption in college basketball, and *Kansas City Star*, for news coverage of a regional flood.

1953   *New York Times*, for its Sunday section called "Review of the Week."

1958   Walter Lippmann, *New York Herald Tribune*, for hs career as a commentator.

1964   Gannett Newspapers, for the program called "The Road to Integration."

1976   John Hohenberg, Columbia University, for his services to the Pulitzer Prizes.

1978   Richard Lee Strout, *Christian Science Monitor*, for career as a commentator and Washington correspondent.

1987   Joseph Pulitzer Jr., *St. Louis Post-Dispatch*, for his years of service on the Pulitzer Board.

Newspaper History Award

1918   Minna Lewinson and Henry Beetle Hough, for their history of the services rendered to the public by the American press. It was the only year in which this prize was awarded.

Bibliography

BOOKS

Bagdikian, Ben H. *The Media Monopoly*. Boston: Beacon Press, 1983.
_____. *The Effete Conspiracy*. New York: Harper & Row, 1972.
Bayley, Edwin R. *Joe McCarthy and the Press*. Madison, Wisc.: University of Wisconsin Press, 1981.
Bonin, Jane F. *Prize-Winning American Drama*. Metuchen, N.J.: Scarecrow Press, 1973.
Broder, David S. *Behind the Front Page*. New York: Simon and Schuster, 1987.
Fischer, Heinz-Dietrich. *The Pulitzer Prize Archive: International Reporting 1928–1985*. Munich: K. G. Saur, 1987.
Hohenberg, John. *The Pulitzer Prize Story*. New York: Columbia University Press, 1959.
_____. *The Pulitzer Prize Story II*. New York: Columbia University Press, 1980.
_____. *The Pulitzer Prizes*. New York: Columbia University Press, 1974.
Isaacs, Norman E. *Untended Gates: The Mismanaged Press*. New York: Columbia University Press, 1986.
Juergens, George. *Joseph Pulitzer and the New York World*. Princeton, N.J.: Princeton University Press, 1966.
Milton, Joyce. *The Yellow Kids*. New York: Harper & Row, 1989.
Rammelkamp, Julian S. *Pulitzer's Post-Dispatch, 1878–1883*. Princeton, N.J.: Princeton University Press, 1967.
Reeves, Thomas C. *The Life and Times of Joe McCarthy*. New York: Stein and Day, 1982.
Reynolds, William Robinson. "Joseph Pulitzer." Unpublished dissertation, Columbia University, New York.
Seitz, Don Carlos. *Joseph Pulitzer: His Life and Letters*. New York: Simon & Schuster, 1924.

Shaw, David. *Press Watch: A Provocative Look at How Newspapers Report the News.* New York: Macmillan, 1984.
Sloan, David W. *Pulitzer Prize Editorials.* Ames, Iowa: Iowa State University Press, 1980.
Swanberg, W. A. *Citizen Hearst.* New York: Scribner's, 1961.
————. *Pulitzer.* New York: Scribner's, 1967.

ARTICLES

Berger, Joseph. "Prize Winners Find Glory Bittersweet." *New York Times,* April 18, 1987.
Blumenfeld, Harold. "The 1980 Pulitzer Prize Pictures: An Insider's Look." *Popular Photography,* July 1980.
Buckley, Peter. "Beating the Odds." *Horizon,* December 1982.
Casey, Constance. "Literary New Orleans." *Publishers Weekly,* May 9, 1986.
Chapnick, Howard. "Behind the Pulitzer Prize Controversy." *Popular Photography,* June 1979.
Clemons, Walter. "The Last Word: The Pulitzer Non-Prize for Fiction." *New York Times Book Review,* June 6, 1971.
Cockburn, Alexander. "Disgusting Award for a Disgusting Paper." *The Nation,* May 7, 1988.
Coulson, David C. "Editors' Attitudes and Behavior Toward Journalism Awards." *Journalism Quarterly,* Winter 1989.
Durniak, John. "The Pulitzer Puzzle." *Popular Photography,* October 1984.
Epstein, Aaron, and Riordan, Patrick. "Playing the Pulitzers." *Columbia Journalism Review,* July/August 1980.
Friendly, Jonathan. "Columbia Journalism School's Future Dividing Administration and Faculty." *New York Times,* March 20, 1983.
Gass, William H. "Prizes, Surprises and Consolation Prizes." *New York Times Book Review,* August 26, 1984.
Grauer, Neil A. "The Great Bloom County Feud: Why Cartoonists Got Mad at the Pulitzer Board." *Columbia Journalism Review,* September/October 1987.
Griffith, Thomas. "The Pulitzer Prizes: Giving and Taking Away." *Time,* May 15, 1978.
Grossberger, Lewis, and Howard, Lucy. "The Pulitzer Prize Hoax." *Newsweek,* April 27, 1981.
Haller, Scot. "Her First Play, Her First Pulitzer Prize." *Saturday Review,* November 1981.
Harwood, Richard. "A Corrupting Mania for Prizes?" *Washington Post,* April 10, 1988.
Hummler, Richard. "Play Author a Prize Bonus Baby." *Variety,* April 6, 1983.
Ireland, Doug. "Press Clips." *Village Voice,* June 24, 1989.
Jaspin, Elliot G. "The Pulitzer Doesn't Always Spell Success." *ASNE Bulletin,* December/January 1981.

Kennedy, William. "How Winning the Pulitzer Has Changed One Writer's Life." *Life*, November 1984.

Konner, Joan. "Winning and Other Triumphs." *Newsday*, April 9, 1990.

Leonard, John. "Pulitzer People Are No Prize." *New York Times Book Review*, May 19, 1974.

Mauro, Tony. "Journal et al. vs. Inquirer: Pulitzer Pile-on." *Washington Journalism Review*, June 1988.

Munson, Naomi. "The Case of Janet Cooke." *Commentary*, August 1981.

Nobile, Philip. "The Pulitzer Surprise." *New York*, April 27, 1981.

O'Donnell, Laurence G. "Reflections of a Pulitzer Prize Juror." *Wall Street Journal*, April 13, 1982.

Poli, Kenneth. "The Pulitzers: Prizes or Products?" *Popular Photography*, September 1978.

Prendergast, Alan. "Of Penguins and Pulitzers." *Washington Journalism Review*, October 1987.

Randolph, Eleanor. "The Pulitzer Pipeline." *Washington Post*, March 4, 1988.

Robertson, Michael. "The Reporter As Novelist: The Case of William Kennedy." *Columbia Journalism Review*, January/February 1986.

Scardino, Albert. "A Pulitzer Prize Can Bring Profits As Well As Prestige." *New York Times*, February 20, 1989.

Shenker, Israel. "Pulitzer Loser Proves Winner in Other Areas." *New York Times*, April 24, 1977.

Sznajderman, Michael. "The Alabama Journal: A Pulitzer and No Future?" *Washington Journalism Review*, September 1988.

Zuckerman, Laurence. "Campaigning for the Pulitzers." *Time*, April 4, 1988.

UNPUBLISHED COLLECTIONS

Joseph Pulitzer Papers, Butler Library, Columbia University.

Index